"Karam and Blow maintain that there is so much more to helping families beyond existing therapy models. This book is about that 'something more,' the common factors that cut across couple and family therapy (CFT) models. They show, for example, how to maximize client factors like motivation and hope. Readers learn how to conceptualize problems systemically, invite alternative views of the presenting problem, disrupt dysfunctional relational patterns, strengthen the therapeutic alliance, expand direct treatment systems, focus on self-of-therapist work and employ regular client feedback. Also, the authors share important best practices in self supervision and treatment planning. Most importantly, as the title suggests, they bring common factors to life.

There is a wealth of wisdom in this book that will improve the readers' therapy and augment their treatment models. What I liked best was the regular reflective questions and learning activities that will encourage critical thinking and personalize each skill. They include, for example, exercises to help one consider therapeutic models that are consistent with one's personality, a hope history inventory and log, a common factors feedback interview, a common factors journal. I loved the many ways the authors engage readers. These activities are perfect for encouraging reflection, class discussion, and self-training. And their case examples illustrate each of their points beautifully. The result is that this book transforms common factors from the margins of CFT to where they belong – front and center – a primary therapeutic focus that will enhance all CFT models and the therapists that employ them."

Fred P. Piercy, PhD, *Professor Emeritus of Family Therapy, Virginia Tech, Former Editor of the* Journal of Marital and Family Therapy

"*Bringing Common Factors to Life in Couple and Family Therapy* offers a refreshing approach to thinking about how to do couple and family therapy more effectively. Karam and Blow provide a down-to-earth guide that enables the reader to meaningfully put common factors research to work using any theoretical model. They engage the reader with practical exercises and examples that bring their ideas to life and inspire real-world applications. Without a doubt, *Bringing Common Factors to Life* will be instrumental in shaping the next evolution of couple and family therapy theory."

Diane R. Gehart, PhD, *Professor, California State University, Northridge*

BRINGING COMMON FACTORS TO LIFE IN COUPLE AND FAMILY THERAPY

With the aim of renewing motivation, energy, and creativity in therapists' clinical work, this book explores how common factors may be utilized to increase effectiveness in couple and family therapy.

Practicing a specific approach or model for couple and family therapy may fulfill many initial therapist needs, but over time it is developmentally normal for your enthusiasm to wane for a specific way of practicing this therapy. This book therefore provides a common factors framework that may help alleviate feelings of "staleness" and reinvigorate your practice. Different from previous theoretical texts about common factors, this practical book will help you construct a personalized plan that will allow you to take charge of your therapeutic development. The authors present helpful strategies and exercises to build on your previously existing therapeutic skill set, stoke curiosity for the work, counter against burnout and frustration and, most importantly, achieve consistently better outcomes for your clients.

This new resource is an essential read for seasoned couple and family therapists who want to improve their clinical skills and personal effectiveness, as well as students and professionals just starting their journey into this type of clinical work.

Eli A. Karam PhD, LMFT, is a systemic therapist, trainer, applied researcher and educator at the University of Louisville, where he is a professor.

Adrian J. Blow PhD, LMFT, works as a couple and family therapy intervention researcher and educator at Michigan State University, where he is professor and department chair.

BRINGING COMMON FACTORS TO LIFE IN COUPLE AND FAMILY THERAPY

Eli A. Karam and Adrian J. Blow

NEW YORK AND LONDON

Cover image: © Alicia Llop - Getty Images

First published 2023
by Routledge
605 Third Avenue, New York, NY 10158

and by Routledge
4 Park Square, Milton Park, Abingdon, Oxon, OX14 4RN

Routledge is an imprint of the Taylor & Francis Group, an informa business

© 2023 Taylor & Francis

The right of Eli A. Karam and Adrian J. Blow to be identified as authors of this work has been asserted in accordance with sections 77 and 78 of the Copyright, Designs and Patents Act 1988.

All rights reserved. No part of this book may be reprinted or reproduced or utilised in any form or by any electronic, mechanical, or other means, now known or hereafter invented, including photocopying and recording, or in any information storage or retrieval system, without permission in writing from the publishers.

Trademark notice: Product or corporate names may be trademarks or registered trademarks, and are used only for identification and explanation without intent to infringe.

Library of Congress Cataloging-in-Publication Data
Names: Karam, Eli A., author. | Blow, Adrian J., author.
Title: Bringing common factors to life in couple and family therapy / Eli A. Karam, Adrian J. Blow.
Description: New York, NY : Routledge, 2022. | Includes bibliographical references and index. | Summary: "With the aim of renewing motivation, energy, and creativity in a therapists clinical work, this book explores how common factors may be utilized to increase effectiveness in couple and family therapy"— Provided by publisher.
Identifiers: LCCN 2022009961 | ISBN 9781138686212 (hardback) | ISBN 9781138686212 (paperback) | ISBN 9781315542737 (ebook)
Subjects: LCSH: Couples therapy. | Family psychotherapy.
Classification: LCC RC488.5 .K 2022 | DDC 616.89/1562—dc23/eng/20220506
LC record available at https://lccn.loc.gov/2022009961

ISBN: 978-1-138-68620-5 (hbk)
ISBN: 978-1-138-68621-2 (pbk)
ISBN: 978-1-315-54273-7 (ebk)

DOI: 10.4324/9781315542737

Typeset in New Baskerville
by Apex CoVantage, LLC

DEDICATION

Both of us would like to dedicate this book to the memory of our friend and mentor Doug Sprenkle, a true pioneer of common factors in couple and family therapy. We started this project shortly after his passing, and his spirit lives both within these pages and in the work we continue to do as academics and systemic therapists. It was Doug who introduced us to each other, and we were both fortunate to have sat under his learning tree for so many years!

I (EK) would like to acknowledge my co-author Adrian Blow for his significant contributions, not only to this book but also to this wonderful profession that we both love so dearly. I admired Adrian's work before I ever met him and have thoroughly enjoyed laughing, learning and collaborating with him over the past decade. I also need to thank my students and clients who helped me innovate and refine many of the ideas in this book. Our ongoing dialogues have challenged me to grow as a teacher and therapist. To my children, Molly and Charlie, thank you for being my inspiration to push through hard times and giving me the joy of being your dad. Most important, I thank my wife, Tracy. Without your tireless effort at home, I would never have been able to focus so much on the work necessary to complete this project. I am lucky to have you as the backbone of our family. You continually remind me what is important, support me and always inspire me to be a better person.

I (AB) would like to thank the many teachers, too many to name, I have had along the way who inspired me to be an effective systemic therapist. I am also grateful for the families whom I have had the privilege of working with in the therapy room – it is always an honor and a privilege to witness your pain, struggles and growth. Thank you, Eli, co-author of this work, for being the initiator of this book and for pushing us to get it done. It has been an honor to work with you. Finally, thank you to my children and my spouse Tina – you all always have my back, and you provide endless support, love and encouragement. I am grateful to each one of you. My wish is that this book will inspire systemic therapists to grow and do effective work with their clients.

CONTENTS

Foreword by Jay Lebow	x
1 Overview/How to Use This Book	1
2 How Change Occurs Part 1: Broad Common Factors of Change	6
3 How Change Occurs Part 2: Narrow Common Factors, aka Common Therapeutic Effects	15
4 Couple and Family Therapy Common Factors	44
5 Choosing the Right Model for You and Your Clients	76
6 Enhancing Client and Contextual Factors	90
7 Mobilizing Hope	127
8 The Talented and Skilled Therapist	145
9 Nurturing the Therapeutic Alliance	179
10 Utilizing Feedback in CFT	201
11 Common Factors Self-Supervision and Treatment Planning	224
Index	245

FOREWORD

I have the privilege of writing the foreword to this wonderful book. Eli Karam and Adrian Blow have written a book that concisely speaks to the most important essential aspects of being a couple and family therapist. *Bringing Common Factors to Life in Couple and Family Therapy* articulates the essential elements of how to be effective as a relational therapist. The client-focused, clinically centered approach to therapy at the core of this book makes so much sense that one might wonder why such a viewpoint hasn't always been at the center of the practice of couple and family therapy.

Yet, the history of couple and family therapy has been complex. Although there were versions of couple and family therapy early in the 20th century, relational centered practice basically has its origins in the systemic revolution of the 1960s and 1970s (Gurman & Fraenkel, 2002). And what a revolution it was. The myopic focus on the inside of individuals of earlier traditions of mental health treatment was challenged in the context of the emerging understandings about systems and, most especially, social systems. Many brilliant theoretical and clinical papers and books were written about those social systems and their processes (Gurman & Kniskern, 1981; Minuchin, 1974). In couple and family, a generation of what were sometimes referred to as "wizards" developed specific methods for intervening that were compelling. Further, their wizardry was often on public display, in "live" observed sessions with families that were both marvelous demonstrations of clinical sensitivity and skill and a precursor to reality television. Everyone wanted to model their clinical practice on these skillful practitioners and learn how to enact such dramatic change.

What followed was an extension of the practice of these first-generation couple and family therapists into manualized models of how to intervene. Ironically, the richness of the practice of the brilliant therapists of the first generation became much more monolithic and limited in the models that emerged. Each model accentuated systemic concepts and one or two specific aspects of working with couples and families. Structural therapists emphasized structure, strategic therapists second-order change, behavioral therapists behavior, experiential therapists emotion and so on. What common ground there was readily became lost in the idiosyncratic vocabularies of the various models, leading to a Tower of Babel where when similarities appeared they could not be recognized.

Even more of a challenge was that the interpersonal skills of these first-generation therapists (those skills that are called *common factors*, which are so apparent in most videos of the pioneers of couple and family therapy) became lost in the descriptions of various theories about why families evolve as they do and how to intervene. This became so out of balance that some systemic therapists even cautioned therapists when the alliance between clients and therapists became too strong (lest this created some sort of dependency on the therapy; Watzlawick et al., 1974). It is important here to highlight that couple and family therapists were not alone in accenting case formulation and the active agents of intervention; very similar patterns emerged in the development of evidence-based individual therapies. Alan Gurman coined a word we should remember to describe these trends, "technolatry" (Gurman & Kniskern, 1978), focused on the technical aspects of therapy and losing track of its relational basis.

It took 3 decades before some balance was restored in couple and family therapy. Eventually, a literature about integrative practice accrued that began to challenge the rigid boundaries presented by treatment models. A major turning point came with the work of Doug Sprenkle, who, with colleagues, began to explicitly write, speak and teach about the role of common factors in couple and family therapy (Adrian Blow and I both co-authored pieces with him about this subject). As Sprenkle and colleagues highlighted (Sprenkle et al., 1999, 2009), there was no doubt that our focus was out of balance. An overwhelming body of research points to the specifics of the intervention model as only one component in treatment effectiveness and, at that, one less important than others such as the alliance between clients and therapist. Further, all bona fide treatments have proven to be successful when practitioners are skillful (Wampold & Imel, 2015). Nonetheless, it also makes little sense to throw out the proverbial baby with the bathwater. Although some argue that treatments make no difference, being skillful at a treatment is very important, because intervention methods are the active agent that propel clients to experience change. Further, clients experiencing the content of therapy as useful becomes, in a circular process, an essential ingredient in clients experiencing the common factors that accrue in a successful therapy. And, at times, there is a treatment approach that is better matched to a specific problem.

Bringing Common Factors to Life in Couple and Family marks our moving into a new era. In this time, while it remains important to learn the skills of specific models, that learning must be paired with learning and practicing a broader set of skills of human relating. Our practice must build on the foundation of establishing a therapeutic alliance, helping to engender hope and overcoming demoralization, as well as a sense of the importance of human connectedness. Some of this falls within the old classic common factors enumerated by Jerome Frank (1963) and others, some within the core systemic factors of couple and family therapy articulated by Sprenkle and colleagues (1999, 2009)and some within "newer" common factors that have more recently been described, such as incorporating client feedback into treatment and attending to client stage of change (Norcross & Lambert, 2018). Ironically, or perhaps simply because of the power of these factors, the manualized treatment models themselves more and more come to include these factors, because it's a no-brainer (confirmed by considerable evidence) that explicitly incorporating these factors into treatment will lead to better treatment outcome. The person of the therapist has similarly become essential to consider, because, as Karam and Blow highlight, therapists always are the vehicle for delivering therapy. And incorporating evidence from qualitative and quantitative research into practice has also become essential to state-of-the-art clinical practice.

So, it is with excitement and optimism about the evolution of the practice of couple and family therapy that I read this book. This is therapy as it should be practiced, accentuating not which model is best but how to bring a therapeutic consciousness to our work as couple and family therapists that includes both attending to common factors and carefully choosing our methods of intervention. As Karam and Blow remind us, the best therapy is the product of therapists refining their skills, furthering their individual development and identifying how they can be most effective in this role to help clients recognize and build on their strengths and find ways to change that which can be changed in the pursuit of a more successful individual and relational life (Lebow, 2014). These therapists are anchored in a set of therapeutic skills they have acquired (and continue to develop), a sense of self as an effective (though not omniscient) therapist and a set of preconscious algorithms for when they do what in therapy (Grunebaum, 1988). However, as Karam and Blow highlight, they remain flexible, engaging in a recursive dialogue with themselves about their practice and in a lifelong process of learning that includes refining their methods (Orlinsky & Ronnestad, 2005). I trust this fine guide will help beginning couple and family therapists to shape a path for their development and therapists further along to reflect on, refine and augment their practice.

Jay Lebow, PhD, ABPP, MFT
Family Institute at Northwestern and Northwestern University
Evanston, Illinois

References

Frank, J. D. (1963). *Persuasion and healing.* Schocken.
Grunebaum, H. (1988). The relationship of family theory to family therapy. *Journal of Marital and Family Therapy, 14*(1), 1–14. https://doi.org/10.1111/j.1752-0606.1988.tb01644.x
Gurman, A. S., & Fraenkel, P. (2002). The history of couple therapy: A millennial review. *Family Process, 41*(2), 199–260. https://doi.org/10.1111/j.1545-5300.2002.41204.x
Gurman, A. S., & Kniskern, D. P. (1978). Technolatry, methodolatry, and the results of family therapy. *Family Process, 17*(3), 275–281.
Gurman, A. S., & Kniskern, D. P. (1981). *Handbook of family therapy.* Brunner/Mazel. http://www.loc.gov/catdir/enhancements/fy0652/80020357-d.html
Lebow, J. L. (2014). *Couple and family therapy: An integrative map of the territory.* APA Books.
Minuchin, S. (1974). *Families & family therapy.* Harvard University Press.
Norcross, J. C., & Lambert, M. J. (2018). *Psychotherapy relationships that work III.* Educational Publishing Foundation. doi:10.1037/pst0000193
Orlinsky, D. E., & Ronnestad, M. H. (2005). *How psychotherapists develop: A study of therapeutic work and professional growth.* American Psychological Association.
Sprenkle, D. H., Blow, A. J., & Dickey, M. H. (1999). Common factors and other nontechnique variables in marriage and family therapy. In M. A. Hubble, B. L. Duncan, & S. D. Miller (Eds.), *The heart and soul of change: What works in therapy* (pp. 329–359). American Psychological Association.
Sprenkle, D. H., Davis, S. D., & Lebow, J. L. (2009). *Common factors in couple and family therapy: The overlooked foundation for effective practice.* Guilford. http://search.ebscohost.com/login.aspx?direct=true&db=psyh&AN=2009-20432-000&site=ehost-live
Wampold, B. E., & Imel, Z. E. (2015). *The great psychotherapy debate: The evidence for what makes psychotherapy work* (2nd ed.). Routledge/Taylor & Francis Group.
Watzlawick, P., Weakland, J. H., & Fisch, R. (1974). *Change: Principles of problem formation and problem resolution.* W. W. Norton.

1
OVERVIEW/HOW TO USE THIS BOOK

Why Read This Book?

You are reading this book for a good reason. Either it has been assigned to you because you are a student learning to be an effective couple and family therapist (CFT) or you are a practitioner seeking to enhance your work with relational client systems. Maybe it caught your attention because of its title and the promise of exploring all of the common factors that account for therapeutic success in CFT. This is not designed to be a book that you will read and put on the shelf; rather, it is one you will customize and participate in through your own self-reflection and integration of common factors in your own work with individuals, couples and families. Even if you are mostly content with your work, the process of reading this book will help you become more aware of what you do that is most helpful to your clients.

After many years of working in a particular style, you may find it becomes harder (not easier) to remain energized and focused on the effective practice of CFT. You may become complacent doing similar interventions or implementing the same therapeutic model over and over again. Whereas practicing a specific approach or model may fulfill many initial therapist needs and provide structure, over time it is developmentally normal for your enthusiasm to wane for a specific way of practicing CFT. An overall feeling of "stuckness" and "staleness" may pervade your clinical work. A common factors framework may help to alleviate these feelings and reinvigorate your practice. After all, it is only through continued renewal activities (e.g., supervision, continuing education, self-study, personal therapy, and other growth experiences) that we keep the momentum going in our professional evolution as systemic therapists.

Regardless of your level of experience or preferred theory, this book is intended to help you:

- Explain the history and guiding principles about what works in CFT and the related common factors.

- Apply examples and explore how to integrate a common factors perspective into your current theoretical orientation.
- Monitor and get feedback on therapist effectiveness by using both practical techniques and user-friendly resources.
- Renew your motivation, energy and creativity in your clinical work.
- Improve your clinical skills and personal effectiveness as a couple and family therapist.
- Become more outcome focused in your work, giving intentional consideration to whether you are effective with your clients and why you are/are not effective.

Chapters 2 and 3 provide an overview of how change occurs in CFT. In addition to learning how common factors operate, the reader will gain appreciation for the empirical underpinnings that anchor the applied information to be presented throughout the pages of this book.

Although much more has been written about common factors in the individual therapy literature, in Chapter 4 we also focus on four common factors that are unique to CFT: (1) conceptualizing difficulties in relational terms, (2) disrupting dysfunctional relational patterns, (3) expanding the therapeutic alliance and (4) expanding the direct treatment system. Though few, these common factors are extremely important and rooted in the ways in which CFT as a discipline is itself distinctive.

Chapter 5 highlights the importance of having a model for doing therapy. Unlike pure model adherents who overemphasize specific ingredients or interventions, we as common factors proponents believe models are important for different reasons. Therapy is helpful largely because the couple's or family's chaos is replaced with the therapist's order (i.e., their model/theory of change). Without a model/theory of change to guide the therapist, the therapist will not know what to attempt to change, how to change it or how to know when therapy is complete. Replacing one person's chaos with another's will not help. Though we contend that a therapist needs to be familiar with many credible models of therapy, we also strongly advocate that a therapist should be flexible within those models. A therapist should not lose sight of the ends (a successful therapeutic outcome and strong alliance) as they focus on the means (i.e., the interventions) and should be willing to abandon the model's means if they are not helping the clients reach desired ends. This chapter helps the reader understand how they originally chose and currently use models in their work with couples and families. The reader will critically examine how their current model fits with both their own worldview and the worldviews of their clients.

Chapter 6 details how to mobilize client factors to unlock powerful individual-, couple- and family-level strengths that may improve therapeutic outcomes. Specifically, we focus on how therapists can engage clients and match their level of motivation. The chapter applies transtheoretical stages of change, an approach traditionally used with individuals, as a lens that can also inform relational therapy. Practical strategies and experiential exercises that target the life and environment of the client that affect the occurrence of change, such as the client's inner strengths, support system, motivation and persistence, are also presented in this chapter. In particular, we focus on how these client factors such as motivation work in a system.

Previous research has shown that the beginning stage of therapy is primarily concerned with a movement from demoralization to remoralization. Hope is a powerful moderator of change in any successful therapy. Without it, both the therapist and family system lack the necessary optimism to maximize opportunities for change. Chapter 7 therefore is devoted to specific strategies and interventions that tap into and build hope within individuals and between couple and family systems.

Chapter 8 is designed to both emphasize and enhance important therapist variables in the process of psychotherapy change. Just as many common factors work through models, models in turn work through therapists. There is consistent evidence that therapists need to adapt to client preferences, expectations and characteristics. We contend that most key changes in therapy are either initiated by the therapist or influenced by the therapist and that a therapist's ability to identify and maximize these change opportunities largely determines the therapist's – and hence the therapy's – effectiveness. Exercises in the chapter operationalize mindfulness and other refocusing skills necessary when couples and therapists get "stuck" or frustrated with complex client systems.

Chapter 9 focuses on the importance of the therapeutic alliance – how it is formed, torn and repaired – and the unique aspects of the alliance in couple and family therapy. Although most therapists think that they are skillful at building an alliance, doing so successfully is a complex task requiring considerable skill, given both the unique alliance needs of specific clients and the pitfalls and intricacies of the multiple alliances in CFT. While the importance of the relationship between therapist and client is interwoven throughout the text, this chapter presents specific strategies and exercises for nurturing the therapeutic alliance.

Chapter 10 builds on previous research about the importance of both giving and receiving feedback in the therapeutic process. In fact, substantial evidence exists showing the degree to which tracking client treatment response benefits clients. It is becoming clearer that clients (particularly if they have trouble engaging) benefit greatly when their response to treatment is formally measured, viewed and responded to by their therapist. The chapter demonstrates how using both formal and informal feedback mechanisms help therapists and their clients to find new and more helpful directions when the therapy is "stuck" or not advancing at optimal rates. The chapter also provides practical guidelines for the reader to begin documenting their own client and therapist practice patterns. By attending to feedback, the therapist's goals shift from becoming an expert in a particular model or therapeutic approach to becoming an effective therapist with specific client systems; that is, helping clients in the best way possible. In this way, we adapt to the client, rather than forcing the client to adapt to our preferred style of working.

Chapter 11 serves as self-supervisory support to therapists as they continue the practice of CFT. A checklist of questions is provided to remind the reader to address important common factor elements in their treatment planning. The chapter offers a practical approach to helping the reader through a self-reflexive review of their client system when they feel stuck or outside supervision/consultation is not readily available. Focusing on each of the common factors explored earlier in the book, this capstone chapter will give you a personalized roadmap to integration and increased therapeutic effectiveness.

Your Personalized Guide to Continued Growth and Development as a CFT

For those CFTs who are committed to self-reflection in order to become the best clinician possible, this book will aid you as you travel your own idiosyncratic journey. This book offers evidence-based and practical guidance on how to become a more effective therapist. Some books preaching specific treatment approaches advocate that getting better at the practice of CFT will require you to change your current model(s) or way of working. Speaking to the contrary, the information presented in the following pages is designed to build upon your existing strengths and passions, not to make you change the "core" of your current clinical identity and preferred theoretical orientation.

It is the kind of book that therapists in solo practice will use, but it is also designed for counseling centers and mental health organizations to purchase for all of their employees to help them reenergize themselves and engage in a form of self-supervision. Although some therapists may be more comfortable integrating the common factors on their own while reading the book, others may wish to process and share what they are doing within the context of their ongoing supervision sessions, staff case consultations or other scheduled interactions with colleagues. It may even be desirable to undertake this process as part of peer supervision or an ongoing support group so that opportunities can be created for talking about what is evoked during the course of reading about the common factors.

We developed many of the exercises in the book as a way to help both our students and us assess and monitor the changes we experience in the therapy room through a common factors lens. Perhaps you have read numerous books about therapy but find that many of the ideas and lessons don't "stick" for very long, somehow are not applicable to your experience of the practice of CFT or are not very practical. Thus, our intention was to create a reading experience that is far more interactive and engaging, one that requires you to personalize the content and respond so that, at the end, you have integrated the knowledge and skills in an organic way, germane to your preferred style of practicing CFT.

This book transforms the best lessons that we have learned from both our clients and psychotherapy research in an applied marriage of art and science. We are both practicing therapists (with a special emphasis in CFT). Although we also teach and do research at universities, we see individuals, couples and families regularly and have the hearts of clinicians. Even after so many decades of practice, we routinely review many of the exercises in this book in a self-reflexive process to sustain or inspire our own personal integration of the common factors into our practice of CFT.

2

HOW CHANGE OCCURS PART 1

Broad Common Factors of Change

How Change Occurs

In this chapter, we provide an overview of how change occurs in couple and family therapy (CFT). This chapter should be read in close conjunction with Chapter 3, because they are companion chapters. We describe in these two chapters nonspecific aspects of treatment that lead to change in a system, including changes in behaviors, cognitions and emotions held by individuals within that system. The reader will also gain appreciation for the empirical underpinnings that anchor the applied information to be presented throughout the pages of this book. Research on change has provided us with convincing evidence that change does occur as a result of general psychotherapy (see Wampold & Imel, 2015). Strong evidence suggests that those who seek help for couple, marital and family difficulties also experience change (Baldwin et al., 2012; Shadish & Baldwin, 2005). However, research has shed little empirical evidence on *how* change occurs because of the therapy process or on which factors are more important in change with specific client systems. CFT is an inherently personal and varied experience, and some therapeutic interventions may lead to differing responses in individuals and throughout the systems in which they live. Therapy never looks quite the same, especially in community practice, because so many factors change from client system to client system. This is especially true as cases become more complex, with more intense presenting problems. While treatment manuals lay out steps for therapy, they all arrive with one stipulation: *that the therapy steps are rarely followed rigidly in sequence*. It is almost always the case that these treatments are delivered through the unique style of the therapist and are matched or adapted to the unique client system that presents for therapy. In this sense, therapeutic change is a uniquely personal experience.

Developing Awareness of Your Assumptions About Change

Homeostasis, the gravitational pull that keeps couple and family systems frozen in a perpetual state of feeling "stuck", is something most clients (and systemic therapists) can relate to. What happens in good therapy to create meaningful change, however, is hard to explain to someone who has not yet experienced it. This change may feel even more powerful when spread across multiple people in a family system in conjoint or relational therapy. Although we strongly believe it is paramount for all CFTs to have a broad understanding of how change occurs in therapy, we also recognize that personal views on how systems "get stuck" and what and who ultimately causes clients to change may vary from therapist to therapist, depending on their clinical background and preferred theoretical orientation. Before we begin our journey into the CFT common factors, please answer the following questions that will help you reflect on your innate views on psychotherapeutic change.

1. How do people or systems become "stuck" or constrained by their problems?
2. How does the process of change occur?
3. How does change occur in systemic therapy? How is this change similar or different to change in individual therapy?
4. Who is responsible for change in systemic therapy?
5. What resources does it take for people or systems to change? What is helpful in this process?
6. What are some constraints to change?
7. How do you measure change in systemic therapy?

Change in human behaviors and conditions is not linear, and questions about the how of change are not simply answered. There are many reasons why people change and overcome difficult life circumstances. Change is mostly not connected to a singular therapy process even though it can be advanced by therapy when individuals choose to participate and are motivated to do the necessary work. Good therapy does not always lead to change, and even bad therapy can lead to positive changes for clients; that is, clients change despite the therapist. Change occurs throughout life and on different occasions. There are many considerations when it comes to change, but the truth is that we are all changing all the time. For example, development is change; we go through developmental processes throughout our lives, and these processes bring about change, some large and rapid, such as those occurring in adolescence, and some slower and more gradual, such as those that occur during the aging process. When individuals and families go through transitions, they change. For example, when a couple has a new child, many changes occur, especially changes in routines and roles. These transitions are often accompanied by high stress and take time before the couple gets to a new normal (usually different to how things once were).

These changes are not insignificant; so, when we think about change connected to psychotherapy, we should not divorce change ideas from changes that are occurring all the time in peoples' lives. Some positive change is simply developmental – things get better with time or things change over time. In other situations, change occurs outside of normative development. In these cases, change involves more, such as when something is done to, done by or occurs in the life of an individual. This may be an unexpected life event (both positive and negative) that leads someone to reflect anew on life and make needed changes. This could be something devastating like a cancer diagnosis or something positive such as a big job promotion. These types of events alter an individual's life and environment and almost always lead to changes of some kind. At times it may be the accumulation of small events that lead to a crisis and to a negative change trajectory; for example, work stress + knee surgery + the breakup of a dating relationship may together collectively leave an individual experiencing incredibly high levels of life stress and feelings of depression. In some cases, things get better with time as the knee heals, as work stress becomes more manageable or the individual becomes more organized and the individual grieves and accepts the loss of the relationship. In other cases, an individual may spiral down into a larger crisis, and change will require something more, such as would occur when someone visits a therapist who can help the client make sense of these three events on their own and collectively and their larger meaning in the individual's life context.

Not everyone arrives in the office of the therapist for the same reasons and in the same way, but often the presentation is precipitated by a crisis of some kind. Psychotherapy is often called upon as a resource when someone is stuck or in spiral or experiencing problems that are causing significant distress. These are times when an individual becomes trapped in a situation and is unable to change out of it for one reason or another. The reason an individual, couple or family comes to therapy may be highly relevant in dictating the process of change. This reason affects an individual's motivation for change and investment in the therapy process. For example, a family who presents in treatment because the adolescent is threatened with expulsion due to fighting in school is likely motivated to prevent the expulsion from occurring. In a different example, a couple who shows up because one of them is having an affair would have the motivation of averting the crisis, but each member of the couple may have different agendas in therapy. This complication of working with multiple members in therapy with competing agendas, a hallmark of family therapy, will be discussed in depth in this book.

If therapists view change as narrow and linear, it will affect everything in therapy. For example, if therapists believe in only one theory or explanation for a problem, the interventions implemented by the therapist may not meet the clinical change needs of the clients. However, if therapists are open to multitudes of possibilities for change, they will be less limited by their preconceived theories and more open to the idea that *change can occur in multiple ways*, an idea we strongly ascribe to. As a result, they will be looking out for opportunities to seize these change opportunities. A major premise of this book is that change is not linear, and change can occur in multiple directions with a wide array of outcomes, many of which are different to the initial goals of the clients.

There is nothing inherently "magical" about a therapist and what they do for clients. Changes can come from how the therapist makes a person think or feel or as a result of different behaviors arising out of the interactions. The truth is that this process is not always simple or quantifiable. In working with couples and families, change is even more complicated. This is due to a process in which multiple members (or at least two) are engaged in the same therapy experience at the same time, trying to change themselves and their interactions with each other. Changes in one individual unavoidably affect the others, and small changes can build on each other and lead to larger changes. This is at the heart of systems thinking, a core foundation for the CFT field. Some changes can lead to sudden and considerable stress in a system, challenges for which effective therapists can provide key support and help.

We are evidence-based practitioners, and common factors thinking is based upon some of the best evidence available. In this book, we want the readers to consider what we know about change and what the best available evidence suggests about the change process from the perspective of CFT. As discussed above, this is only a narrow part of change in the life of families. When clients show up in therapy, *we advocate for you to use the best evidence available to conduct your work* but to approach this use of evidence with *flexibility* depending on the clients and their context, as well as on feedback from the clients about the therapy process.

The APA Presidential Task Force on Evidence-Based Practice (2006) views evidence-based practice as "the integration of the best available research with clinical expertise in the context of patient characteristics, culture, and preferences" (p. 273). The common factors approach argues that much of what makes one treatment approach effective is common to other forms of effective treatment (Sprenkle & Blow, 2004a). All credible approaches (what Wampold, 2001, termed "bona fide approaches") have the potential to bring about change with clients. However, we need to consider what change approaches are best for specific clients, with specific presenting problems, in unique contexts. Our goal in this chapter is to provide you with a big-picture overview of change that results from CFT and the role of key therapy processes, with a focus on broad common factors of change. Chapter 3, a companion chapter, will focus on narrow elements of change in therapy.

Common Factors of Change

Over the last 30 to 40 years, a great deal of literature on therapy change has emerged, broadly referred to as the common factors of change. Michael Lambert came out with an influential estimate (his best guess) of how he thought about change in therapy from a broad common factors perspective (Lambert, 1992). He said that client factors and extratherapeutic events were responsible for up to 40% of change, that the therapeutic relationship was 30% responsible, that 15% of change was connected to the hope and expectancy generated in therapy and that only 15% of change could be ascribed to specific models and techniques used in therapy. These estimates, even though not statistically derived, heavily influenced thinking about therapy change (see Hubble et al., 1999). Bruce Wampold's book the *Great Psychotherapy Debate*, and its subsequent edition, took a different view of change (Wampold, 2001; Wampold & Imel, 2015) when it came to estimating important contributors to positive therapy outcomes. His work is statistically derived through meta-analyses of studies of psychotherapy. Wampold concluded that the total change variance that can be ascribed to therapy is around 14%. Wampold and Imel concluded:

> ... the average client receiving therapy would be better off than 79 percent of untreated clients, that psychotherapy accounts for about 14 percent of the variance in outcomes, and for every three patients receiving psychotherapy, one patient will have a better outcome than had they not received psychotherapy. (p. 94)

This conclusion suggests that therapy, for many, is efficacious. Meta-analyses of CFT suggest that treatments operating from a systemic perspective are similarly efficacious (Baldwin et al., 2012; Shadish & Baldwin, 2002, 2005). While therapy explains 14% of change variance, this also means that a large amount of change can be ascribed to *non-therapy factors*; that is, client/extratherapeutic/ contextual factors and other unexplained change factors account for up to 86% of change.

Wampold (2001) went on to break down the 14% of change ascribed to psychotherapy treatment. In breaking this down, he estimated that therapist effects range from 6% to 9%; the therapeutic alliance from 5% to 7%; expectancy, hope and allegiance up to 4%; and models/techniques only 1%. This analysis highlights the complexities of the therapy change process and the challenges in making conclusions. There is no doubt that this process is much more complicated when it comes to CFT and the multiple combinations of additional factors at work when therapists add additional individuals and systems into the therapy process (Wampold, 2001). So, while these estimates are of strong interest, *they should not be overinterpreted* in thinking about therapy change. All ingredients are important in their own way.

The literature points to different kinds of common factors (Sprenkle & Blow, 2004a), mainly according to two groupings. First are broad factors that are part of most kinds of therapy. These include client factors, therapist factors, the therapeutic alliance and hope and expectancy. The second are what can be termed *narrow common factors* or *common therapeutic effects* (see Chapter 3). The narrow view refers to nonspecific aspects of treatment models and therapeutic effects, such as creating changes in meaning, which are found in many models under different names (Sprenkle & Blow, 2004a). These include how clients view problems, feel about problems and behave in relation to problems. In addition, there are common factors attributable to the CFT field.

Broad Common Factors

Client Factors/Extratherapeutic Events

Clients bring a wide range of characteristics and experiences to the therapy room that always affect therapy. These can be positive, negative or both. These could be innate traits like determination or motivation or external factors such as the events occurring in a client's life context and circumstances. Someone living in poverty has many more challenges than someone raised and living in physical comfort. Some extratherapeutic events (discussed in detail in Chapter 6) occur by chance (e.g., winning the lottery, getting a cancer diagnosis), whereas other variables occur naturally in the life of some clients (e.g., social support). These variables are present in the life of the client whether they attend therapy or not. Even though they are independent of the treatment process, they influence treatment, and certainly therapists can make the most of these factors by using them for therapeutic leverage (see Chapter 6 for examples of leveraging client factors and contexts). Wampold and Imel (2015) ascribed 86% of change to non-therapy factors, a sizeable amount.

Therapeutic Alliance Factors

The therapeutic alliance is a critical component of all therapy. In CFT, alliance formation and maintenance are complex and entail a therapist forming multiple alliances and balancing these alliances in a way that allows therapy to progress in a positive direction (discussed in detail in Chapter 9). The alliance establishes the space in which the work of therapy can occur. Bordin's (1979) theory of the alliance includes three key components: *the bonds* that exist between the therapist and clients, *the goals* that the therapist and clients agree on for therapy and the *comfort between therapist and clients on the tasks/activities* that are used in therapy to achieve therapeutic goals. The alliance, when working with couples and families, includes other components, because the therapist needs to have an alliance with each member of the family in terms of the bonds, goals and tasks. In addition, the alliance in family therapy includes components such as safety, shared sense of purpose and engagement in therapy (Friedlander et al., 2006). Finally, therapists who are effective are able to closely monitor and repair this alliance when things go awry in therapy. The alliance is the vehicle through which clients engage in the therapy process. Wampold and Imel ascribe 5% to 8% of change to alliance factors.

Models/Techniques

Every therapist has training in specific models and techniques (choosing a model is discussed in detail in Chapter 5). These are theories or maps that guide therapists in treatment. There are many different models that guide CFT practice, and the majority of these, especially the newer models, are excellent, supported by evidence and practical. We use several of these models in our own work. Models/techniques can be considered to be strategies, activities or rituals that help clients to heal. However, the research on the importance of models and techniques suggests that only about 1% of change in therapy can be attributed to these specific models and their related techniques (Wampold, 2001). This is not to say that they are not important, as common factors are operationalized through a therapy model or theoretical approach (Frank & Frank, 1991; Sprenkle & Blow, 2004b; Wampold, 2001). It should also be noted that head-to-head studies of bona fide treatments suggest that these treatment approaches are about equally effective (Sprenkle & Blow, 2004a; Wampold & Imel, 2015).

Expectancy, Placebo and Allegiance

Going to therapy is not easy for most people. It is anxiety provoking, to say the least, to go to a therapist whom one does not know very well and then to take risks in sharing personal life problems. However, the very act of going to a therapist brings about an expectancy effect that suggests to the client that things are possibly going to get better (discussed in detail in Chapter 7). Therapists also do things that make clients feel more hopeful, such as encouraging them or reassuring them. When clients feel more hopeful, or believe that therapy will help, they are likely to be more motivated to work on their life situations and change. Wampold and Imel (2015) ascribed about 4% of change to these factors.

Therapist Effects

Who the therapist is has been shown to be more important than the model or technique delivered by the therapist (Blow et al., 2007). The therapist is a crucial component of any therapy (discussed in detail in Chapter 8). In working with couples and families (often difficult cases), the person of the therapist is crucial, and it takes great skill in managing the multiple personalities and data points that arise in this kind of therapy (Blow & Karam, 2017). There is evidence showing that some therapists are more effective than are others. These effective therapists form better therapeutic relationships with clients (Blow & Karam, 2017), process therapy moments more effectively and achieve better outcomes. These therapists seem to be more competent regardless of their gender, age, training background, license type or experience. Wampold and Imel (2015) ascribed 4% to 9% of change to these therapist factors.

Common Factors Unique to CFT

The CFT field has factors that are unique to systemic therapies (discussed in detail in Chapter 4). These were first described in Sprenkle et al. (1999). These factors include conceptualizing difficulties in relational terms, expanding the therapeutic alliance, expanding the direct treatment system and interrupting sequences/patterns of behavior. The idea of relational conceptualization is possibly the most foundational CFT concept as CFTs attempt to keep the whole system (or systems) in view, regardless of the number of people present in the therapy room or the presenting problem.

Conclusion

In this chapter, we introduce the reader to broad common factors of change, each of which has an entire chapter devoted to it in this book. These factors transcend therapy models and are used to some extent by all therapists. They are ingredients of change that require mastery by all therapists and just becoming expert in each of these factors will significantly enhance treatment outcomes. As we point out in this chapter and throughout this book, these factors are operationalized differently when it comes to working with couples and families. The introduction of more members into the therapy process adds additional layers of complexity that present challenges for CFTs. Dealing with these complexities will be described in detail in chapters to follow.

References

APA Presidential Task Force on Evidence-Based Practice. (2006). Evidence-based practice in psychology. *American Psychologist, 61*, 271–285.

Baldwin, S., Christian, S., Berkeljon, A., & Shadish, W. (2012). The effects of family therapies for adolescent delinquency and substance abuse: A meta-analysis. *Journal of Marital and Family Therapy, 38*(1), 281–304. https://doi.org/10.1111/j.1752-0606.2011.00248.x

Blow, A., & Karam, E. (2017). The therapist's role in effective marriage and family therapy practice: The case for evidence based therapists. *Administration and Policy in Mental*

Health and Mental Health Services Research, 44(5), 716–723. https://doi.org/10.1007/s104 88-016-0768-8

Blow, A. J., Sprenkle, D. H., & Davis, S. D. (2007). Is who delivers the treatment more important than the treatment itself? The role of the therapist in common factors. *Journal of Marital and Family Therapy, 33,* 298–318.

Bordin, E. (1979). The generalizability of the psychoanalytic concept of the working alliance. *Psychotherapy, 16,* 252–260.

Frank, J. D., & Frank, J. B. (1991). *Persuasion and healing: A comparative study of psychotherapy* (3rd ed.). John Hopkins University Press.

Friedlander, M., Escudero, V., & Heatherington, L. (2006). *Therapeutic alliances in couple and family therapy: An empirically informed guide to practice.* American Psychological Association.

Hubble, M., Duncan, B., & Miller, S. (Eds.). (1999). *The heart and soul of change.* American Psychological Association.

Lambert, M. (1992). Psychotherapy outcome research: Implications for integrative and eclectic therapists. In J. Norcross & M. Goldfried (Eds.), *Handbook of psychotherapy integration* (pp. 94–129). Basic.

Shadish, W., & Baldwin, S. (2002). Meta-analysis of MFT interventions. In D. Sprenkle (Ed.), *Effectiveness research in marriage and family therapy.* American Association for Marriage and Family Therapy.

Shadish, W., & Baldwin, S. (2005). Effects of behavioral marital therapy: A meta-analysis of randomized controlled trials. *Journal of Consulting and Clinical Psychology, 73,* 6–14.

Sprenkle, D., & Blow, A. (2004a). Common factors and our sacred models. *Journal of Marital and Family Therapy, 30,* 113–129.

Sprenkle, D., & Blow, A. (2004b). Common factors are not islands—They work through models: A response to Sexton, Ridley, and Kleiner. *Journal of Marital and Family Therapy, 30,* 151–158.

Sprenkle, D., Blow, A., & Dickey, M. (1999). Common factors and other nontechnique variables in marriage and family therapy. In M. Hubble, B. Duncan, & S. Miller (Eds.), *The heart and soul of change: What works in therapy* (pp. 329–360). American Psychological Association.

Wampold, B. (2001). *The great psychotherapy debate.* Lawrence Erlbaum.

Wampold, B., & Imel, Z. (2015). *The great psychotherapy debate: The evidence for what makes psychotherapy work* (2nd ed.). Routledge.

3

HOW CHANGE OCCURS PART 2

Narrow Common Factors, aka Common Therapeutic Effects

In addition to broad common factors of change discussed in Chapter 2, there is a group of factors that are more narrow and used in different ways, depending on the approach to working with clients but that achieve the same effects in therapy. These narrow factors will be referred to as *therapeutic effects*; they are outcomes that cut across models, although each model uses different change strategies or change mechanisms to achieve these outcomes. These three broad effects include (1) changing the thinking (shifts in attributions, meanings and views of the problem or situation), (2) changing the doing (shifts in behaviors that lead to shifts in problems) and (3) changing the experience (related to shifts in emotions or in experiencing of the problem, relationship or situation; see Sprenkle & Blow, 2004, for a discussion).

What Are Therapeutic Effects?

Therapeutic effects refers to both large and small outcomes in therapy that move the client(s) in the direction of their desired optimal goal. While the overall goal of therapy can be a large therapeutic effect, smaller steps toward the overall goal can also be thought of as therapeutic effects in their own right. Sprenkle and Blow (2004, p. 120) cited an exercise example used by Tallman and Bohart (1999) to describe this process:

> Many people go to health clubs to achieve the goal of cardiovascular fitness (think, good psychotherapeutic effects). The health club offers them a variety of pieces of equipment to achieve this end—elliptical trainers, treadmills, stationary bicycles, and stair-stepper machines (think, therapy models). If the goal of cardiovascular fitness is successful, it matters considerably more that the health club clients motivate themselves to get out of bed, get to the club, use the machines, and stick with the program, than it matters which particular machine they choose to achieve the goal. However, this does not mean that the machines are not helping achieve cardiovascular fitness. It is important to remember that there are many

DOI: 10.4324/9781315542737-3

pathways to cardiovascular health, just as there are many therapy models that can be used to achieve desired therapeutic effects.

In the above illustration, motivation, showing up at the club, choosing a machine and developing a program are all important outcomes that need to exist to some extent in an individual who has the ultimate goal of cardiovascular fitness. Consider the example in the text box that illustrates this process.

> **Case Example 1**
>
> An individual goes to see her doctor, and the doctor tells the individual that she needs to exercise physically in order to prevent heart disease. The woman decides that she is going to join an athletic club that offers a wide range of fitness options. These include swimming, a track, a weight room, a room with a number of different exercise machines, aerobic classes and recreational sports such as tennis and racquetball. Her goal at the athletic club is to achieve physical fitness. There are a number of options available to help this individual obtain her goal of physical fitness (heart health). There would be some criteria (structural) that she would have to meet. For example, she would need to attend the athletic club on a regular basis. She could not just go once a year. She would also need to pick activities that increased her heart rate to a point where the exercise was helpful. She would also need to sustain this activity for a period of time during which her attendance provided her with sufficient exposure to the athletic club benefits; for example, she could go to the club four times a week and participate in an aerobic activity each time. The optimal aerobic activity may need to be decided on through a process of trial and error considering her preferred exercise and the exercise that realized the best health benefits. There are many combinations of activity available to her to help her achieve her goals. The key health benefit is obtained through regular exercise that increases her heart rate sufficiently.

Similarly, in therapy, the ultimate goal of clients (often a mental or family health focus) has many smaller effects that occur along the way that help clients realize their larger and ultimate goal(s). Similar to the cardiovascular illustration (see text box), there are many therapy models, strategies and change principles that can lead to the desired therapeutic effects, and these will vary according to the presenting problem and the unique characteristics of the client including culture, learning style and comfort with emotions, to name a few. While effects may be common for all clients (e.g., changing their views of a problem or parts of a problem), the optimal therapeutic strategy used to achieve these effects differs from client to client, family to family, and according to preferred ways of working and comfort of the therapist. However, when a therapist has a clear idea of a desired effect, they would ideally choose to utilize a strategy (pathway) to achieve this effect that they are comfortable using *and* that fits the client's preferred way of learning/experiencing in therapy. It is unlikely that one step on one pathway will lead to the ultimate desired goals; rather, the small steps (outcomes) along the way are additive and together build change momentum.

Another way we think about effects is in terms of how an individual learns new material in an educational context. It is well documented in education that there are unique learning styles that vary among individuals. The desired outcomes in education are that a student achieves comprehension of a body of knowledge and that they are able to use this knowledge in applied ways in their field of labor. How students best gain this comprehension may vary and depend on the individual student; their preferred learning methods may include one or more of the following: didactic lectures, role plays, observation of videos, small-group activities or online group interaction, to name a few. All of these instructional methods are different strategies used to help individuals achieve mastery of a topic. While not always feasible in an educational setting, ideally instructors should match their teaching methods to the preferred learning styles of students. While this does not always occur, many students are still able to learn material when the method used is not their most preferred. We can all identify with enduring a long, boring, dry lecture. While we may not all prefer this style, we all have learned from this method, but it may not be the *best* way that we learn. It also may not be the best way to keep us engaged with the material or motivated to learn. Further, it is unlikely that students learn all of the material in one class period or by reading one article. It usually takes several classes, much reading, practical application and other learning methods for students to master a topic. The goal of learning is to grasp a concept or subject (the desired effect). For some students, such as those with learning disabilities or attention problems, special provisions may need to be made. Knowledge acquisition is also a process, with one piece of knowledge learned serving as a foundation for future knowledge. There are also contexts that allow for more optimal learning (e.g., high-cost private schools versus a school situated in an impoverished developing country) and instructors who are able to inspire students in different ways.

Therapy is no different. There are broad structural goals that individuals set out to achieve, but there are large and small effects that help these individuals in their change trajectories. Some interventions may help achieve some outcomes but others are needed, such as in the case of a student who learns some materials in a lecture but who learns other material by meeting one-on-one with the instructor. For example, in couple therapy, there are many ways to achieve the desired goal of relationship happiness (a construct that is highly individualized to each couple). For some it may entail creating more of an emotional connection, whereas for others it may entail more talking, and for others, more physical intimacy. One effect most couple therapists try to achieve is to have a couple lower their "walls" and be more vulnerable with each other. In emotionally focused couple therapy (Johnson, 2004), this is called a *softening*. Softenings can be big (like a relationship breakthrough that changes how the couple functions) or minor (a small risk with one's partner). There are many ways to achieve softenings in relationships, and they often occur naturally in the course of a relationship without any kind of intervention from a therapist. They can occur through shifts in the couple's *thinking*, and they can also occur through shifting how each member of the couple experiences their partner by having each share more of how they are feeling about aspects of their relationship.

We will describe below three major effects in therapy – changing the viewing, changing the feeling (experiencing) and changing the doing. However, there are many smaller effects that lead to these larger effects, and, in reality, therapeutic effects often encompass all three. There are strategies or change mechanisms that lead to these effects. Case 2 in the text box provides an illustration on how changing the feeling (experiencing) and changing the viewing (meaning) in a couple relationship can shift relationship dynamics.

Case Example 2

A couple is caught up in a rigid cycle of interaction. Both parties in the relationship are well defended and the level of connection is low. The therapist reframes this interaction, using attachment language, as one in which each is afraid to "let the other in" because they might end up hurt (e.g., their partner would not respond in a caring way) and so they do not take risks with each other. The new frame (way of seeing the problem) is not only more palatable but may allow each member of the couple to lower their defenses with each other. Lowering of these defenses allows the couple to feel more connected to each other (a new emotional experience), first in small ways and then in larger ways over time. These new experiences of the relationship, even though small, may lead the couple to do

> new things for each other; for example, go on a walk together (change of behaviors). In this regard, small softenings in the relationship, accompanied by shifts in viewing their problem, are important effects that connect to a larger mechanism of change for them. This shifts how each partner views the other and their own role in the relationship. Over the course of several sessions, the therapist does several more of these reframes. This has the effect of shifting how the couple comes to view and understand each other. As a result, they begin to take more risks with each other. Suddenly, they are sharing more feelings with each other. Over time, these sharings grow and are deeper and more intimate. The couples' views of each other shifts and their experiences of each other change, and they now feel more connected to each other. This change trajectory is made up of small changes in viewing each other and their problem and in experiencing each other in their relationship.

We propose that to maximize the effectiveness of therapy, therapists ideally work to target key effects that lead to ultimate change and that the pathways/strategies used to reach the outcomes are the ones that best fit the unique client(s). Therapists use strategies they are most comfortable in delivering and that the clients feel comfortable trying. These strategies are modified based on honest feedback from clients (see Chapter 10). In this regard, the therapist should be persistent and open to new ideas, because it is likely that first attempts will fail. There are several core therapeutic effects (key ones are described below) and hundreds of strategies to achieve these effects. If therapy is to be ultimately successful, it needs to achieve a series of proximal outcomes that are repeated over time and that become somewhat stable (e.g., clients develop and stabilize new patterns and sequences of relating to and interacting with each other).

Different Kinds of Therapeutic Effects

Therapeutic effects are *desired outcomes*, which entail both proximal (intermediate) and distal (ultimate) outcomes. Distal outcomes point to larger outcomes in therapy, whereas proximal outcomes are smaller effects that take place within a client system that added together bring about distal outcomes (Blow & Distelberg, 2006). Not all therapeutic effects are equal. The ultimate effect of therapy (change as defined by the client or some stakeholder in the therapy process) is not the same as smaller effects along the way. As a result, we conceptualize some therapeutic effects as distal (ultimate) outcomes and others as proximal (close or intermediate) outcomes.

Distal Outcomes

Most of our thinking about change in therapy focuses on distal outcomes, and these are usually the focus of research studies. First sessions usually focus on the ultimate goals of therapy and how to achieve these goals. Research studies seek out outcomes that measure some large change variable; for example, the couple is satisfied in their relationship, the couple did not divorce, the adolescent did not get expelled or the addict stopped using and did not relapse. However, these are not the only relevant outcomes, and, as we argue, these distal outcomes are likely the cumulative effects of smaller proximal outcomes that are realized throughout the therapy process (Blow & Distelberg, 2006).

Proximal Outcomes

These are smaller outcomes that occur throughout therapy and that keep the change process moving in a productive direction and collectively achieve change momentum. For example, early on in therapy with a family, an initial outcome that the therapist works to achieve is client engagement in therapy. This engagement consists of clients showing up for therapy sessions, buying in to therapy (and trusting the therapist) as a means to help them with their problems and having some level of motivation to work to change. The ideas of clients showing up for sessions, client buy-in, the therapist's influence and client motivation can all be conceptualized as smaller effects (outcomes) that together lead to a larger proximal outcome of engagement in therapy (Blow & Distelberg, 2006).

Pathways

Important to the idea of proximal and distal therapeutic outcomes are pathways. *Pathways* refers to the strategies that a therapist and client can use together to achieve desired therapeutic effects. *The question is not what the best strategy is for all situations but rather what the best strategy (pathway) is to achieve a specific outcome (both proximal and distal) with a specific client system, in such a way that it has a sustained influence on the client system.* A good example of this can be found in Pinsof's (1995) *Integrative Problem Centered Therapy*. In this approach, the therapist works with the client system to rigorously define the problem and the system constraints that maintain the problem; the therapist and client system then proceed to come up with a number of different ways (hypotheses) to solve the problem. Essentially, his approach maps out the desired effect in collaboration between the therapist and client system early in treatment and then systematically tries to achieve the effect using credible therapeutic strategies.

We conceptualize these systematic strategies as pathways to desired effects (ideally agreed on between the therapist and client). If these are not agreed upon, the therapist may need to convince the clients to give it a try or patiently wait until an optimal point in therapy when the pathway can be implemented (e.g., when the clients are more ready to accept the intervention).

In another example, we take the case of evidence-based medicine where practitioners are encouraged to come up with one question that effectively describes a way to achieve a desired outcome. The therapist can then move to determine the best pathway to achieve this outcome (Patterson et al., 2004). Patterson and colleagues (2004) advocated for the use of evidence-based medicine in couple and family therapy (CFT) training practices. They defined evidence-based medicine as an approach that combines results from empirical studies, clinical wisdom and client preferences that results in optimal care for clients. The core of evidence-based medicine is the question (or desired effect) the practitioner comes up with in relationship to the problem. The question that all CFTs should be trained to ask and answer is "What are the treatment effects necessary to help this client resolve their specific presenting problem?" This is similar to the hypothesizing suggested in multisystemic therapy, in which therapists hypothesize about the best strategies to meet the short- and long-term therapy goals (Blow & Distelberg, 2006).

Patterson et al. (2004) proposed five steps that are useful in guiding evidence-based clinical work: (a) converting information into an answerable question, (b) finding the best evidence to answer the question, (c) critically examining the research, (d) integrating the evidence with clinical expertise/experience and clients' uniqueness and (e) evaluation of the effectiveness of the intervention. Therapists can ask "What are the proximal and distal treatment effects that need to occur in order to help this client resolve the presenting problem?" A follow-up question could be "What pathways do I as the therapist need to take (in consultation with the client) in order to help this client achieve this effect?" Therapy (if it is to be ultimately successful) needs to achieve a series of proximal outcomes that build on previous outcomes and that lead to the ultimate outcome of therapy. The fit of this pathway with clients is important, as Lebow and Jenkins (2018) concluded: "A client is apt to be more willing to take the kinds of risks that therapy demands if the path toward change is in tune with his or her character" (p. 61).

How They Work Together

While we describe the process of effects and strategies to achieve these effects in a somewhat cookbook fashion, it is never that systematic; rather, these processes work in essentially a series of iterations. In essence, change is cyclical. At the end of their paper arguing for a common factors position in CFT, Sprenkle and Blow (2004, p. 126) stated:

> ... we think that a common factors lens will force us to think more about *therapeutic effects* than therapeutic strategies or techniques. Therapeutic effects are what take place in a therapeutic system that leads to a positive outcome. For example, if looking at one's problems in new way ... is a therapeutic effect, there are probably hundreds of ways to achieve the same effect—including reframing, positive connotation, prescribing of the symptom, externalizing the problem, rewriting one's life story, and so on. Indeed, the emphasis on strategies and techniques as opposed to effects has probably led to the proliferation of therapy models and the mistaken assumption that specific models, strategies, and techniques are primarily responsible for therapeutic change.

We know very little about a sequence of therapeutic effects that lead to desired change in CFT. It is conceivable that therapists achieve a sequence of effects that could feasibly lead to negative changes for a client. This might be especially true when working with couples or families. For example, a couple comes into therapy because one partner (Mary) is thinking about leaving the relationship but the other (Jared) is invested in staying. The therapist herself is going through ambivalence in her own relationship. When Mary talks about her unhappiness, the therapist validates her feelings and inadvertently implies that a non-married life is not that bad and that sometimes as people grow, they change, and their relationship no longer works for them. When Jared talks about his concerns of ending the marriage and his concerns about their children, the therapist reframes his concerns as "fears of the unknown" and says that children can thrive despite divorce. This brief example illustrates how the therapist quickly shifts the views and feelings about divorce, making this more of a realistic possibility for both. These small effects (shifts in thinking) with both parties can create more momentum towards the proximal outcome of divorce. In contrast, the effects can work in the opposite direction with different interventions by the same or a different therapist.

Another example of an effect is the change in meaning of a problem in the life of a family. CFT has multiple techniques that allow meanings to shift – reframing, positive connotation, prescribing the symptom, externalization of the problem, rewriting a story, validation of a client's experience and others – that all allow for a shift in the meaning of a problem. There is not one correct way to shift meanings; rather, it is only important that meanings are shifted in a way that lead to more substantive changes. Many families are unable to see the way out of their situations. Shifts in meaning not only serve to change how they view their problems but also empower clients, reduce negativity and open up space for new directions in which to change. Consider the effect that many approaches achieve when they change how individuals think about their specific problem or situation. Examples of this occur by means of the miracle question in solution therapies, the challenge to cognitive distortions in cognitive therapies and the focus on unique outcomes in narrative therapies.

Another example in CFT of a common effect is differentiation of self (Bowen, 1978). Differentiation of self is an outcome that is said to occur when an individual is able to separate intellectual thought processes from emotional reactivity. Numerous techniques and models allow this effect to occur. Bowen (1978) promoted the idea of sending clients on a family of origin journey and used genograms to facilitate this process. Schwartz (1995) saw this as occurring when the self of the client emerges through the separation of extreme parts, and dialectical behavior therapy (Linehan, 1993) achieves this by helping clients have a new relationship with their emotions.

We believe that when we talk about model and techniques, we need to emphasize the effects far more than the strategies, in that there are many effective ways in which to achieve the exact same effect. We also believe that it is the emphasis on strategies as opposed to effects that has contributed to the proliferation of models. In Figure 3.1, we visually depict the main effects that a therapist is attempting to achieve along with smaller pathways to these effects. This is not a comprehensive list but rather an example of how these processes/mechanisms are reflected in therapy. For example, we believe that an important outcome in couple therapy is that each party is able to take personal responsibility for their role in the cycle. While there are times when one party is "more guilty" than the other in causing relationship problems— for example, in the case of infidelity or interpersonal violence – in general, for shifts to occur in couple's work, each party needs to take a measure of responsibility for the problems. This is a major effect we are trying to realize in working with couples and is likely a characteristic of all couples work. It may start with small acceptances of responsibility and then grow into larger steps with time. There are mini steps leading to this larger outcome, and the larger effect is developed by smaller steps along the way. The acceptance of personal responsibility may occur through many strategies including if the therapist challenges the client, if the clients are able to process communication in the here and now, through using reflective listening and "I" messages, or if the therapist interrupts negative cycles of blaming. These may look different depending on the couple and their presenting issue, but if a therapist keeps in mind that they are trying to achieve this effect, then they can be considering ways in which to achieve this end. Therapists should consider the best effects for each presenting problem and unique client configuration. Then the therapist can ask questions like, "What are the best

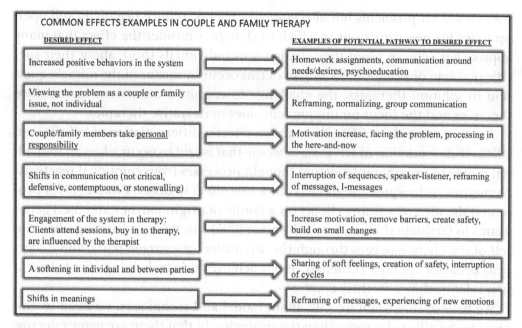

Figure 3.1 **Common effects examples in couple and family therapy.**

pathways to each effect?" "Which pathways are best for this particular client?" "What cultural or contextual factors stand in the way of this particular client system?" "What specific steps does one need to take to get there?" "Are we making progress toward this effect and, if not, what needs to occur?"

Major Effects

In working with couples and families, change becomes complicated as effects manifest differently in each individual. When multiple family members, or at least two members, are engaged in the same therapy process at the same time, changes in one individual unavoidably affect the others, and small changes can build on each other and lead to larger changes. Therapeutic effects can quickly multiply as they impact everyone in the family. In general, as stated earlier, there are three primary therapeutic effects and many pathways to achieve these effects.

Key Therapeutic Effect: Changing the Viewing

Couples and families need to change how they *view* the problem. This is a key common factor/common effect/family therapy principle, and it can be operationalized as follows:

> *If a member of a couple or family can have a new way of thinking about the problem that brought them to therapy and the relation of that problem to their couple/*

family, this will change the way in which they engage in therapy and in which they talk to each other about their problems. This process alone will lead to changes in the system.

A great deal of CFT is built on the idea that problems exist because individuals come to view problems through the wrong lens. This leads to incorrect attributions ascribed to a family member and to spiraling interactions that constrain all in the family. In a conflictual marital relationship, a spouse may view the other spouse as controlling. This is a highly negative view of a partner and is not the ideal way to live out a relationship. There are different ways of thinking about these behaviors, and shifting this view can shift their dynamic. Through an attachment lens, they can be viewed as "fears" that a spouse would leave the relationship for someone else. Through a poverty lens, they can be viewed as concerns about going back to having nothing. And through an intergenerational lens, they can be viewed as differences in family of origin experiences. All of these explanations could be accurate and valid from a certain point of view. Merely looking at these interactions from a different point of view shifts the meaning of the problem and creates space for the couple to dialogue about it in fresh ways.

In another example, when working with an acting-out adolescent in a family context, members usually have different ways of viewing the problem. The adolescent could be thought of as a "bad egg" or a "rebel" or as someone "trying to tear the family apart". This is a label that sets up instant polarization within the family as individuals work to change or fix the problem child. The parents can be viewed as "out of touch", "controlling" or "mean spirited". Like the example about couples, all effective family therapy approaches operate from the principle that members of the family need to come up with a different view of the problem. There may be many ways in which this principle could be realized. One common approach to changing the views of problems in families is through the technique of reframing (Sexton & Alexander, 2003), which will be expounded upon below.

The effect of changing the viewing involves shifts in cognitions and, related, in how an individual comes to view their own self, family members, problems, and life situations. Essentially this shifts the meaning an individual ascribes to the difficult life position and leads to new realizations and ways in which the individual views life. Changing the way that clients see their problems and their situation is a way to change the meaning that the problem has in their lives. This occurs when therapists facilitate clients gaining insight (understanding, new meaning) about interactional processes within themselves and the family, between the family and other systems and across generations (Wampler, 1997). In CFT there are key outcomes that are important in changing the viewing, and here we discuss five critical outcomes (a shared view of the problem, engagement in treatment, changes in meaning, building of safety, and creation of a shared sense of purpose) and three key strategies to achieve these outcomes (reframing, psychoeducation, circular questions).

CHANGING THE VIEWING: A SHARED VIEW OF THE PROBLEM

All CFT approaches work to change how the members of the system view the problem they are dealing with in their lives. Differing theories propose varying ways in which a system shifts how it views problems, their cause and their meaning. This entails coming up with a view of the problem that is less pathologizing and that is situated within the larger family, community and cultural context. For example, in working with troubled adolescents, a key goal is to not pathologize the adolescent for his or her behaviors and through this process, making things worse by creating resistance and defensiveness. Rather, the goal is to shift the explanation of the problem and the means of its resolution to the family/system level. This means that the family members share responsibility in the problem's existence as well as in solving the problem. For example, in working with couples, when blame is focused on blaming one individual in the relationship, a therapeutic imbalance results, setting up a foundation for defensiveness and resistance. As a result, in couples work, a key outcome early on is to help couples to share blame and responsibility for the situation in which they find themselves and to come to see the problem as a part of their dance. Even in situations where one member of a couple is guilty of hurting the relationship badly, such as in the case of infidelity, the therapist is still focused on seeing the resolution to the problem as a joint endeavor. In emotionally focused therapy (EFT), therapists are focused on helping the couple to focus on the dance of the relationship and each member's role in the dance, rather than focusing on one member specifically (Johnson, 2004). Sexton and Alexander (2002, p. 125), proponents of the well-studied functional family therapy, described this well:

> In the engagement and motivation phase, a family-focused problem definition can be constructed through the conversation of therapy. A family-focused problem definition is one in which everyone in the family has some responsibility and thus, some part in the problem. However, no family member bears the blame for the state of affairs in the family. The difficult goal is the reduction of blame while each one retains a sense of responsibility for his or her own actions.

CHANGING THE VIEWING: ENGAGEMENT IN TREATMENT

Many approaches to family therapy overtly and explicitly focus on engagement in treatment early on. While engagement can be conceptualized through a behavioral lens, it is also an attributional construct, meaning that clients sign on as willing participants in a therapeutic process, they are motivated to attend treatment sessions, they see therapy as a means to help them with their problems and they trust the therapist to help them with their problems. Engagement is a sign that clients have changed how they think about therapy and are ready to work. It is more than just showing up. For example, the first treatment phase in functional family therapy (Sexton & Alexander, 2003) is engagement/motivation. Clients are engaged through this model when negativity between family members is lessened. This can occur when clients blame each other less for their problems, for example. This also occurs when clients see their problems as something belonging to the whole family as opposed to just one member. Engagement also occurs when clients are comfortable in terms of the therapeutic alliance, which means that they feel connected to the therapist, they are comfortable with the tasks of therapy and they agree on the goals set for therapy.

Therapists may question whether or not clients are engaged in treatment. One way is to simply ask them using both formal and informal feedback mechanisms. Engagement has truly occurred when all clients in the system sign on as willing participants in a therapeutic process and are ready to work together on the issue that brought them into therapy. This means that family members come to view themselves as a part of both the problem and its solution. It occurs when family members, especially resistant family members, are open to the influence of the therapist. In order to achieve engagement, the therapist needs to work to change the family members' perceptions of the process of therapy. In this way, the therapist uses self to help clients relax and come to see therapy as a resource for change. Many contextual factors can help, and the therapist may use professionalism, humor, dress, office setting, empathy and many other "use of self" strategies to win the trust of clients. A key effect the therapist is seeking in engagement is that the clients trust the therapist and view the therapy process as a means to help them with the situation they are facing. The clients are motivated to attend therapy, and when they show up, they are willing to work.

Friedlander et al. (2006) defined *engagement* as the client *viewing treatment as meaningful*; that is, a sense of being involved in therapy and working together with the therapist, that therapeutic goals and tasks in therapy can be discussed and negotiated with the therapist, that taking the process seriously is important and that change is possible. We will discuss some alliance-building strategies that engage families in later chapters, but it is important for therapists to have some of the following ingredients in the therapy:

1. Create a collaborative partnership that involves clients in all facets of therapy (Bertolino, 2010). Facilitate conversations in which clients' ideas and perspectives can be expressed, heard and understood.

2. Communicate acceptance of their values and perspectives through language and interaction.
3. Engage clients in the development of goals and ways of achieving those goals.
4. Utilize continuous feedback mechanisms to learn and incorporate clients' experiences of therapeutic processes.

CHANGING THE VIEWING: CHANGING MEANING

Another key task in changing the viewing of problems and their context is achieved through changes in meaning or attributions about therapy and about their problems. Change in meaning occurs in successful therapy and is a key desired effect in many therapies. This occurs when therapists facilitate clients gaining insight (understanding, new meaning) about interactional processes within themselves and the family, between the family and other systems and across generations (Wampler, 1997). Cognitive changes occur when the therapist provides explanations for problems, gives a rationale or hypothesis as to what might be going on, offers interpretations and provides information. It may also involve shifts in hopefulness and seeing obstacles in the future as surmountable. By providing information and offering insight, reframes, interpretations, explanations or rationales (pathways), meanings slowly begin to shift for clients. If we can change the meaning of an event or experience, we can also help the client to change the way they feel about the event and the behaviors that go along with this.

CHANGING THE VIEWING: SAFETY IN THERAPY

Safety is a key variable in CFT. While it can be conceptualized as a feeling (and it is a feeling; e.g., "I feel safe with my therapist"), it is also a cognitive construct (e.g., "I believe therapy is a safe place and that my therapist has my best interests at heart"). Invariably, clients come to therapy feeling stirred up or activated by the prospect of being in therapy. Through a variety of explanations and alliance-building strategies, clients begin to relax and believe that therapy is a place where they can work on their problems and achieve their therapeutic goals. The therapist will say things to clients that reassure them and put them at ease. Sometimes the therapist may explain the process of therapy or provide a rationale for activities of therapy. These types of explanations shift how clients feel about the therapy process. When clients believe that they are safe in therapy, they are more relaxed and are more willing to be open in their self-disclosures and more willing to take risks to achieve their goals. This is a key goal of family therapy. In their work on this topic, Friedlander and colleagues (2008) described safety in therapy as follows:

Although safety is necessary in all treatment, in conjoint therapy safety is also affected by how vulnerable a client feels with other family members. Clients who are comfortable in this context may express painful feelings, ask each other for direct feedback, reveal secrets, or encourage others to speak frankly, assuming that family conflict can be exposed without lasting harm. Clients who feel threatened may show their anxiety, anger, or defensiveness by avoiding interaction with other family members, shutting down, or threatening to leave the room. (p. 76)

Friedlander et al. (2006) defined *safety* as

... the client viewing therapy as a place to take risks, be open, flexible; a sense of comfort and an expectation that new experiences and learning will take place, that good can come from being in therapy, that conflict within the family can be handled without harm, that one need not be defensive. (p. 216)

Safety means that an individual can authentically explore issues in an open and nonjudgmental way. While safety is important in any kind of therapy, the importance is multiplied when we add family members to the process and ask them to be vulnerable with each other. The need for safety within the therapeutic environment is a unique and critical element of family therapy. Safety is not always easy to achieve, especially when family members come to therapy with a history of fighting, hurt feelings and negativity. In this sense, creating safety can be a daunting task for the therapist because the family has conflicting perceptions of the problem, raw emotions and differing motives for therapy. While these will be discussed in detail in a later chapter, there are alliance-building strategies that help promote safety (adapted from Bertolino et al., 2010).

1. Give family members a clear explanation of all aspects of the treatment context that relate to confidentiality.
2. Encourage family members to talk about aspects of the therapy that may intimidate them.
3. Address any signs of discomfort in the moment (e.g., "How do you feel about coming to therapy today?").
4. Accommodate therapy to the family's sociocultural or religious values.
5. Normalize fear and anxiety.
6. Remove blame and judgment in the family.
7. Reframe problems in systemic terms (i.e., problems belong to all).

8. Interrupt negative sequences of toxic interactions and, through this, provide family members with a new experience of their relationships with each other.
9. Connect to unique family culture (no assumptions).
10. Control the intensity and pace at which emotionally difficult material is discussed.
11. Contain, control and convert conflict into something constructive.

CHANGING THE VIEWING: CREATION OF A SHARED SENSE OF PURPOSE

The fifth important view that family members need to succeed in therapy is a shared view of where they are going, both in therapy and as a family outside of therapy. A shared sense of purpose is a key construct used in Friedlander and colleagues' (2006) depictions of the therapeutic alliance. This depiction suggests that when more than one family member is in the room, these members need to be mostly agreed on the purpose and focus of therapy. This is similar to the goals dimension of the therapeutic alliance. It is integrally related to the view that clients have of therapy and of their family. Friedlander et al. defined a shared sense of purpose as

> family members seeing themselves as working collaboratively to improve family relations and achieve common family goals; a sense of solidarity in relation to the therapy (we're in this together); that they value their time with each other in therapy; essentially, a felt unity within the family in relation to the therapy. (p. 126)

We propose that just the act of getting family members on the same page about their joint purpose may in and of itself be sufficient to bring about lasting change. For example, if a family comes in to therapy because an adolescent wants more freedom in the form of no curfew, a therapist may achieve resolution of this issue by getting family members to agree on a shared sense of purpose that includes keeping everyone safe, respectful relationships, and a set of negotiated rules that all members of the family agree upon.

In CFT, family members typically have conflicting views of the need, purpose and goal for therapy, and research suggests that divergent views of the goals of therapy among family members can result in poor treatment outcomes (Friedlander et al., 2006; Robbins et al., 2003; Symonds & Horvath, 2004). There are several ways in which a therapist can encourage family members to create a shared sense of purpose. These include promoting mutual support and caring within the system, facilitating conversations that allow clients to ask each other's perspectives, praising clients for respecting each other's point of view and emphasizing commonalities among perspectives on the problem or solution. These all have the effect of shifting the ways in which family members think about their situation. During the first sessions, therapists must take the differing problem narratives and differing ideas on the goals and tasks of therapy held by each therapy participant and reframe these as goals that all parties agree on as the focus of therapy along with general agreement on the key tasks needed to achieve these goals.

Strategies to Change the Viewing

KEY STRATEGY 1: REFRAMING

In our view, reframing or reattribution is a key intervention strategy to helping clients to shift the viewing of problems. The idea behind reframing is literally to provide a new way of looking at a situation that makes it more palatable and easier to engage with. For example, core CFT models all use reattribution techniques to shift how clients view situations. In emotionally focused therapy for couples, therapists reframe behaviors within the attachment bonds of the relationship. Instead of saying that a husband is a "control freak", EFT therapists would frame this behavior as "he is afraid of losing you" or "he feels insecure", frames that are much more palatable and approachable. In brief strategic family therapy, an adolescent who wants to have her own way can be labeled as "rebellious" or "deviant", but skilled family therapists are able to shift the thinking of a family away from these types of labels into ones that are much less activating of polarizations between family members. As will be explained below, a skilled family therapist will help the family see that the girl's behavior is not deviant but that her self-assertion is developmentally appropriate as she grows up and forges her own identity. This new attribution allows family members to relax more and have more productive conversations with each other about changes needed to improve the lives of all.

Reattribution is an important construct in the change process. It is at the heart of individually oriented evidence-based approaches such as cognitive behavioral therapy and is a core construct in evidence-based CFT approaches. This is a particularly powerful intervention when the thinking of multiple family members is changing during the process. Key skills for reattribution include reframing, relabeling and normalizing of situations. Attributions are at the heart of how we go about making meanings of our lives and the situations that we find ourselves in. Reattribution of the intent and meaning of family problems is very helpful, especially when more understanding is provided as to the intentions behind emotions or behaviors.

When events, emotions and behaviors are reframed, an alternative route (pathway) to emotional expression is created (Sexton & Alexander, 2002). New possibilities for acting or relating emerge from this process. Positive reframes are able to reduce negativity around family interactions. It must be remembered that when families/couples get embroiled in negative spirals, these escalate and create a negative climate within the system. Shifts created due to reframing build on each other over time, creating change outcomes. Good reframes also create confusion and in this way provide distance and protection from the automatic negative processing and relational patterns that exist in families; in this sense, they are a way to interrupt familiar negative sequences.

In CFT, therapists always ask, "What can/should be reframed?" While there is no precise answer to this question, it is important that therapists who work with systems use reattribution strategies to change family dynamics to the extent that family members are able to relate to each other in fresh and new ways. Negative and blaming statements, destructive behaviors of family members and the implied intention and purpose of family members' behaviors (as implied from another) are all fair game for reframing.

THE PROCESS OF REFRAMING

Reframing begins by validating the family member's existing frame of the problem. The therapist then proposes an alternative frame and checks in with this person and the rest of the family about the fit of this frame. The goal of reframing is to get all members of the family on board with a new view of the problem. This view shifts the dynamics of the family and allows for family members to work together in different ways.

Validation is important in reframing in that clients are less defensive when the therapist suggests a different way to view their situation through the reframe. The therapist works to validate, for example, the client's viewpoint, emotions, positions and description of an event. It is important that clients feel as if their frame of what is wrong is understood. In the case mentioned earlier where the husband's behaviors made the wife feel as if he is a "control freak," the therapist validates the point of view of the spouse first: "I understand that you feel controlled by your husband when he keeps asking where you are going." It helps if the validation recognizes the impact of painful and negative behaviors on the family: "I can see how those behaviors make you feel stifled and trapped in this relationship."

Validating statements are supportive, and the therapist should work to describe the event or behavior in a warm, direct, clear and nonblaming way. Validation needs to be in such a way that it supports and engages all members of the family.

The *reframe* is provided by the therapist after the validation feels complete; that is, after all members of the family feel understood. After this has occurred, the therapist presents a new frame to the problem, behavior or event. The therapist draws the frame from experience in therapy, knowledge of relationships/families and the context of the situation. There is not one correct reframe. More important, it is ideal if the frame, especially the first reframe attempt, is close to one that the family is able to accept. With the reframe, the therapist presents an alternative explanation, theme or meaning to the event/behavior/problem. It is critical that the reframe be plausible and believable to each of the clients and that it is a good fit with the clients' views of the world. There are three directions of reattribution/reframing:

- Changing the meaning (helpful if the therapist can give noble or well-intended motives to negative behaviors).
- Challenging the family by suggesting a potential different direction.
- Linking family members together (creating a family focus)

Checking/evaluating the fit of the reframe is the next crucial step. The impact of the reframe on the family must be evaluated. At this point the therapist needs to listen carefully to the clients' responses: what fit, what did not, what was missing, what could be added. The point is that the initial frame is not the final frame. Rather, it is an initial hypothesis put forward by the therapist. The checking/reevaluating part is incredibly important as the initial frame develops and grows through a collaborative conversation into something that does fit for the family. It is worth emphasizing here that there is no right reframe. The therapist makes an informed guess, checks it out with the client and uses the feedback from the client to expand the reframe.

Reframing suggests an alternative that focuses responsibility from the other/event to an understandable and nonpathologizing aspect of an individual. There are many examples of reframing. While we do not have space to list them all here, the therapist should use creativity in coming up with new frames for the situation. Anger can be framed as the hurt an individual is experiencing because of what is going on in the family. In another context, anger implies loss and can be framed as a response to loss. Nagging signifies that the relationship is of great importance. Pain interferes with listening. An adolescent's argumentativeness can be viewed as is identity formation. Therapists use various lenses to inform their reframing; for example, an attachment lens, a developmental lens, a life context lens. We think it would be useful for therapists to keep a running list of good reframes.

- What are good reframes for child/adolescent behavioral difficulties?
- What are good reframes for couple/marital difficulties?

- What are good reframes for difficult parent–child dynamics? For example, criticism, control, hostility.
- What are good reframes for individual mental health? For example, depression, anxiety.

The bottom line is that reframing is so effective because it occurs with more than one family member (often several) and affects all of their thinking. It truly is a fantastic way to change the view of the situation.

KEY STRATEGY 2: PSYCHOEDUCATION

The decision to pose an intervention in an educational format is used throughout the therapy process by all CFT approaches but primarily after engagement in treatment has occurred. However, the degree to which psychoeducation is used within therapy varies from model to model. Psychoeducational interventions include support, education and skills training and are designed to change how clients think about problems. They may include brief statements about a topic or longer lectures or mini-lectures about an issue families are dealing with in their lives. Psychoeducational approaches draw from the best evidence available to enlighten individuals more about their topic. Whole approaches to CFT include psychoeducation at the core; for example, psychoeducation for families where a member has a major mental health condition like schizophrenia, psychoeducation for families where a member has a physical illness such as cancer or approaches such as relationship education that provides couples with core materials about strengthening their relationship. Psychoeducation achieves a number of goals related to changing the viewing, including reducing stigma, providing a different way to look at a situation, equipping the client with accurate information and understanding the course of a difficulty if it is not treated. We describe three approaches to psychoeducation here: (1) brief statements in the here and now, (2) targeted education for a specific condition and (3) homework and other client-directed activities. It should be noted that psychoeducation usually occurs once clients are engaged in the process and the therapist has credibility.

PSYCHOEDUCATION: BRIEF EDUCATIONAL STATEMENTS IN THE HERE AND NOW

We contend that therapists are continually influencing clients in the here and now and shaping their thinking about their problems. This education can be revealed in direct statements or in more indirect ways such as when the therapist asks a question that has information embedded. These statements are not long statements and usually last less than a minute, but over time they have a powerful impact on a client. As an example, consider a couple who presents for therapy because their child is having emotional outbursts. After assessing the situation, the therapist realizes that the parents are constantly arguing in the presence of the child and that this triangulation in conflict is contributing to the child's emotional reactions. In her conceptualization, the therapist decides that she will find ways to educate the couple about this issue. She decides that she wants to find the opportune moment to intervene, in a way that does not activate the defenses of the couple and does not lead to them feeling blamed. This would be unhelpful and may lead the couple to premature dropout, a scenario the therapist is determined to avoid. Toward the end of the second session the couple begin to argue with each other about their parenting and the child becomes increasingly agitated. The therapist uses this as her moment to intervene. Turning to the child, she asks if he would step out of the room for three minutes. After he leaves and is out of earshot, she turns to the couple and says,

> Research on children is abundantly clear that when children witness their parents arguing, it has toxic effects on the child. This is because children feel pulled to take sides, and this creates an internal conflict. It seems clear to me that you have some things to work out in your relationship, and some of the attempts to work those things out may become tense. I am here to support you as you work out those issues. However, based on what we know from research, I have one request, and I believe this will really help your son: that you take your disagreements to a private place where your son does not know about them. This might be in your bedroom when he is asleep, or in the therapy office. Can you agree to this?

In this brief psychoeducation, the therapist makes a powerful statement in the here and now. Her statement occurs at an optimal time in the therapy process. Having the child leave for the intervention punctuates the point the therapist is attempting to make. These types of psychoeducational interventions are important in changing how clients view their problem. This intervention helps the parents to see that they are a part of the child's difficulties but also that with relatively little effort in setting an appropriate boundary, they can protect their child from their arguments.

PSYCHOEDUCATION: TARGETED EDUCATION FOR A SPECIFIC CONDITION

There are numerous approaches to treatment that can be characterized as primarily psychoeducational. Perhaps one of the most well-known approaches is family psychoeducation for schizophrenia and psychoses (McFarlane, 2016). This approach to treatment incorporates education of family members about needed supports for their loved ones. Many studies of this approach show overwhelming support for its effectiveness in preventing relapse and in improving the life and well-being of the individual diagnosed with schizophrenia. There are numerous other similar approaches. For example, Saltzman and colleagues (2011) developed a comprehensive psychoeducation program for families going through deployment in war time. In this approach, family members are provided with practical information about deployment and its related stressors and strategies that family members can use to interrupt negative and toxic family processes during this time of stress. This approach helps family members know what to expect in the process and provides them with guidance on how to react and deal with difficult deployment-related situations. Information allows family members to head off problems by implementing positive routines and processes early on and for members to feel more in control of their circumstances.

Another series of psychoeducation-based approaches focuses on relationship education, an area that aims to strengthen couples' relationships. For example, the Prevention and Relationship Education Program (PREP) has been used with military couples to strengthen their relationships (Allen et al., 2015). PREP is a psychoeducational prevention program for couples that is disseminated in a couples' group format. This approach provides numerous relationship education components that help couples to strengthen their relationships. Many studies of PREP showed that it is an effective way to strengthen intimate relationships (see Markman & Rhoades, 2012; Markman et al., 2022, for a review of the research). The three approaches mentioned are all well studied, with strong evidence of effectiveness. These approaches set out to change how individuals view their situations by providing evidence-based information.

PSYCHOEDUCATION: HOMEWORK AND OTHER CLIENT-DIRECTED ACTIVITIES

Many clients read books, watch videos or participate in Internet platforms, sometimes at the therapist's recommendation. While not all clients like to do this kind of extra work, many clients, especially those who are motivated, are continually searching for answers to their predicament, and it is wise for therapists to influence the material they consume, because there is so much information available and not all of it is reliable. These materials consumed outside of weekly therapy sessions influence clients' lives, relationships and decisions. In the CFT field, numerous resources exist on relationships, deepening intimacy, parenting and the like. These resources can be used as an adjunct to therapy. One concern lies in online forums where clients may be getting advice for their dilemmas that are counterproductive. Adrian, for example, has worked with numerous couples dealing with infidelity. There are many Internet chat forums for clients facing this situation. Some clients take part in these discussions as an adjunct to their therapy. Many are helpful to clients by providing additional strategies to help them manage this stressful situation. Others are less helpful, with content that stirs up anxieties and insecurities, in some cases promoting hostile and litigious approaches to resolving the issue, all which undermine the healing process. In these cases, changing the viewing of problems and thinking differently are highly dependent on the sources of information clients are accessing. We strongly advocate for therapists to be vocal in their support of evidence-based resources and vetted materials and to let clients know about this early in the process. Therapists can also provide recommended readings and other materials to clients at the outset of therapy, especially as they relate to the presenting problem.

KEY STRATEGY 3: CIRCULAR QUESTIONS

Circular questions are another tool CFTs use to change how their clients come to view their situations (Tomm, 1987a, 1987b, 1988). These questions target clients' cognitions and challenge how clients see themselves and their relationships and the influence of their behaviors on their relationships. Often clients are unaware of how their behaviors affect each other. Circular questions are key questions asked in therapy that not only elicit information from clients but also get clients to understand how their behaviors affect each other. Having clients talk about the answers to the questions helps new insights to emerge among therapy participants. Circular questioning highlights each individual's own role in the situation and how their behaviors may influence others. Ryan and Carr (2001) studied the effects of circular questioning as used by Tomm on the therapeutic alliance. They concluded that on both individual and systemic levels, circular questions lead to a better therapeutic alliance than linear questions. Circular questions are questions that are used to gather information in an exploratory fashion and "are based on the assumption that everything is somehow connected to everything else" (Ryan & Carr, 2001, p. 68). The goal of this style of questioning is to reveal patterns that are reoccurring in the family rather than the cause of problems. This seems to take the focus off blame in the system and leads to less nondefensiveness, significantly changing how clients come to view their situation. Circularly focused questions are seen to be more respectful. Tomm (1987a, p. 3) concluded, "Yet, many questions do have therapeutic effects on family members, (directly) through the implications of the questions and/or (indirectly) through the verbal and nonverbal responses of family members to them." These questions are directly targeting clients' thinking systems and creating different ways to think about or view situations. These questions can be provocative and disruptive to clients' internal systems, especially when they are answered in each other's presence. For example, a traditional linear question may ask, "How long has your father had problems with his memory?" A circular question, on the other hand, gives much more opportunity to expand the scope and see how different member of the family system interact and view the issue at hand. Phrased in a circular manner, that same question may look something like "How has your family been impacted by your father's memory problems?"

Key Therapeutic Effect: Changing the Doing
(Behavioral Skill Building)

Behaviors change when therapists facilitate new actions or intervene to help clients change interactional patterns or dysfunctional sequences, modifying boundaries and changing family structures, learning new skills, becoming more supportive of each other and learning to empower self and others. Behavioral regulation is often unique in CFT in that these factors often involve multiple family members. While intervening at the cognitive or emotional level often results in changes in behaviors, this effect refers to specific things that therapists do to modify behaviors directly. One strong example of this in CFT is when the therapist directly intervenes in the process of interaction between family member; that is, interruption of the process. Many systemic models working with couples and families have an explicit aim of interrupting maladaptive processes/interactions within a system (Minuchin, 1974; Szapocznik & Hervis, 2020). This idea is based upon the assumption that maladaptive sequences of interaction keep people stuck in unhelpful ways of living. There are multiple ways to achieve this, such as boundary making, increasing differentiation in one family member, focusing on times when the pattern did not occur or interrupting a pattern in the here-and-now. At times it may involve something the therapist says in the moment in therapy, such as directing lines of communication between family members; on other occasions it may involve teaching of specific skills such as parenting, and sometimes it may involve something a therapist directs a client to do outside of therapy.

Behavior change is seen as both proximal and distal therapeutic effects. From a proximal outcome perspective, smaller behavior changes have additive effects that gather momentum and, over time, lead to distal outcomes. Some approaches may shift seating in the therapy room. In other cases, the therapist may act like a director of traffic, telling people when to talk and to whom. In other cases, the therapist is working to put parents in charge in families. These effects are determined through a clear and in-depth conceptualization of the problem (see Chapter 4). This conceptualization should guide the therapist in deciding what is maintaining/exacerbating the problem within the system structure and the priorities for intervention.

Key Therapeutic Effect: Changing the Feeling (Experiencing)

This occurs when therapists facilitate clients in regulating or experiencing emotions and making emotional connections with themselves, the therapist and (most important) each other. A key component of changing the feeling is to give system members a new experience of their relationships in the moment (i.e., in the here and now). Examples of affect regulation include getting couples to express the underlying (primary) emotions underneath angry/defensive exchanges within emotionally focused therapy. In EFT, when the therapist helps couples to express the (primary) emotions underlying angry/defensive exchanges, couples are able to experience each other in new ways and a shift occurs in their pattern of interaction. Of course, the initial shifts should only be seen as proximal effects, but when this occurs repeatedly, they will likely lead to distal effects. Affective regulation or experiencing occurs in unique ways in CFT when it involves multiple family members. This essentially results in a new experience of relationships in therapy (Sprenkle et al., 1999). When working with couples and families, emotions are commonplace.

Principles of Change

Principles of change have been proposed as important in CFT (Blow et al., 2007; Christensen et al., 2005). Principles of change are similar to common factors. We think of principles as "truths" or "values" that relate to what is important to achieve in therapy. As Blow et al. (2007) stated, "Principles are concentrated 'truths' of therapeutic change, applicable to a wide variety of clinical circumstances and present across diverse models of therapy" (p. 309).

Consider the following example.

> A family presents to you in therapy. They have been referred to you by the elementary school. Two of their children are in this school, a second grader and fourth grader. They are having numerous problems in school, including poor grades, horseplay and failure to concentrate due to tiredness. The principal who provided the referral describes them as pleasant children but out of control. The therapist meets with the parents and children for a 2-hour assessment and quickly determines that this family is one where there are no clear rules or consequences for breaking rules, that the parents disagree on the rules and that the children are staying up until midnight each night watching TV. The therapist uses one word to describe this family: chaotic.

Before you read on, stop and answer the following question: "What are some principles (think values, truths) that would help this family?" When we work with families that are chaotic, key principles that we consider are (a) Are the parents in charge? (b) Do children in this family have predictable routines such as bedtime and mealtime? (c) Do children have clear and appropriate consequences that are fairly and consistently enforced by the parental subsystem? (d) Are the parents in agreement on rules and their consequences if they are broken? These questions speak to four clear principles we consider as we approach this type of chaotic family system. We have the value/belief/principle that children thrive when they have leadership from parents/parental figures who are going to provide day-to-day guidance for the family and that these parents are in agreement with how to approach their parenting. If they are somehow undermining each other, that is a recipe for more chaos. We also hold a value/belief/principle that boundaries are critical in families and are especially needed in chaotic systems. These boundaries cannot be too loose or too rigid. These boundaries define crucial family structures and routines. We believe that children do best when they develop within a predictable structure. Finally, this structure needs to be enforced with consequences. The way to implement these principles can vary across cases. However, this example around parenting illustrates how we view principles of therapy. These principles help in the conceptualization of the problem; that is, chaos is prevalent in this family system because of inconsistencies in parenting and unclear consequences. The ways in which these are operationalized clinically by a therapist may vary. For example, the well-studied Parent Management Training Oregon (PMTO; Forgatch & Patterson, 2010) approach to parenting uses role-playing to illustrate the importance of concepts in therapy. It is also important to note that even though, in general, we subscribe to these principles around parenting and optimal family functioning, they also change depending on client context and how these principles play out in this context. For example, if we are working with an immigrant family from Mexico, we would also consider issues of language and culture in adapting to a US system, financial stress, and time constraints. These would change if we were working with a single parent or if we were working with a divorcing couple. However, the larger principles would still exist; that is, children do best when they grow up in a context with clear and consistent rules that are enforced by loving parents who agree with each other on the rules and enforcement of the rules.

Some principles may arise out of our experience about what works in therapy or from our own personal family backgrounds. We think of principles of change as not connected to one model of therapy but rather as transcending models. In the above example of parenting, we would expect all parenting approaches to incorporate those principles in some way. In this sense, principles of change are similar to common factors.

Principles for Couples and Families

Therapists all develop their own lists of principles. These are rooted in who the therapist is, their cultural background and the therapist's own values. These should optimally be rooted in evidence; for example, there is a large body of research showing that children thrive in a loving but structured environment. We can think of many examples where inaccurate or biased principles can cause difficult situations for couples or families. One example is if a therapist believes that a couple should ideally stay together no matter what the situation. In this scenario, the therapist could end up reinforcing abusive relationships. In this case, a principle would be better modified to reflect that the therapist believes that, in general, couples with children are better off if they find a way to stay together, except in cases where there is abuse or persistent untenable violations of the marital contract (e.g., infidelity). Ideally, therapists should take time to become overtly aware of their beliefs and values and list in writing the principles that guide their work. They should also evaluate these principles for biases and values that may clash with those of their clients (principles are often rooted in personal values).

Conclusion

In this chapter we provided an overview of some common processes in CFT. Change occurs as a result of therapy, but the reasons why change occurs are multifaceted. In the chapters to follow, we will go deeper into change processes and ways in which therapists can maximize each change variable.

References

Allen, E. S., Rhoades, G. K., Markman, H. J., & Stanley, S. M. (2015). PREP for strong bonds: A review of outcomes from a randomized clinical trial. *Contemporary Family Therapy, 37*(3), 232–246. https://doi.org/10.1007/s10591-014-9325-3

Bertolino, B. (2010). *Strengths-based engagement: Creating effective helping relationships*. Allyn & Bacon.

Bertolino, B., Blow, A., & Timmons, S. (2010). *Strengthening the alliance in couple and family therapy*. American Association for Marriage and Family Therapy.

Blow, A. J., & Distelberg, B. (2006). *Common factors in four evidence-based family therapy approaches* [Paper presentation]. National Council on Family Relations Annual Conference, Minneapolis, MN, United States.

Blow, A. J., Sprenkle, D. H., & Davis, S. D. (2007). Is who delivers the treatment more important than the treatment itself? The role of the therapist in common factors. *Journal of Marital and Family Therapy, 33*, 298–318.

Bowen, M. (1978). *Family therapy in clinical practice*. Jason Aronson.

Christensen, A., Doss, B. D., & Atkins, D. C. (2005). A science of couple therapy: For what should we seek empirical support? In W. M. Pinsof & J. Lebow (Eds.), *Family psychology: The art of the science* (pp. 43–64). Oxford University Press.

Forgatch, M. S., & Patterson, G. R. (2010). The Oregon Model of Parent Management Training (PMTO): An intervention for antisocial behavior in children and adolescents. In J. R. Weisz & A. E. Kazdin (Eds.), *Evidence based psychotherapies for children and adolescents* (2nd ed., pp. 159–178). Guilford.

Friedlander, M. L., Escudero, V., & Heatherington, L. (2006). *Therapeutic alliances in couple and family therapy: An empirically informed guide to practice.* American Psychological Association.

Friedlander, M. L., Lambert, J. E., Valentín, E., & Cragun, C. (2008). How do therapists enhance family alliances? Sequential analyses of therapist–client behavior in two contrasting cases. *Psychotherapy: Theory, Research, Practice, Training, 45*(1), 75–87. https://doi.org/10.1037/0033-3204.45.1.75

Johnson, S. M. (2004). *The practice of emotionally focused couple therapy* (2nd ed.). Brunner-Routledge.

Lebow, J. L., & Jenkins, P. (2018). *Research for the psychotherapist: From science to practice* (2nd ed.). Routledge.

Linehan, M. (1993). *Cognitive behavioral treatment of borderline personality disorder.* Guilford.

Markman, H. J., & Rhoades, G. K. (2012). Relationship education research: Current status and future directions. *Journal of Marital and Family Therapy, 38*, 169–200. doi: 10.1111/j.1752-0606.2011.00247.x

Markman, H. J., Hawkins, A. J., Stanley, S. M., Halford, W. K., & Rhoades, G. (2022). Helping couples achieve relationship success: A decade of progress in couple relationship education research and practice, 2010–2019. *Journal of Marital and Family Therapy, 48*, 251–282. https://doi.org/10.1111/jmft.12565

McFarlane, W. R. (2016). Family interventions for schizophrenia and the psychoses: A review. *Family Process, 55*(3), 460–482. https://doi.org/10.1111/famp.12235

Minuchin, S. (1974). *Families and family therapy.* Harvard University Press.

Patterson, J. E., Miller, R. B., Carnes, S., & Wilson, S. (2004). Evidence-based practice for marriage and family therapists. *Journal of Marital and Family Therapy, 30*(2), 183–195. https://doi.org/10.1111/j.1752-0606.2004.tb01233.x

Pinsof, W. (1995). *Integrative problem-centered therapy.* Basic.

Robbins, M. S., Turner, C. W., Alexander, J. F., & Perez, G. A. (2003). Alliance and dropout in family therapy for adolescents with behavior problems: Individual and systemic effects. *Journal of Family Psychology, 17*(4), 534–544. https://doi.org/10.1037/0893-3200.17.4.534

Ryan, D., & Carr, A. (2001). A study of the differential effects of Tomm's questioning styles on therapeutic alliance. *Family Process, 40*(1), 67–77. https://doi.org/10.1111/j.1545-5300.2001.4010100067.x

Sackett, D., Straus, E., Richardson, W., Rosenberg, W., & Haynes, R. (2000). *Evidence-based medicine: How to practice and teach EBM* (2nd ed.). Churchill-Livingston.

Saltzman, W. R., Lester, P., Beardslee, W. R., Layne, C. M., Woodward, K., & Nash, W. P. (2011). Mechanisms of risk and resilience in military families: Theoretical and empirical basis of a family-focused resilience enhancement program. *Clinical Child and Family Psychology Review, 14*(3), 213–230. https://doi.org/10.1007/s10567-011-0096-1

Schwartz, R. (1995). *Internal family systems therapy.* Guilford.

Sexton, T., & Alexander, J. (2002). Functional family therapy for at-risk adolescents and their families. In F. Kaslow & T. Patterson (Eds.), *Comprehensive handbook of psychotherapy, cognitive–behavioral approaches* (Vol. 2, pp. 117–140). John Wiley & Sons.

Sexton, T., & Alexander, J. (2003). Functional family therapy: A mature clinical model for working with at-risk adolescents and their families. In T. L. Sexton, G. R. Weeks, & M. S. Robbins (Eds.), *Handbook of family therapy* (pp. 323–350). Brunner-Routledge.

Sprenkle, D., & Blow, A. (2004). Common factors and our sacred models. *Journal of Marital and Family Therapy, 30*, 113–129.

Sprenkle, D., Blow, A., & Dickey, M. (1999). Common factors and other nontechnique variables in marriage and family therapy. In M. Hubble, B. Duncan, & S. Miller (Eds.), *The heart and soul of change: What works in therapy* (pp. 329–360). American Psychological Association.

Symonds, D., & Horvath, A. (2004). Optimizing the alliance in couple therapy. *Family Process, 43*, 443–456.

Szapocznik, J., & Hervis, O. E. (2020). *Brief strategic family therapy*. American Psychological Association. https://doi.org/10.1037/0000169-000

Tomm, K. (1987a). Interventive interviewing: Part I. Strategizing as a fourth guideline for the therapist. *Family Process, 26*(1), 3–13. htttps://doi.org/10.1111/j.1545-5300.1987.00003.x

Tomm, K. (1987b). Interventive interviewing: Part II. Reflexive questioning as a means to enable self-healing. *Family Process, 26*(2), 167–183. htttps://doi.org/10.1111/j.1545-5300.1987.00167.x

Tomm, K. (1988). Interventive interviewing: Part III. Intending to ask lineal, circular, strategic, or reflexive questions? *Family Process, 27*(1), 1–15. https://doi.org/10.1111/j.1545-5300.1988.00001.x

Wampler, K. (1997). *Systems theory and outpatient mental health treatment* [Paper presentation]. Inaugural AAMFT Research Conference, Santa Fe, NM, United States.

4
COUPLE AND FAMILY THERAPY COMMON FACTORS

Introduction

In the larger field of psychotherapy, research aimed at uncovering the common factors of therapy models that account for change has blossomed over the past 3 decades, while similar research in couple and family therapy (CFT) is still in its childhood. Although much more has been written about common factors in the individual therapy literature, in this chapter we focus on common factors that are *unique to couple and family therapy*. While there may be many candidates, we settle on four factors that have consensus among CFT common factors scholars as shared across CFT theories: (1) systemic conceptualizing of the problem, (2) disrupting dysfunctional relational patterns, (3) expanding the therapeutic alliance and (4) expanding the direct treatment system. While few, these common factors are extremely important and rooted in the ways in which relationship therapy is itself distinctive from other approaches to working with clients. These four factors are unique to CFT and reflect the core identity of the CFT profession; that is, what is distinct about CFT separate from nonsystemic individual therapy and what is common across all CFT models.

There is a considerable overlap between common factors in different presentations of therapy, including both individual therapy and CFT. For example, the alliance is a key variable in all kinds of psychotherapy, as is a competent therapist. The question then can be asked, "What ingredients of change are distinct to the couple and family therapy field?" This is a key question for this book and for the differentiation of the CFT approach from other ways of providing treatment. CFTs work with complex family systems. We contend – and evidence supports our view – that working with these cases requires a high level of therapist skill and a different way of thinking than individually oriented theories. CFTs conceptualize problems in their context, considering their systemic constraints and prioritizing interventions based on this conceptualization. As the family shifts over time, therapists are required to be nimble and move responsively to address new and emerging issues in the family.

DOI: 10.4324/9781315542737-4

> **Case Example 3**
>
> This case example will be used to guide your thinking in considering key CFT common factors. A family presented in therapy requesting help with their 7-year-old son. It was the mother, Sarah, a 34-year-old, who made the appointment and who showed up for the initial intake session on her own. She reported numerous problems in the family but that her son Jason was the main concern. When pressed in session to say more about other problems, Sarah stated that she had suffered from anorexia for about 17 years. She reported that in the last 2 months she had a relapse of symptoms and that she was struggling to eat enough food and was losing weight. She reported that her husband, William, was in the military and had returned 4 months previously from a wartime combat deployment. He had some posttraumatic stress symptoms, had sleep difficulties and had struggled to adjust to the bustle of their home environment. She reported that he had also developed an issue with porn use, which made her feel even more "ugly" and inadequate. In addition to the 7-year-old (Jason), there was one other child in the family, a 15-year-old daughter, Ava, who, in Sarah's words, was an "over-functioning" female adolescent, who had maintained straight As in school even amid family stress. According to the mom, Jason, the identified patient, had many problems in school, including poor grades, reported attention deficit hyperactivity disorder (ADHD, an inability to concentrate) and frequent detentions for fighting. It was his latest violent incident that led her to seek help; he had tipped over a desk in the classroom, causing concern for the teacher and class peers.

In approaching clinical work with this case, a therapist or a therapeutic team could take many different approaches. A separated and individual approach would prioritize individual therapy with the child. This therapy could include play therapy, talk therapy or group therapy, and this is a common way these types of cases are treated. In addition, other members of the family would be good candidates for individualized treatment. The mom certainly would benefit from therapeutic support for her anorexia symptoms, and the dad could use treatment for his possible PTSD and adjustment to civilian life post deployment. These individualized treatments could include prescribing medications that are commonly used for the issues these family members are wrestling with. It would also be common to add additional providers to the team. In this case it would not be uncommon to have up to five therapists – individual therapists for Jason, Sarah and William; a marital therapist for the couple; and a family therapist for all in the system. These five providers, and possibly psychiatrists, would come at a hefty financial cost, a high level of emotional strain and scheduling challenges. While this approach could bring relief and healing to this family, it could also lead to a situation where providers worked on individual issues without considering the larger context and inadvertently pushed family members away from each other, creating additional stress and less support within the family. In this conceptualization of the problem and its treatment, individual work is primary, with family/couple therapy an adjunctive specialization. While this approach may provide some help, it may also work against the goals of the entire system. For example, the wife could complain to her therapist about her "angry husband" with PTSD who undermines her parenting. From an individual therapy perspective, it is natural and normal and appropriate for a therapist to validate this concern and maybe even suggest action away from the marriage. The therapist might say, "I am saddened to hear that your husband is so angry; maybe you should consider a separation?" or "You know you don't have to tolerate his behaviors, right?" Responses like this or something similar are not uncommon in individual therapy. Even if the therapist does not overtly state these words, nonverbal responses by the therapist communicate a great deal. An individual therapist is tuned in to validate the concerns raised by their clients. However, the individual therapist is hampered in understanding and treating the relational issue with only one person in the room. In this sense, the therapist is in a bind: either support the concerns of the spouse and undermine the marriage or try to take the husband's point of view and thus invalidate the client. Neither of these options is ideal. Below, we will provide alternative ways of working with a case like this or similar cases, with systemic thinking at the forefront.

Systemic Conceptualization of Problems

Systemic conceptualization of problems is a critical ingredient in the CFT approach to therapy, especially when it comes to working with couples and families (Sprenkle et al., 1999). CFT therapists make sense of/understand symptoms and behaviors within families/relationships, cultures, and contexts. Relational conceptualization occurs when the therapist can step back and consider all of the forces at play in *developing, exacerbating, and maintaining* the presenting problem (and related problems). The therapist uses this conceptualization information to come up with ways to intervene in the system and to shift dynamics in the direction of positive change. In this sense, conceptualization of the problem in systemic terms is an *assessment mechanism* in which the therapist develops an explanatory map of the problem and its existence. It is also a *guide for intervention* in that hypotheses about what interventions are needed for change occur at the conceptualization level and the therapist uses these conceptualizations to inform interventions. As the therapist tests or follows each hypothesis through intervention, information from these efforts is fed back into the conceptualization of the problem, which is then refined or modified. Systemic conceptualization is a foundational CFT principle and a key building block of systems theory; it gives the CFT profession its unique identity and is the most foundational concept as CFTs attempt to keep the whole system (or systems) in view, regardless of the number of people present in the therapy room or the presenting problem.

Sprenkle et al. (1999) first proposed the systemic conceptualization of problems as a CFT common factor. They contended that most CFTs view mental health problems "within a complex web of reciprocal influences involved in the complaint" (p. 345). Critically, CFTs conceptualize presenting problems in terms of the context in which they exist. Working within a *systemic conceptualization* framework changes how treatment plays out in a complex case such as the one described above, how the therapist thinks about the case and how they might intervene. If multiple providers are involved, there would be communication among providers and shared goals for treatment, keeping the goals of the system front and center – goals derived from the conceptualization. The conceptualization of the problem is a core feature of the CFT profession. It is what makes CFTs unique and differentiates CFTs from other disciplines of mental health. Wampler and colleagues (2019) contended that a key defining feature of the profession is in how therapists go about conceptualizing the cases with which they work. They contended that CFT is not as much a modality of intervention (who is in the room) but rather a conceptualization of a problem in its context. After careful assessment of this context, the CFT trained therapist develops interventions that are delivered in collaboration with the client(s) and that are congruent with the conceptualization of the problem. This way of approaching therapy means that a therapist cannot be restrained by one narrow way of thinking. Instead, the therapist is open to possibilities. The most important question a therapist asks with this conceptualization is what strategies are needed to create therapeutic effects that relieve the symptoms and the problem(s).

Problems always present in a context. This context is both *historical* (i.e., where one comes from) and *experiential* (where one is situated in the present). One way to describe a relational conceptualization of problems is when therapists can take several factors into account and consider how each may be related to the presenting problem. Once a relational conceptualization of a problem exists, the therapist can begin to intervene in collaboration with the individual, couple or family.

How to Conceptualize Problems Systemically

It is important for therapists first to let clients know that the first two to three sessions will involve coming up with a conceptualization of the problem and how the problem and its resolution are connected to the life contexts of the individual (identified patient). It is important from a therapeutic alliance perspective that therapists have permission from clients to do this assessment/data collection and that this be a joint process (i.e., the therapist will not just give them a diagnosis about what they think the problem is). The more thorough this can be, the more rigorous the conceptualization. This initial conceptualization changes as new information comes to light or as early interventions do not work. At a basic level, therapists are asking clients curious questions and then noting responses to these questions. Responses are assessed by considering details noted, emotional reactions, and overall levels of engagement around topics. It is important that therapists be highly active and engaged in the conceptualization process. They ask questions, they probe, they ask about affect noted, they check in with clients, they note responses and they probe more. They are trying to get a rich description of the context. They are attempting to answer: "What is going on in the context of this particular client with this particular presenting problem, and how is this context related to the difficulties these clients are experiencing? How might the historical context affect these clients?"

Those who work using a CFT lens know that getting a good conceptualization of the presenting problem is a key first step to therapy. This conceptualization should occur regardless of the theoretical orientation of the therapist. The "how" to arrive at a solid conceptualization entails taking several factors into account. Table 4.1 describes several considerations in achieving a conceptualization of the problem. The specific content areas to gain information from that lead to this conceptualization are especially useful during the early stages of therapy but can be explored at any point along the way. The steps to conceptualization may vary depending on the specific case. The first steps in a comprehensive systemic conceptualization include an in-depth assessment that involves interviewing members of the system together about their views of the presenting problem and related factors that brought them to therapy. It may also be necessary to interview members alone and in some cases in dyads. For example, when working with couples, we will always interview members of the dyad alone to assess for individual points of view, deepen the alliance with each individual and rule out issues that will be toxic for couple therapy, such as secret infidelity and interpersonal violence. It is important that the therapist have an approach for dealing with these types of secrets. Some therapists have individuals sign "no secret" contracts (these can also unintentionally serve to silence secrets), while other therapists are prepared to hold secrets, encouraging clients to share them with their partners when the time is right. When working with families, we will always meet with the parents alone to assess issues that they are concerned about without children present. We also use this time to assess issues in the parents' relationship with each other that might get in the way of effective parenting.

At times we will meet with children alone as well, and decisions to do this vary on a case-by-case basis depending on the age of the child and the presenting problem. For example, we will almost always meet alone with children

Table 4.1 **Considerations to Arrive at Systemic Conceptualization of the Problem**

- **Interview** each member of the **family together** in the room about their **view of the problem** and why they are seeking treatment for the problem at this time.
- If necessary, **interview members of the family alone** or in **key subsystems** about their **views of the problem** (e.g., it is common practice for couple therapists to have individual interviews with each member of the dyad; in working with families, it is common practice to interview the parents without children present).
- **Obtain a history of the presenting problem**. When did it begin? What was going on when it began? Who knew about the problem? How was the problem revealed/discovered?
- Assess **attempted solutions to the problem**. What has the family tried to do to solve the problem? What has worked? What has not worked? Have the attempted solutions made things better or worse?
- **Larger System Considerations**
  - **Neighborhood** consider things like safety, social supports, available resources.
  - **Children** consider things like schools, peer groups, discrimination, extracurricular activities, bullying.
  - **Adults** consider things like employment, friendship, discrimination, extended family support, financial resources.

- **Genogram.** Obtain key historical information about the family. Ideally this should include three generations. While genograms can take a long time to get detailed information, we advocate to get the following information at a minimum:
  - Family members across three generations (parents, grandparents, siblings, children)
  - Nodal family events – marriages, divorces, untimely deaths, illnesses, catastrophic events, immigration
  - Any family secrets; e.g., infidelity, imprisonments, sexual abuse, mental health problems
  - Religious beliefs
  - History of substance abuse
  - History of racism, oppression, cultural expression.
  - Predictable and unpredictable family development events
  - Traumatic events
  - Pertinent information related to specific presenting problem; e.g., sexual history in a sex therapy case
- **Family/relationship timeline (related to genogram information)**
  - Couples – how they met, dating history, relationship history
  - Families, relocations, additions, losses
- **Family interaction observation.** It is important to observe and carefully consider how family members interact with each other (process). This includes the sequence of interactions, who talks the most, who is quiet, what are the emotions present during the interaction, who interrupts the interaction, how it escalates, how it deescalates, and the like.

in a stepfamily to give the children the opportunity to have a voice around issues that may concern them. Because of intense loyalty issues in stepfamilies, children are not always comfortable sharing their concerns in the presence of a parent or stepparent. We also usually meet one-on-one with adolescents to deepen our alliance with them and give them an uninterrupted voice about the predicament that led to seeking help. It should be noted that any individual sessions can serve to undermine systemic processes, and therapists should hold these sessions sparingly, with full transparency with the other clients in the system.

In addition to these interviews, we formulate our conceptualization of the presenting problem through observing interactions between family members. It is important early in therapy not to let these get out of control or escalate too far, because we don't want clients to become discouraged by repeating the same old patterns that they do at home in therapy. However, we let families know that it is important that we can get to know them better by observing their interactions with each other. This requires that when the therapist meets with the family they include as many members as possible present in person so that the therapist can witness and experience firsthand the system's processes as they play out in the present.

In addition to views/observations of the presenting problem, we are interested in the developmental history of the problem over time. This history is important in understanding more about what may have precipitated the problem. We seek to obtain information about the history of the presenting problem from the time it first appeared until the present. We also spend time inquiring about attempted solutions to the problem, including the utilization of other therapy services. We want to get a handle on what has worked, what has not worked and reasons behind these successes or failures. Every case that presents in therapy has a problem history that led to the need for treatment. At times the problem is really the problem, whereas at other times clients are still trying to figure out all aspects of the problem or what underlies the perceived problem. It is important for therapists to spend time figuring out details of the problem, operational definitions of the problem and historical factors related to the problem. We also want to know what precipitated their seeking out therapy services at this time. Key questions include:

- When did you first notice the problem?
- What about the problem led you to seek therapy?
- When is the problem worse?
- When is it not as bad?
- What have you done to solve the problem?
- Who in your context knows about the problem/is connected to the problem?

- Has anyone else in your family had the same/similar problems in the past?
- What happened that resulted in you seeking help for the problem at this time?

We almost always spend time early on gaining genogram and relationship history information. This may vary on a case-by-case basis. For example, if a family comes in with a big crisis going on, we may delay this information collection until a more optimal time, or we may choose to gather very basic genogram data early on, enough to inform our conceptualization. However, this type of delay is not ideal and should be rare. While obtaining sufficient information to arrive at a suitable conceptualization may be more difficult when clients present with these high levels of distress, therapists should resist the urge to shortchange the systemic assessment while at the same time not neglecting to triage urgent symptoms (at times, it is a balancing act).

Ideally, we would like to have a good amount of information about the history of the family/system (up to three generations) and for couples, the history of the relationship, previous relationships, and nodal events in those relationships. Table 4.1 highlights multiple areas we inquire about in this process. We also believe that therapists need to have some understanding of the extended family context. While the extent of this context may vary from case to case, we believe that any long-term therapy requires a therapist to have knowledge of three generations. See Timm and Blow (2005) for a full description of genograms and questions to ask about in order to get accurate and important information. At a minimum, we want to know all of the important individuals across generations, including names, ages, relationship status, deaths, cause of death, cultural factors, mental health issues, substance use and misuse, relationship dissolutions, history of violence, history of infidelity, immigration events, employment and other nodal life occurrences. Nodal events are important and relate to the development of the family as a system. We ask, "Are there any events that occurred in your past that were difficult/notable for your family as a whole?" Examples of these include premature deaths, fortuitous events, family tragedies, illnesses and the like.

If the person is in an intimate relationship, it is important to assess for relational data as it may be connected to the problem. Key couple questions include:

- The history of the relationship.
- How the relationship started and under what circumstances.
- Levels of commitment in the relationship.
- What it is like living in the relationship.
- Ongoing difficulties in the relationship (e.g., frequent fighting).

- Major threats to the relationship (e.g., violence, infidelity, threats of divorce).
- The history of prior intimate relationships for each individual.
    - What were these relationships like?
    - How long did they last?
    - Why did they end?
    - What were the nodal events that stood out in these relationships?

In a family, relational questions are different. We ask:

- Who is close to who in the family?
- Who has a strained or nonexistent relationship?
- Where do tensions exist in the family?
- Who is in charge in the family?
- Is there a clearly defined family leadership structure?
- Are family leaders on the same page?
- Do members of the family share the same rules, and are these rules enforced in similar ways?
- What kinds of boundaries exist in the family?
- Are family members overly close to or overly distant from each other?
- Which members of the family are related to/involved with the presenting problem?
- What is going on in the family when things are better/worse with the presenting problem?

Finally, we realize that individuals and families are embedded withing larger systems. All family members spend considerable time in their neighborhoods and communities, and depending on the context, these can be a source of distress or a resource. Children spend a great deal of time with their peers, in their schools and with their recreational/sporting teams. Adults spend a great deal of time in their places of employment. These contexts can all affect what is going on in the family. A child who is bullied at school may act out at home. A parent who is harassed in the workplace will have difficulties focusing at home. We assess for the larger system and how it may be influencing the family system and each individual within the family. In addition to current relationships, family and historical family situations, therapists need to be aware of the larger culture as well.

- What is going on in this culture?
- What kind of neighborhood is a family living in?
    - Is it safe?
    - Is it violent?
    - Are there resources to support the life of the system?

- Is a family a victim of racism or discrimination of some kind?
- What type of school do the children attend?
- Where do the parents work and what is the context of this employment, and how is it related to the presenting problem?
- How much stress are members of the family under?
- What types of positive supports exist for the family?

Determining the Systemic Conceptualization

Once we have collected the information described above, the next step is to utilize it to inform the initial conceptualization of the problem. Experienced therapists can come up with this conceptualization quite quickly based on their knowledge of theory and their experiences in working with similar cases. For novice therapists, consultation with a supervisor may help greatly in the conceptualization. We advocate for therapists to share some of their conceptualization with the family. While it is too technical to share everything that the therapist is thinking, we like therapists to share an initial conceptualization and plan in simple terms; it is important to connect the plan to the interventions that will take place next.

> **Case Example 3 Conceptualized**
>
> Using the above case example, we illustrate how to approach conceptualization. The therapist spent time assessing the family together as a group, exploring their contributions to the issue in the first three sessions (the first session was with Sarah alone). In the additional two sessions, the therapist met with William alone (to balance out the time with Sarah), the parental unit alone and the whole family. In the couple meeting, it quickly became apparent that there were tensions in the marriage related to porn use and the increase in eating disorder symptoms. In the individual meetings with parents, the therapist assessed the extent of William's PTSD and its impact on the family and Sarah's eating disorder symptoms. In the whole family session, the therapist was able to listen to every member's point of view as well as observe how family members interacted with each other. The therapist's initial conceptualization was that the family lacked structure related to the dad's deployment to war, which exacerbated his difficulty returning home and integrating into the family, and the additional layers of stress triggered Sarah's management of her eating disorder. The therapist summarized this to the family as follows:
>
>> You have all been through a great deal as a family. There have been many losses and transitions that you have had to deal with as a family.

> These have stressed everyone out. I am suggesting that we meet together for at least the next three months to work on establishing more structure and routines in your household. This will take some work on each of your part.
>
> [To the couple only]: Your relationship has been through a great deal due to the separation and the stress you have been under since William returned home. William has been struggling to get into sleep routines with adapting back to civilian life. He has been struggling to get his use of porn under control. Sarah has been managing her own concerns related to her body, her eating and her identity. Intimacy has been difficult. In addition to working with the whole family, I propose that we spend sessions working on intimacy issues in your relationship. It will also be good to get you both on the same page in your approaches to parenting. This is a common struggle that families face after a deployment.
>
> These therapist suggestions are that the initial steps in treatment would involve couple sessions interspersed with family sessions. The couple sessions would focus on the marriage relationship and underlying marital issues, helping the couple provide support for each other and working on co-parenting by getting the parents on the same page with regard to family rules and routines. The family sessions with both children would work on routines and on the implementation of the parenting plan worked on in couple sessions. Depending on symptom severity, the therapist could decide to refer the individual issues (PTSD and eating disorder) to individual therapists. If this occurs, it is essential that the therapist have regular communication with these providers about the goals of the system (ideally these other providers are also systems thinkers).

Conceptualization Informs Intervention

From early on in treatment, the therapist works to help the family come up with a shared view of the problem based on case conceptualization on the part of the therapist. Therapists form hypotheses about change based their initial conceptualization. For the above case, one initial part of the conceptualization is that the family lacks structure and that this stems from the parental unit not being cohesive in their approach to parenting. This lack of cohesion could stem from many hypothesized sources – the deployment, tension in the marital relationship, parents overwhelmed by their own issues, bad parenting role models or other reasons. These reasons may all be uncovered in the subsequent work. The conceptualization involves the therapist making sense of all of the information and the conceptualization *suggests the best strategy* and *priorities for interventions*. Once a therapist has obtained important information through observing and experiencing family dynamics, they must figure out what to do with this information. Along the way, the therapist should have begun to form some idea of how the problem development and maintenance is related to the overall systemic context. A big part of a systemic conceptualization of problems is that therapists can know what information is important to ask about and then, once answers are provided, what information among those answers is essential to the amelioration of the problem. Contextual information is always interesting, but it is not always relevant in conceptualizing or treating the presenting problem. Skilled therapists should avoid tangents and stay focused on the most important tasks that will lead to problem resolution.

Systemic conceptualization includes making sense of all of the information and using it to establish treatment priorities. Once a conceptualization is in place, interventions are then used to test the hypotheses consistent with a model the therapist is proficient in using. This is an important consideration in that there are many starting points for therapy depending on the therapist's theoretical persuasion. For example, an individual therapist might prioritize seeing the child individually and keep the parents out of therapy altogether, other than short updates. A psychoanalytic therapist would want to see Jason multiple times a week in individual treatment and would largely exclude the parents. In our view, this intense individual work would not be the most effective approach to treatment, especially given everything that this family is dealing with at the current time.

The Initial Conceptualization Is Not Static

It is important to note that the *conceptualization shifts as problems are resolved, new information emerges, clients give additional feedback or interventions fail.* For example, in the above case, the therapist initially conceptualized the core problem as lying primarily in the parental subsystem, and this informed the early intervention focus. As the therapist worked with the family, it emerged that Jason was being severely bullied in school and that William had been frequenting strip clubs. This new information provided new information to add to the initial conceptualization. It suggested new areas to intervene, and it ratcheted up the urgency of intervening in the couple relationship. Conceptualization (and treatment) then shifted to include the therapist intervening in the school system by directly by talking to the teacher/principal and through empowering the parents to do the same. It also included working on marital betrayal and trying to save the relationship by intensifying the frequency and focus of couple sessions.

> **Case Example 3 Summary (from beginning to end)**
>
> The therapist let the family know at the outset that she was going to spend the first three sessions getting to know their whole family, understand their history and collaboratively work with them all on the most promising approach to treating their situation. Of most concern to the therapist, when presented with this case, was the wife's worsening anorexia symptoms and threats to the marriage due to the porn use. Second were the PTSD symptoms of the husband, which, although not extreme at the time of intake, seemed to have the potential to be triggered in a short amount of time. The child's ADHD was also of concern in that grades were affected, and the therapist's initial conceptualization was that these problems were a result of inconsistent parenting and multiple life transitions related to a disjointed parenting model based on the husband's absence and difficulties reintegrating post deployment. The initial treatment consisted of couples work focused on putting up barriers to porn use and increasing accountability in the relationship, addressing anorexia symptoms before they worsened (these were addressed in the context of the couples work) and increasing intimacy and parenting cooperation in the marriage. The therapist decided not to involve individual therapists but kept this as an option. When the two new pieces of information came up about the visits to strip clubs (a clear violation of the marital agreement) and bullying of the child at school, therapy reached a crisis point – a make or break juncture in the therapy. The therapist needed to be active in both of these situations, assessing the extent of betrayal and engaging teachers and the principal at the school to address the bullying concerns. Couples treatment lasted for 6 months, whereas the family sessions only required eight sessions. During these family sessions, a focus was on loss and transitions faced by family members, family rules and consistent and appropriate enforcement of these rules. Early in the couples work, rigid boundaries were established between William's use of porn and strip clubs. During the couple sessions, William's PTSD symptoms decreased due to the routines in the family life and the avenues to discussing issues in the relationship. He was able to disclose to Sarah during sessions some traumatic memories of war

> that Sarah was able to listen to with deep compassion and without judgment. These treatment decisions required skill in assessment and conceptualization, particularly at the front end, and then skills in prioritizing treatment, in consultation with the clients. Additional shifts in the case conceptualization and related treatment occurred late in therapy. When the husband stopped watching porn and emotional intimacy increased in the relationship, William began to pursue Sarah for more physical intimacy. This pursuit brought about an emotional crisis for Sarah around her body fears related to anorexia symptoms and intimacy. This heightened tension became a focus of several sessions focused on increasing secure attachment in the relationship, and successfully navigating this moment led Sarah to have increased acceptance of her body and William to feel more satisfied in their intimate relationship.

This case example is illustrative of many of the points we make in this chapter. First, the complexities of this case required a high level of therapeutic presence. It required a therapist to be able to see problems in relation to all parts of the system and how difficulties experienced by the clients emerged at key life cycle stages and transitions – in short, a systemic conceptualization of the problem. This conceptualization is separate from any specific theory a therapist ascribes to, although it is informed by systems theory in general and knowledge of developmental and family therapy theories. It required a therapist who was competent in understanding theories that would inform the complexities of the work (based on the initial conceptualization). This required knowledge of individual theories related to anorexia and PTSD, as well as couple and family theories related to the couple and family dynamics. The right conceptualization dictates strategies of action implemented in collaboration with clients. In the above case, individual/group work with William's PTSD in parallel to the couple/family work might have been another feasible strategy if the couple intervention was not successful. This conceptualization of the problem and then subsequent prioritization of interventions requires therapists to be highly collaborative with their clients, clearly communicative and highly flexible in changing when interventions based on the initial conceptualization do not appear to be working or as new crises arise.

Disrupting Dysfunctional Relational Patterns

Disrupting dysfunctional relational/systemic patterns was originally identified as a common factor by Sprenkle et al. (2009). Family therapists have long recognized and stressed that the patterns of interaction or sequences of relating in systems are a key component of problem formation and resolution (Breunlin et al., 1992). The idea that there are patterns of interactions within systems is a core concept in family therapy thinking. Not all patterns of interaction are problematic, and they are important to healthy family functioning (e.g., routines). At other times, they are a core part of the problem and maintain dysfunctional problems in systems. This common factor is integrally related to the systemic conceptualization of the problem. The conceptualization points to areas for intervention, but it is the disruption of the process of the system that moves change in the positive direction. Ideally these relational patterns are disrupted in the present time – that is, the here-and-now – but they can also be shifted with carefully structured interventions with individuals or parts of families (see Table 4.2 for some common family therapy approaches to interrupting system patterns).

Before we begin to talk about our common factors lens to viewing the disruption of dysfunctional relational patterns, refer to Table 4.2 to see how traditional family therapy approaches have used model specific language and techniques to end up at a similar outcome.

Family Process

To be effective in disrupting system patterns, it is important that CFTs have an intimate knowledge of family process if they are going to work with systems. When families come to treatment, they are most interested in finding resolutions to their problems and are focused on the content of their problems versus the process (Nichols & Schwartz, 1998). Common across all schools of family therapy are mechanisms to interrupt the process. This may look different depending on the model used and the presenting issue. For example, some models use interventions such as boundary making, "I" statements, circular questions, strengthening of the hierarchy and interrupting communication patterns to shift *how* family members relate to each other (see Table 4.2). *Process* is contrasted with *content*. Content involves the actual words, ideas and information exchanged. Content is not to be ignored, and sometimes it is critically important to focus on the content; for example, suicidal thoughts, abuse, violence. However, knowledge of content does not change the process; that is, how family members relate to each other. Clients will work very hard to pull therapists into the content, but effective therapists who work with systems keep bringing the process to the forefront so that important therapeutic change moments can occur.

Process can be defined as the "nature of the relationship between interacting individuals" (Yalom, 1995, p. 130). Therapists who are process oriented are concerned not only with the verbal content of a client's utterance but with the *how* and the *why* of the utterance. In group/systems therapy, one searches for

Table 4.2 Five Examples From Family Therapy Models of Disruption of Dysfunctional Relational Patterns in a System

Description of Interruption Intervention	Effects Achieved Within System	Theoretical Roots
Boundary making. This is a classic technique developed by Minuchin (1974) that interrupts negative sequences by establishing a boundary. Examples of this include stopping someone from speaking, creating rules for interacting or changing physical space such as chairs in a therapy room.	Setting a boundary stops an interaction in its tracks. System members are forced not to relate in their same familiar ways, because they are unable to transcend the boundary. Therapists can be instrumental in setting boundaries in sessions, or they can empower clients to set boundaries in their lives outside of therapy.	Structural family therapy
Coaching. Coaching is a classic Bowen family therapy concept (Bowen, 1978) where the therapist works in session with a client (often an individual). The goal of coaching is to help individuals to change themselves as they enter their relationship/extended family systems. The goal is that these individuals would engage with their systems without emotionally cutting off from them or giving in to the pull of the system. In this regard, then, by changing how they relate in the system, the individual disrupts system patterns.	Changing the way an individual relates in this system forces all members of a system to engage differently. For example, if an adolescent is continually triangulated into their parents' conflictual relationship, the therapist would coach the adolescent to set boundaries around triangulation, forcing the parents to talk to each other. McGoldrick and Carter (2001) laid out three steps: 1. System mapping. 2. Helping an individual learn about their role in the system. 3. Reentry into the system in an authentic way, while changing the role an individual has in old system patterns.	Bowenian family therapy
Restructuring experiences and interactions. When system members attend therapy, they bring with them a way of relating to each other that is displayed in repetitive and entrenched cycles of interaction. The goal of therapists is to bring the experiences/ interactions into the here and now of therapy and to shift things in therapy so that system members have a new experience of their relationships with each other.	Restructuring in sessions allows system members to have a new experience of their ways of relating to each other. This new experience/way of relating shows system members an improved way of relating to each other (different to their negative cycles). These new ways of relating translate into new interactions outside of sessions (see Johnson, 2004).	Emotionally focused therapy; symbolic experiential therapy

(Continued)

Table 4.2 (Continued)

Description of Interruption Intervention	Effects Achieved Within System	Theoretical Roots
Shifting the meaning of behaviors in a cycle. A key way in which family therapists interrupt the cycle of behaviors is by shifting the meanings of behaviors that drive the cycle. There are several ways to change the meaning (attribution) of behaviors. Reframing, as detailed in this book, is a common approach. Other approaches including a focus on exceptions to problems or alternative stories that disprove the problem narrative.	Shifts in the meanings of interactions provide individuals with new attributions to attach to the behaviors of system members. For example, in emotionally focused therapy, when the therapist frames "controlling behaviors" as originating from positions of fear, insecurity or hurt, it has the power to shift the ways individuals relate. Instead of being repelled by controlling behaviors, an individual can move toward hurt feelings. This shifts how system members relate to each other (see Johnson, 2004).	All family therapy approaches use strategies to change the meanings of behaviors
Implementing new behavioral routines in a system. Shifting interaction patterns can simply be having system members implement new routines. Simple interventions such as couples going on a weekly date night, families eating dinner together or families going on walks in the evening can all serve to shift typical interactions.	While behavioral routines may not be the complete long-term intervention, in the short term they serve to help family members have new interactions with each other (see Christensen et al., 2020).	Behavioral systemic interventions

the process not only behind a simple statement but behind a sequence of statements. We can assume that processes of interaction are somewhat similar across contexts. Communication occurs in sequences of interchanges, and it is these sequences that illuminate important patterns of interaction. It is important to identify sequences of interaction within a family. These occur during the conceptualization phase mainly by observing family members as they interact with each other. The therapist is also actively engaged in asking circular questions about these interactions; for example, "When dad yells, what do you do?" These types of questions help to map out the sequencing of behaviors, and it is these sequences that are ideally interrupted.

How to Identify Process

If CFTs are going to successfully interrupt maladaptive patterns in a system, they must be adept at identifying the process of interaction between members of the system. It is this process that the therapist then targets for disruption. It is essential that the therapist be tuned in to what is going on between family members. The therapist must be able to intentionally seek out the process. In this, it is essential that the therapist be able to separate themselves out from what is going on in the system; that is, if the therapist inserts themselves too much into the system, they will misunderstand/misread the process. Process-oriented therapists start out by noticing everything that goes on in their interactions with members of the system. This starts out from the first contact; for example, who makes contact first and how does this unfold. We note nonverbal data; for example, seating arrangements (e.g., who chooses to sit where, who sits together, who sits near and far from the therapist), presentation in therapy (e.g., dress, timeliness), engagement with the therapist (e.g., eye contact, posture, looking at watch, yawning) and engagement in therapy (e.g., no-shows, excuses for not attending). Therapists must be process detectors, noting what people say and what they avoid. Avoidance may be indicative of important topics that some members of the system may not want to discuss. Process can be illuminated when members are added or removed from the group. For example, a parent may be animated and engaged when the other parent is absent but be completely silent when they are seen together. We find that emotions are a key window into process. Emotions, especially intense emotions, tend to activate automatic processes in systems. When emotions intensify, we pay particular attention. If one family member starts to cry, what happens? Who is concerned? Who acts to comfort? Who grows silent? These are all clues into the process between family members. Process invariably is the same or similar around these emotional dynamics between family members, no matter the content. The pursuing family members will pursue, the peacemakers will try to make peace and conflict avoiders will avoid conflict across content situations. One important aspect about the process is that it is not essential for therapists to know the *why* of the process; they don't need deep insights initially into why system members are interacting with each other in a certain way. Rather, as will be expounded upon below, therapists need to be prepared to reflect on or point out the process. This is usually best done in a curious and questioning way. For example, the therapist can say, "I noticed when your mom started to cry, you became silent and did not seem to move in your chair for a while. I may be wrong, but it seems like something big was going on inside you".

How to Utilize Process: Illumination and Use of the Here and Now

It is not enough to observe the process. Therapists must intervene in the process to shift family dynamics. Yalom (1995), who has written extensively about process in group therapy, advocated for two phases in working with process in the here-and-now. In the first step, he described the *activating phase*, a time in the therapy where the therapist's primary task is to move the family/group into the here-and-now. This is a subtle shift, and it involves moving the group away from discussion of content material related to issues outside of the immediate concern of the group and instead helps the system members to focus their attention on their relationships with each other or what is going on in the therapy room *in the present*. This entails system members becoming more *aware* of what is going on *in the present moment* and tuning in to their *experiences* of each other in the present. The second phase involves *process illumination*, a time in which the therapist focuses on the process of what is going between members of the system. In this process, the family/group reflects on itself and its dynamics. Yalom suggested that the family/group doubles back upon itself in a self-reflective loop and examines the here-and-now behavior that has just occurred. In this process, system members gain insight into their behaviors in relation to each other and how their behaviors affect each other. A third phase, indicative of family therapy, is what we call a *process action phase*. During this phase, the therapist guides family members to shift their process or ways of relating to each other. This shift in process provides family members with a *new experience* of their relationships with each other. This is not an experience that replicates old behaviors but rather one that provides them with insights into a new way they can relate to each other. For example, in emotionally focused therapy (Johnson, 2004), the therapist provides a context where couples can experience new relationship dynamics as the therapist helps couples take risks with each other, share vulnerabilities and respond to them in caring and attuned ways. These new experiences occur in session, represent a new way of relating for the couple, and become a foundation for a new way of interacting with each other into the future. The therapist will push/encourage clients to shift their process by, for example, taking risks to share vulnerable feelings with each other. This sets up a partner to respond to what is shared. This process of helping one individual to share vulnerabilities and the other to respond to the vulnerabilities in attuned and responsive ways has a significant impact on how the couple experiences their relationship. This focus on process shows clients what their behavior is like and how their behaviors make others feel. It provides a new experience of how their relationship can be. This shifts familiar ways of relating, provides hope for the future and ideally translates into the relationship outside of the therapy room.

Intervening in the here and now (experiential) entails a move away from a historic focus into the present moment and how people are relating in the here-and-now. All major evidence-based family therapy models focus on the experiential; that is, they bring key system members together in the same room and work to change the experiences that these system members have with each other by changing how they relate with each other. The here-and-now is ahistoric (although never truly ahistoric). The goal is rather to use the past inasmuch as it offers insight into how to system members relate to each other in the present (Yalom, 1995).

Therapists should not only be able to identify the process but should also be able to interrupt, shift or deepen the process. To do this, the therapist intervenes in a way that gives family members a new experience of their interactions together in the present moment by bringing the experience into the moment and through having system members engage with each other in the moment. This "in the moment engagement" is built on by the therapist, who guides the system members into an alternate experience than they would usually experience, one in which the therapist can guide them to new ways of relating through deeper and more positive interactions. These shifts in the moment translate into larger shifts in their relationships with each other outside of therapy. The systemic therapist is focused on steering the process of therapy into the here-and-now at every opportunity and have system members process and enact what is going on in the moment in the session. System members do not report on what happened in the past; rather, the therapist has them discuss in the present what their concern is with each other. Rather than the therapist asking a husband, "Tell me about the fight you had with your wife last week", the therapist directs the husband as follows, "Tell your wife what was going on for you last week when you had that fight". This is a significant shift in the interaction. The therapist is not being reported to but rather is a witness to the couple discussing the fight together in the present. This is a substantial change in the dynamic of the couple and in the dynamic of therapy. The therapist works to facilitate a process commentary (a self-reflective loop) in system members by having them reflect on their interactions together. In this way, the therapist helps clients to *experience* their relationship with each other differently and has them step back and *reflect on* their relationship with each other. Sometimes the process reflection occurs when the therapist instructs system members to do something together and then instructs them to reflect on that experience. On other occasions, the therapist may simply ask an open-ended question and then use silence to drive clients deeper into their experience. For example, the therapist may say, "That was a pretty powerful statement that raised everyone's heart rates; what was going on for each one of you during that interaction?" (followed by silence). Silence can be a powerful process tool at this point. Carl Whitaker, a family process founder, stated that silence drives people back onto their own internal resources (Whitaker, 1976).

To illuminate process, it is of high importance to focus on affect. There are two important considerations in this regard. First, the therapist should notice and ask about the feelings of system members present in the therapy room. Therapists should ask these individuals about how they are feeling and should push them for feelings and not cognitions. Sometimes clients will answer a feeling question by providing a thought, and therapists must reorient them to respond with a feeling. It is also important that the therapist monitor their own internal feelings during the therapy process. A therapist's internal feelings are an important guide for what is going on in the therapy and can instruct the therapist on what is occurring in the room. It should be emphasized that if the therapist has many unresolved issues, they may get the process wrong because it will become about them and not about the system members they are working with and for. If therapists have done their own work and their own emotional issues are largely under control, they become ideal process consultants. When this occurs, the therapist can trust their feelings and intuitions about what is going on between members. These are feelings that therapists come to trust after living through many similar experiences in therapy or in their own families. These feelings can be like a stethoscope is to a doctor. We see many feelings as important to therapists in identifying process. For example, any emotion the therapist is feeling can be important to the therapist; for example, boredom, anger, frustration. The therapist does not even need to understand what they are feeling but only needs to have enough awareness that they are feeling something. This can be important in informing the therapist and can be reflected back to the client when the moment presents itself. For example, the therapist who is constantly feeling bored with a client can ask themselves, "Why am I always so bored with this client? What is that about them that brings up boredom?" The therapist can also ask the client in a diplomatic way, "When you are telling these stories, I have a difficult time following them. I wonder if others feel that way as well?"

The therapist can be an obstacle to process illumination. For example, if a therapist is uncomfortable with intense emotions, they may steer the therapy away from this intensity through tangential questions or humor (often unintentionally). Therapists need to actively reflect on their own role in identifying and interrupting process. Therapists should reflect on themselves and whether anything was occurring internally that prevented them from asking tough questions, avoiding emotions, challenging clients or staying engaged in the process. Therapists may find themselves inadvertently protecting themselves or certain clients from discomfort. Unfortunately, a focus on the process will always lead to uncomfortable feelings in the room, and these are almost always healthy and will help system members change and grow. Clients may not like the therapist who is pushing them, and these reactions may lead to negative responses toward the therapist. However, if the therapist has a sound alliance, they can work through these negative reactions.

Becoming a good process therapist takes skill. Therapists ideally focus on process and make comments and reflections on the process from the outset of therapy. These comments and reflections tune family members into process, allowing them to begin to shape their thinking in systemic ways. The timing of process comments is important. The best timing for process statements occurs around emotions aroused in the room when the therapist interrupts the process and has the family stop and reflect. A process focus shifts and deepens the intensity of therapy and, in our view, a process focus works best when some emotional intensity is present in therapy.

Interrupting the Process

Therapists can use many different strategies to interrupt the process. They need to be able to *interrupt without alienating* system members. We categorize these process interruptions in three groups: behavioral, cognitive and emotional. Davis and Piercy (2007a, 2007b) concluded that therapists help clients to both disrupt their process and then later reflect upon their respective parts in the negative interactional sequences using a combination of behavioral, cognitive and affective interventions (see Table 4.2 for examples).

Behavioral shifts in the process occur when the therapist disrupts behaviors in the present. This can be as simple as allowing system members to speak in turn or when the therapist has given them explicit permission to speak. At times, all communication may need to go through the therapist. Other times, the therapist is "directing traffic" and in this role prevents system members from interrupting each other. Therapists may exclude members from a conversation (e.g., meet only with parents) or change the way seating occurs in the room. All of these are examples of shifting the process through behavioral means.

Cognitive interruptions to the process occur primarily when the therapist gets members to reflect on and gain insight into the process and their role in the process. This may entail the therapist asking members to stop and reflect on what is occurring in their interactions with each other. In this regard, the therapist alters how family members think about their interactions with each other.

Emotions drive process, and process becomes automatic because of emotional intensity; they pull system members in. To shift process related to emotions, the therapist has system members reflect on how they are feeling during an interaction and then share these in appropriate ways such as by using "I" statements. An example would be asking a child to share what they were feeling when the parents were arguing. In emotionally focused couple therapy, the process is shifted by having members of the dyad share different (and more palatable) feelings with each other. For example, instead of having individuals share anger, the therapist helps the individual to share their hurt feelings behind the anger or to describe what was going on that made them feel angry. Sharing hurt feelings without attacking makes emotions easier to respond to and allows system members to move closer to each other and be more responsive to each other; in this regard, the process shifts from combative anger to more connecting interactions.

Interrupting Patterns When the Here-and-Now Intervention Is Not Possible

It is not always possible to get all key system members into the same room together. Intervention is easier if all system members attend sessions. However, there are many reasons why individuals do not attend, including distance barriers, distrust of therapy, financial resources and simple unwillingness to be a part of therapy. Even though it is more difficult, it is possible for therapists to change maladaptive interactional patterns with only one or a few system members present. Most important, an individual can change their own role in negative sequences of interaction. When working with individuals or small groups in a system, therapists should work to help these individuals gain insight into the negative patterns of interaction and not to engage in them. For example, an individual can be coached not to engage in interactions that are negative and act differently. McGoldrick and Carter wrote a seminal article on coaching in a system when working with just one person (McGoldrick & Carter, 2001). They contended that if one person is able to change their emotional functioning in a system, the whole system will eventually change. They describe several steps to working with just one individual. The first step is to help the individual to gain insight into the dynamics of the system in which they are embedded.

This insight will help the individual see *what* needs to change. The second step is to help the individual to *understand their own role* in the system and in the negative cycle. Every individual in a system plays a role in negative interactions, and everyone should change to shift these dynamics. Third, they argued that an individual should engage in the interactions in ways that are different than what they did before. The therapist helps the individual to engage differently in the cycle of interaction in the system. The therapist helps the client understand the system and the reactions of the system to their new interactions. Often this work is intense, and clients are reluctant to follow through because of the intensity. McGoldrick and Carter (2001) suggested that there are three steps in this process: (1) the change, (2) the system's reaction to the change and (3) helping the individual deal with the system's reaction to change. These steps can take a lengthy period and entail the therapist helping a client engage differently with their system and then sustain the engagement so that change becomes permanent. Shifting the role of one person in the system can lead to new structures in the system and improved functioning for all (Foote et al., 1985). For example, if a parent chooses to change their approach to parenting, this can occur without the approval of the adolescent or the other parent. Now the parent may need help in dealing with the reactions of the adolescent or the other parent, but important shifts can occur with changes in just one of these members.

Expansion of The Therapeutic Alliance

The therapeutic alliance is historically made up of three key variables (see Chapter 9 for a in-depth focus). First are the *goals of the alliance*, meaning that the client and the therapist are on the same page in terms of the goals of therapy. Second is a *connection* (bond) between the therapist and client and whether this bond is sufficient to be conducive to the work of therapy (i.e., whether the client feels connected enough to the therapist to engage in therapeutic work). Third are the *tasks of therapy*, including the clients' and therapist's comfort with the activities engaged in during therapy, activities usually initiated by the therapist that foster the work of therapy. In CFT, the therapist must be able to manage alliances with more than one individual at the same time.

Different from individual work, the therapist must be able to form alliances with multiple people at the same time, keep them all engaged in the process, and treat them equitably. In short, the therapist needs to be seen as a trusting and caring ally for all concerned. Chapter 9 goes into detail on the alliance, but we will discuss nuances related to the expanded alliance here as well. The expanded therapeutic alliance accounts for the complexity of the different interpersonal subsystems relevant to the therapy. Sprenkle et al. (1999) referred to the expanded alliance as follows:

> When more than one person is involved in the direct client system, the expanded therapeutic alliance may be a common factor unique to CFT. If, for example, a husband and wife and two teenage children participate in therapy, each of the four individuals will have an alliance with the therapist. In addition, each subsystem (parents, marriage, partners, and siblings) will also have a subsystem alliance with the therapist, which is more than the individual alliances. Further, the entire client system will have an alliance with the therapist that may be more than the individual and subsystem alliances combined. (p. 348)

It is important to consider the many different combinations of the therapeutic relationship that exist in working with couples and families. This makes the therapeutic relationship in CFT not only unique but also complex and important. Pinsof (1994) referred to four interpersonal levels of the therapeutic relationship that are possible in working with couples and families.

The individual relationship. This relationship exists between the therapist and members of the family as individuals. It is the one-on-one relationship that the therapist can establish with each individual member of a family independently. Further, these independent relationships are different, with some been stronger than others. The therapist, through their humanness, will find themselves drawn to certain family members and repelled by others. This has a lot to do with what the therapist brings to the therapy room regarding issues such as their own birth order, family of origin and current life crises.

Subsystem relationships. In working with couples and families, one aspect the therapist must deal with is having relationships with different subsystems within the larger system. These relationships can significantly support or undermine the process. It is quite common for subsystems to stick together against an external "foe." The therapist is treading on sensitive territory when members of subsystems gang up against them. If it is a powerful subsystem that has a say over the continuation of therapy, it is likely that therapy will end. Different subsystems include the parental subsystem, sibling subsystem, gender subsystems and extended family subsystems such as aunts, uncles or grandparents. Who to have to stronger relationship with will be discussed in detail in Chapter 9, but it is important to note at this juncture that there are usually subsystems in a family that hold more sway in the family with whom the therapist needs to have the strongest relationships.

The whole-system relationship. Not only does the therapist have a relationship with each family member independently and with combinations of these individuals in the form of subsystems but the therapist also has a relationship with the family unit or couple as a whole. This is ultimately the client whom the therapist is helping; they are seeking good outcomes for everyone in the family and in this regard for the family as a whole.

Within-system relationships. *Within-system relationships* refers to relationships that exist within the therapeutic system, such as alliances and coalitions that are both overt and covert in the therapeutic system. The therapist who remains unaware of these might run the risk of alienating family members or misunderstanding resistances. Within-system alliances are the alliances that system members have with each other. Within-system alliances examine how system members who present in therapy are doing in terms of the bonds, tasks and goals they have with each other, and system members should develop a strong working alliance within their relationship. It is particularly important to get most system members on the same page in terms of the goals and tasks of therapy, and the therapist should continually monitor the alliances that members have with each other. For example, if individual members shift their goals for therapy, they are no longer on the same page and will work against each other.

Pinsof (1995, p. 67) concluded that "Each alliance level and locus influences, through mutual causality, every other level and locus." He went on to say that

> ... different aspects of the alliance are more influential in the overall outcome of therapy. . . . [The] key determinant of which subsystems contribute most to the variance in the total alliance is the amount of power the subsystems have to facilitate adaptive changes within the patient and therapist systems. (Pinsof, 1995, p. 68)

In other words, when working with large systems, therapists need to be aware of *how power is distributed in systems related to the alliance.*

Rait (2000) suggested that the skilled couple and family therapist must be adept at "developing and maintaining a functional therapeutic milieu that continually balances the therapist's relationship with each family member, as well as various coalitions within the family" (p. 213). It is the task of the therapist who works with multiple family members to address the unique needs of an individual in a family and to connect with that family member while at the same time keeping the other family members engaged in the process and not polarized to the therapist or to the specific family member with whom the therapist connects. It might also be necessary for the family therapist to challenge family members' beliefs or actions. This can activate hidden loyalties, and the therapist might find themselves confronted with family members' anger. It is not uncommon for family members who are add odds with each other and who seek help for their difficulties to suddenly present a united front when confronted by an external threat such as the therapist, even when the external threat is their best chance at getting help for their problems.

The CFT therapist must learn to manage the therapeutic relationship in a context of vulnerability, emotionality, conflict and threat when there is more than one system member in the room, each feeling a different aspect of the conflict or threat (Rait, 1998). Rait (1998) aptly noted that

> . . . with regard to managing changes in this evolving, multifaceted alliance over time, the contemporary literature has been notably silent. As any therapist walking the tightrope between battling family members or competing coalitions knows, the most formidable clinical challenge involves not simply building these alliances, but also sustaining them over the course of therapy. (p. 173)

Chapter 9 is devoted to the alliance and details building alliances with important systems beyond the immediate client system (e.g., schools), and we refer you there to read more on the expanded therapeutic alliance.

Expansion of the Direct Treatment System

CFTs expand their work and extend their engagement beyond direct treatment systems. The *direct client system* includes the members of the client system who are related to the presenting problem and who are directly involved in therapy at any point in the process. These are the clients or family representatives who are present in the therapy room. The *indirect client system* consists of members of the client's system who are related in some way to the problem (and possibly its resolution) but who are never directly involved in the therapeutic process. When the therapist does not consider the indirect system the client interacts with on a day-to-day basis and the inherent power in this indirect system, the therapist may find themself battling to keep the influence they have with the client from a relationship perspective (Pinsof, 1992). The involvement of the indirect treatment system can be conceptual or can involve additional work to engage the indirect system in some way. An example of conceptual thinking about the indirect treatment system would be when a minority family is experiencing racism in a community; although the therapist may be powerless to directly shift racist behaviors in a short time, the conceptualization of this indirect influence on the family is of high importance to how the therapist goes about working with the system. An engagement of the indirect system would occur in the example of reaching out to teachers of a child struggling with academics.

Multiple partners may exist outside of treatment depending on the case and the presenting problem. For example, in working with troubled children, it is not uncommon for therapists to need alliances with key players in the life of the child, including schoolteachers, other treatment providers (e.g., psychiatrist), child protective services workers, attorneys or case workers. Or, in a collaborative healthcare context, therapists may need to have relationships with physicians, physician assistants and nurses. The therapist must be able to build and maintain alliances that will help the family obtain the best treatment possible. These members of the indirect therapeutic system may have a large influence on therapeutic outcomes. Expanding the direct treatment system involves the therapist influencing these systems or advocating for client well-being within these systems. Medical family therapists, for example, have made great strides in working in medical settings and in influencing the medical outcomes of clients. They achieve this by working with multiple medical personnel involved in a case.

While the examples above discuss involving community stakeholders, the treatment system can be expanded to include additional members of the client's family system. In these cases, family therapists push to involve more people than the immediate client(s) directly in treatment in order to enhance the treatment (Pinsof, 1995). These include persons not physically present in treatment but who affect the problem in important ways. For example, after doing family-of-origin work with an adult son, the client is ready to work on his relationship with his aging mother. The therapist expands the system to conduct this dyadic session, as the mother moves from the indirect into the direct client system. There are also indirect patient systems that include those individuals who do not engage directly in treatment but who can affect treatment in some way. These individuals are often hard to engage or take additional work on the part of the therapist, but once they are engaged, they can impact treatment in a large way.

As Sprenkle et al. (1999) noted, therapists who expand the direct treatment system see the impact of therapy as occurring when the therapist engages with a live system and the immediacy of that system that plays out in the here-and-now. This is only possible when these individuals are present together at the same time and the therapist can intervene in the process that emerges. Pinsof (1995) suggested that (1) therapists will learn more about clients and their problems if they meet as many key members in their system and context as possible; (2) alliances will be stronger in these systems if the therapist has taken the time to meet and engage these systems through face to face contact; (3) when work is done in the collective and everyone present is impacted by the work, the greater a resource they can be; (4) major breakthroughs are more powerful when they have more witnesses; and (5) the therapist will have a more accurate understanding of the problem maintenance structure by being part of the system in therapy.

Before deciding to expand the direct client system, it is important to consider the following questions:

- How does the referring client (the client who calls for help) narrate their problems and ask for help?
- Is the problem relational?
- What theoretical rationale are you using to justify expanding the system to others beyond the immediate client system?
- How does the referring client respond when you tell them about your attempt to expand the direct client system?

We provide three key steps to engaging the indirect treatment system in therapy.

Consent and Rationale

It is important that the client system be onboard with expanding the direct treatment system. There is likely to be resistance to this idea initially. Clients who consider including extended family in treatment or schoolteachers, for example, may find themselves filled with anxiety. As a result, it is of high importance for therapists to have their complete consent to reach out to players beyond their immediate system. It is also important for therapists to provide a strong rationale for this so that clients can see how this is connected to them and their personal growth. Below are some example statements therapists can make to expand the treatment system.

- **School involvement:** "I am asking your permission to contact the schoolteacher and principal. It might seem strange to you that I would reach out to them directly but there are two large benefits to this. First, I will get to hear their side of the story directly from them, and their viewpoint is often invaluable to successful treatment. Second, I will be able to advocate on your behalf with the school leadership".
- **Inviting extended family to sessions:** "We have been working together now for some time, and we have discussed how hurtful your mother has been to you at times in your life. I think it is time we invited your parents to one of your sessions. I know that this creates a lot of anxiety in you,

but we will learn a lot in our time together with them, and in my experience, this is often an opportunity for growth".
- **Inviting co-parent to therapy:** "I know you are no longer together with your son's father, but a lot of our sessions revolve around how you wish he would change. I am wondering if we could strategize together about ways we can involve him in treatment so that he will be a co-parent who is a resource to you and to your son".

Building an Alliance With the Indirect Treatment System

In the same way as it is important to build alliances with all members of the system, it is essential that the therapist build a working alliance with the indirect treatment system. Therapists need to present themselves as allies versus someone who will cause stress. In the above example of inviting parents to session, they may feel very threatened by the prospect and be afraid that the therapist would confront them in ways that are not helpful. The therapist should thus present themselves in as supportive a way as possible. It is also ideal if the therapist can describe the clear goals for the work and the methods that would be used to achieve the work. The therapist can say,

> Your daughter has been struggling with some issues, and she needs your support. We would like to meet with you for three sessions. In these sessions, she will read some insights to you from her journal and ask for your reactions. We are not setting this up for you to feel blamed for anything. Our goal is to find ways for you to be an even bigger source of support to her.

In cases where therapists are working in systems such as schools or healthcare centers, the therapist may need to have a positive relationship with the system as a whole.

Collaboration

Although built into the previous two steps, the entire work with the indirect treatment system is conducted through the lens of collaboration. When working outside the direct treatment system, any individual may be important to treatment. For example, in working with schools, the therapist will need to gain the trust and buy-in of many entities within the school, including administrators, teachers, school counselors and the like. They all have a unique view of the situation, and the therapist should first learn their viewpoints before trying to change them. The therapist should be positioned as a resource who can facilitate a better way for all. In medical family therapy, the therapist is positioned as the driver of collaborative care, serving as the therapist with the family and as a collaborator between the family and medical professionals (Tyndall et al., 2012). The therapist in these contexts has to be able to form and maintain relationships with key players and facilitate conversations between them, often in a short period of time.

Conclusion

In this chapter we reviewed common factors unique to CFT. Becoming an expert in each of these areas will help the therapist be more effective in working with systems and in achieving the best changes for the client system.

References

Bowen, M. (1978). *Family therapy in clinical practice.* Jason Aronson.

Breunlin, D., Schwartz, R., & Kune-Karrer, B. (1992). *Metaframeworks: Transcending the models of family therapy.* Jossey-Bass.

Christensen, A., Doss, B. D., and & Jacobson, N. S. (2020). *Integrative behavioral couple therapy: A therapist's guide to creating acceptance and change* (2nd ed). W. W. Norton.

Davis, S. D., & Piercy, F. P. (2007a). What clients of couple therapy model developers and their former students say about change, part I: Model-dependent common factors across three models. *Journal of Marital and Family Therapy, 33,* 318–343.

Davis, S. D., & Piercy, F. P. (2007b). What clients of couple therapy model developers and their former students say about change, part II: Model-independent common factors and an integrative framework. *Journal of Marital and Family Therapy, 33,* 344–363.

Foote, F., Szapocznik, J., Kurtines, W., Perez-Vidal, A., & Hervis, O. (1985). One-person family therapy: A modality of brief strategic family therapy. *NIDA Research Monograph, 58,* 51–65.

Johnson, S. (2004). *The practice of emotionally focused couple therapy: Creating connection* (2nd ed.). Brunner-Routledge.

McGoldrick, M., & Carter, B. (2001). Advances in coaching: Family therapy with one person. *Journal of Marital and Family Therapy, 27*(3), 281–300. https://doi.org/10.1111/j.1752-0606.2001.tb00325.x

Minuchin, S. (1974). *Families and family therapy.* Harvard University Press.

Nichols, M. P., & Schwartz, R. C. (1998). *Family therapy: Concepts and methods* (4th ed.). Allyn and Bacon.

Pinsof, W. M. (1992). Toward a scientific paradigm for family psychology: The integrative process systems perspective. *Journal of Family Psychology, 5,* 432–447.

Pinsof, W. M. (1994). An integrative systems perspective on the therapeutic alliance: Theoretical, clinical, and research implications. In A. O. Horvath & L. S. Greenberg (Eds.), *The working alliance: Theory, research, and practice* (pp. 173–195). John Wiley & Sons.

Pinsof, W. M. (1995). *Integrative problem-centered therapy.* Basic Books.

Rait, D.S. (1998). Perspectives on the therapeutic alliance in brief couples and family therapy. In J. Safran & C. Muran (Eds.). *The therapeutic alliance in brief psychotherapy* (pp. 171–191). American Psychological Association. doi: 10.1037/10306-007

Rait, D. S. (2000). The therapeutic alliance in couples and family therapy. *Journal of Clinical Psychology, 56,* 211–224.

Sprenkle, D., Blow, A., & Dickey, M. (1999). Common factors and other nontechnique variables in marriage and family therapy. In M. Hubble, B. Duncan, & S. Miller (Eds.), *The heart and soul of change: What works in therapy* (pp. 329–360). American Psychological Association.

Sprenkle, D., Davis, S., & Lebow, J. (2009). *Common factors in couple and family therapy: The overlooked foundation for effective practice.* Guilford.

Timm, T. M., & Blow, A. J. (2005). The family life cycle and the genogram. In M. Cierpka, V. Thomas, & D. Sprenkle (Eds.), *Family assessment: Integrating multiple perspectives* (pp. 159–192). Hogrefe.

Tyndall, L. E., Hodgson, J. L., Lamson, A. L., White, M., & Knight, S. M. (2012). Medical family therapy: A theoretical and empirical review. *Contemporary Family Therapy, 34*(2), 156–170. https://doi.org/10.1007/s10591-012-9183-9

Wampler, K. S., Blow, A. J., McWey, L. M., Miller, R. B., & Wampler, R. S. (2019). The profession of couple, marital, and family therapy (CMFT): Defining ourselves and moving forward. *Journal of Marital and Family Therapy, 45*(1), 5–18. https://doi.org/doi:10.1111/jmft.12294

Whitaker, C. (1976). The hindrance of theory in clinical work. In P. J. Guerin (Ed.), *Family therapy: Theory and practice.* Gardener Press.

Yalom, I. (1995). *The theory and practice of group psychotherapy* (4th ed.). Basic Books.

5
CHOOSING THE RIGHT MODEL FOR YOU AND YOUR CLIENTS

Overview

How do you know if you are choosing the right model for yourself and your clients? On the surface this may seem like a simple question, but for many systemic therapists the answer could be quite complex and multifaceted. Deciding on a model is a filtering process that requires discipline, clinical experience and time. It is completely developmentally normal to try several models before you find the right fit. Numerous variables influence choice of one model over another, such as personal worldview, the culture of your training program, your family of origin, past/present romantic relationships and your own personal therapy, not to mention the characteristics and preferences of your clients. Through both personal life and clinical experiences with different client systems, your tastes may change over time. It could also be expected that through these experiences, you may discover limitations with your original model of choice after experiencing frustration or failure in the therapy room. In this chapter we will help you develop a self-reflective process to understand how purposeful model selection for you and your clients may serve to potentiate powerful common factors in couple and family therapy.

Let's first start by defining what we mean by the term *model*. A model is a conceptual framework that provides a theory-driven outline for (a) generating hypotheses about the client system, (b) formulating a rationale for using specific interventions and (c) evaluating the ongoing therapeutic process.

The Importance of Models

Clients often enter therapy overwhelmed and unsure of where to go or what to do with their problems. They need direction and structure to first understand and then make changes in their lives. Much like clients need a credible pathway to change, therapists need similar organizing frameworks. Therefore, we believe that you must have some type of model to guide your therapy. A model serves as a coherent, organized "roadmap" that therapists use to get where they are going with their clients. Your choice of model guides virtually all of your clinical decisions. Good models clearly articulate an explanation for dysfunction along with interventions to create alternative thoughts, feelings and actions for our clients. Although distinct in application and language, couple and family therapy (CFT) theories are similar in that all use interpersonal, systemic models to guide relational therapists through the process of understanding client problems and developing solutions. Additionally, learning models may have some merit because they can create confidence and avoid *syncretism*, a type of haphazard selection of techniques and interventions that often resembles what is referred to as an undisciplined, "seat of the pants" style of therapy (Karam et al., 2015).

As opposed to a potential radical stance on common factors that would completely diminish the value of models, we see merit in learning as many specific CFT theories and approaches as possible (Blow et al., 2007; Sprenkle & Blow, 2004a). After all, common factors are not islands unto themselves but, rather, they work through models (Sprenkle & Blow, 2004b). Only when we learn several models really well can we see the similarities that exist between them. Reading this book and completing the practical exercises throughout these pages will help you use your existing systemic framework or favorite CFT model to potentiate powerful common factors empirically linked to therapeutic success.

Empirical Evidence and Model Selection

Over the past several decades, our profession has attempted to compete with the other major mental health disciplines by advancing the science behind the art of what we do. To better answer the important question about research's impact on model selection, we first need a scientific way to compare outcomes across models. Meta-analysis consists of a set of statistical techniques for quantitatively aggregating and summarizing the results of numerous psychotherapy outcome studies. It serves as a convenient evaluative tool for you to review the evidence for and against the practice of CFT and provides the empirical rationale behind our moderate common factors approach.

In their influential meta-analysis, Shadish and Baldwin (2003) concluded that couple and family therapy clearly works, both in general and for a variety of distinct presenting problems. More specifically, they concluded:

- CFT models are absolutely efficacious when compared to no treatment at all.
- CFT models are at least as efficacious as other modalities, such as individual therapy, and may be more effective in at least some cases.

There is little evidence for differential efficacy among the various CFT models, particularly if mediating and moderating variables are controlled. Therefore, while there is strong evidence for the effectiveness of certain approaches, there is not yet strong evidence for the relative effectiveness of the various evidence-based models vis-à-vis each other. Knowing this information from these CFT meta-analyses helps systemic therapists to realize they need not make a premature commitment to the superiority of any one model.

What if I use a classic CFT model (e.g., Bowenian, experiential) that is neither evidence based nor included in these meta-analyses? Does this mean that these models are not effective? Do not despair! Given that CFT is used for an extremely wide range of presenting problems, many without a clear diagnostic definition, it is not feasible that there will be evidence for every application of the approach to treatment. To the extent that such models are (a) based on sound theoretical and systemic principles, (b) organized and coherent and (c) implemented by competent therapists with allegiance to the approach, they would most probably (but not certainly) be proven to be just as effective as their empirically supported counterparts. Given that many of our classic models have no data to support their claims, you could also study similar next-generation CFT models that have excellent empirical support as to their effectiveness with specific populations (Sprenkle, 2012; Sprenkle & Blow, 2004a). For example, those therapists learning an evidence-based model like emotionally focused therapy (EFT) should be able to see the commonalities between this approach and the work of its nonempirically validated experiential predecessors, such as Satir (1988) and Whitaker and Keith (1981). We would advocate that you learn the approaches to problems you work with that have the best current evidence available. For example, if you work with couples, we would advocate that you learn EFT, integrative behavioral couple therapy, or the Gottman method, approaches that have all been well studied.

Learning Models

Singular Training: Pure Model Mastery

If you discovered family therapy prior to the 1980s, chances are that you were originally trained in a related mental health discipline (i.e., social work, counseling, psychology). Early CFT pioneers trained their fervent followers not on college campuses but at free-standing institutes throughout the United States in single-school, pure model approaches. If you were in the market for a family therapy education, you might have felt both excited and confused, as there were many establishments to choose from, each purporting to teach "the absolute truth", including the Philadelphia Guild Guidance Clinic, the Bowen Center for the Study of the Family in Washington, DC, the MRI Brief Therapy Center in Palo Alto, the Ackerman Institute of New York and Haley & Madanes' Family

Therapy Institute of Washington, DC, just to name a few of the early meccas of CFT training. As a student at any of these centers, however, you were only taught one model: the proprietary approach of the model developer. For example, a family therapy trainee at the Philadelphia Guild Guidance Clinic would be trained entirely in structural family therapy, without any exposure to popular alternatives at the time, like the experiential models of Satir and Whitaker or the transgenerational theories of Bowen or Nagy.

This type of pure model training is believed to provide the beginning therapist with a deeper theoretical appreciation for how peoples' problems originate and are ameliorated through model-specific techniques and interventions. Students learn to apply the model, in both theory and practice, to different presenting problems and family constellations. It could be argued, however, that it is more difficult to see commonalities between approaches or learn openness and flexibility later on in your career if you have only prioritized one pure model for a long time.

Concurrent Training: Minimal Competence With Multiple Models

In stark contrast to this pure model mastery approach, the concurrent model of psychotherapy training that exists in most modern-day, university-based CFT programs teaches models simultaneously and focuses on minimal competency on a wide range of CFT theories and approaches. As often displayed in a family therapy theory course, this sequential approach to training can be referred to as "the model of the week" style that conforms to the time available for instruction and the structure of the course. Proponents of a concurrent approach to learning CFT models stress that this style emphasizes the interconnection of change processes in systemic therapies and primes young therapists for critical thinking and the ability to compare/contrast models from the onset of their training (Karam et al., 2015). A potential downside of concurrent training, however, is that the exposure to each model is too brief to make an informed decision about goodness of fit. You could easily feel overwhelmed by the multitude of model choices available to systemic practitioners. Even if you find a model you like on paper, you may feel lost in the therapy room when attempting to put the theory into practice without continual training and supervision. Furthermore, the model therapists prefer may end up being a poor fit for specific clients. Of note is that some of the most well-researched evidence-based models are not taught in any depth to new trainees. Some of this has to do with branding of models by developers as well as lack of training in these models by CFT faculty.

Integrative Training: Merging Models and Techniques

Integrative training allows a great range of choices in treatment and therefore great flexibility in working with different client systems and presenting problems. Many systemic therapists claim that their orientation is integrative or eclectic, but what does that really mean? Is there a rationale behind why and when they integrate, or do they flexibly mix and match interventions and models without much thought? Both integration and eclecticism involve the application of theoretical concepts and interventions that cross pure model boundaries. While some seasoned practitioners pick up an integrative stance informally after many years of clinical experiences with couples and families, other systemic therapists are formally trained to be purposeful in their integration during their graduate school experience.

There are four formal pathways to integrative training: (1) assimilative integration, (2) technical eclecticism, (3) theoretical integration and (4) common factors (the focus of our book). Assimilative integration is an approach in which a solid grounding in one theoretical approach is accompanied by a willingness to incorporate techniques from other therapeutic approaches. In technical eclecticism, the same diversity of techniques is displayed but without a unifying theoretical underpinning. Theoretical integration provides a metatheory or, in other words, a theory about how to combine theories. It prescribes a logical order of operations of how, when and why models should be integrated. This style of training promotes teaching integration from the beginning, providing a specific guiding framework that therapists will gradually grow into as they deepen their knowledge of different models and theories over the course of their psychotherapeutic careers (Norcross & Goldfried, 2005).

BRINGING THE COMMON FACTORS TO LIFE: TRAINING AND MODEL SELECTION CHECKLIST

How were you originally trained in CFT?

☐ *Major focus on one particular model*
   Model name_____

☐ *Minimal exposure to multiple models*

☐ *Integrative training*

What initially influenced your choice of model? (Check all that apply and circle the most influential factor.)

☐ *Professor/supervisor*   ☐ *Your own personal therapy*

☐ *Early clinical experiences*   ☐ *Research evidence*

☐ *Family of origin*   ☐ *CFT coursework/curriculum*

☐ *Your personality*   ☐ *Other: _____*

How did your graduate training experience influence your theory development process? How did it either allow you space or limit your ability to explore different models?

_____
_____

How did your postgraduate clinical experience and supervision influence your choice of model?

_____
_____

Are you still practicing CFT in a manner similar to how you were originally trained?

☐ *Yes*
☐ *No*

If you answered "no", how has your preferred model or theory changed over the course of your career? What factors necessitated these changes?

_____
_____

Model Selection and Worldview

Your Own Worldview

We are who we are, shaped by both nature and nurture. Every therapist has a unique outlook on life, commonly referred to as a *worldview*, which influences the types of models we are attracted to. Whereas personality traits are innate and relatively stable over the life course, a worldview is not necessarily something we are born with. Rather, this personal perspective on life is shaped by time and experience. Articulating a worldview usually requires making decisions, though not necessarily in an explicitly conscious way, about what governs behaviors, thoughts and feelings about the human condition. Self-awareness is essential in this articulation process of a worldview. Once aware of your own beliefs and values, you can move to adopting a CFT approach that not only serves family systems in intentional ways but also complements who you are as a unique individual.

We presumably experience a more "natural" fit with some orientations than with others. Believing that we are naturally attracted to therapeutic models whose underlying story about the human condition closely matches our own, we propose that CFT is enhanced by therapists who have explicitly chosen to guide their practice based on models with congruent worldviews (Blow et al., 2007). For example, I (EK) grew up as a sensitive kid very attuned to my feelings and concerned about how others felt about me. I was also greatly impacted by the death of my father when I was a child. Based on my genetic "hard-wiring," my family-of-origin experience and what I learned in my human development classes, I believe that our early caretakers and parental figures provide the blueprint for which we judge all future relationships. Without a proper blueprint, people may become stuck and unable to form healthy relationships. Through safe and healing reparative relationships, however, I also strongly believe that these same people with faulty blueprints can overcome previous relational deficits and wounds to go on to have more secure and fulfilling connections in their adult romantic partnerships and friendships. Given this worldview, coupled with my sensitive personality traits, I am naturally drawn to attachment-based, experiential CFT models, like EFT.

Allegiance refers to the therapist's belief that they are doing will be effective for the client system they are treating. You must assess whether or not you believe in the theory and then determine your ability to convey that conviction to the clients so that they may "buy in" as well. Therefore, if the personal worldview of the therapist does not coincide with the theoretical underpinnings of the model, the therapist may experience some degree of dissonance or resistance when attempting to integrate it into their practice of CFT. For example, consider a therapist who is very collaborative in both her approach to therapy and her overall worldview. She believes that a therapist should never claim to be an "expert", that people are not defined by their problems and that clients ultimately have the strength and self-determination to discover their own solutions. Usually drawn to various postmodern, social constructivist approaches, this therapist is having trouble implementing paradoxical directives from strategic family therapy that were recommended to her during her peer supervision. She feels uncomfortable presenting herself in an expert role and being less than transparent with the family she is working with.

Your Client System's Worldview

Much like ourselves as couple and family therapists, client systems bring to the therapeutic experience their own personal preferences and unique concerns, expectations and values. Some scholars have suggested that clients can retain their own worldviews while still being open to a model-derived conceptualization by their therapist. The clients might also accept parts of the therapist's explanation while rejecting other elements that don't seem to fit for them (Simon, 2012). We firmly believe, however, that CFT works best when therapists can match their way of working to the worldview of clients as long as the therapist is able to practice with authenticity (Blow et al., 2012; Vargas & Wilson, 2011). The inclusion of your client system's worldview and values in this discussion about model section acknowledges that the effectiveness of your therapy is likely to be increased when it is responsive to the system's values and preferences. However strong the empirical evidence for a specific model, it is unlikely to bring about the desired changes for a couple or family if it does not address their particular needs or if it is not in accord with their worldview. Research also demonstrates (Sprenkle & Blow, 2007; Blow et al., 2012) that utilizing the client's theory of change and worldview may strengthen the therapeutic alliance, increase client engagement and overall enhance therapeutic outcomes.

CFTs are trained to ask every member of a family system about the problem that brought them to therapy and their treatment goals during an initial session. To learn clients' worldviews, however, we must go beyond these traditional inquiries and be curious enough to ask a complementary series of foundational question in an intentional way. These questions seek a clear understanding of how clients view relationship problem formation and resolution. Questions that target a client's theory of change, core values and beliefs will aid the therapist in both understanding and adapting to the particular client's worldview. After asking the right questions, you then should listen closely to the client's language and use the exact words that they choose to describe both the human condition and their unique dilemma. We are not advocating for you to passively accept the views of your clients about change but rather that you engage in an active, generative exchange with them about their predicaments and ways in which change can occur. Honoring the client's worldview occurs when you encourage and nurture the client's ideas for change or when you select a technique or intervention that fits the client's beliefs about their problem(s) and the change process.

Worldviews are valence free – neither right nor wrong. While it is important for couple and family therapists to identify their own, they must do so without judgment of others' contrasting worldviews, especially their clients. For example, is a client who values dependence on their spouse wrong? No. However, you must both understand and respect the value and how it may affect your own theoretical orientation and the work with the client system. When working with multiple family members in a system, you must remember not to assume that each client shares the same worldview. Take, for an instance, a father who values independence and self-reliance. In family therapy, the dad often gets frustrated with his wife, who believes there needs to be more nurturing and parental assistance at home with their unconfident teenage son. Therefore, you should evaluate client worldviews on an individual level, rather than a family level, and in the process be mindful about the assumptions you make about the personal worldviews of your clients.

Bringing the Common Factors to Life: Worldview Self-Reflection

We have developed some questions to help you explore how worldview influences both your theory of change and the model selection process. Articulating your own values, life philosophy and view of couple and family therapy is an important step in solidifying your professional identity. However, to truly adapt a common factors framework to this process, you must also identify the views, values and life philosophies of your client systems.

CHOOSING THE RIGHT MODEL

Worldview Self-Reflection

For You:

What are the principles and values that are central to who you are?

_____
_____
_____
_____

How did your family of origin experience influence these principles and values?

_____
_____
_____
_____

What are the models that most align with these principles and the values that you described? How are they related to your principles and values?

_____
_____
_____
_____

How would you describe your personality? Which models do you feel more or less drawn to as a result of your personality? Why?

_____
_____
_____
_____
_____

How specifically does your preferred model fit or not fit with your ideas about how people change in CFT?

_____
_____
_____
_____

Which models help you to contextualize your family of origin in a meaningful way? How have these models enhanced your understanding of your role in these important familial relationships?

_____
_____
_____
_____
_____

Do you feel drawn toward a particular model based on your experiences in current or past relationships (romantic, children and friendships)? Explain.

_____
_____
_____

If you are currently in therapy or have been in therapy in the past, how has your experience affected your model selection process and how you view change?

_____
_____
_____
_____
_____

For You & Your Clients:

- *What values and beliefs are central to your identity?*

_____
_____
_____
_____

- *What have been the strongest influences on your family's beliefs and values (e.g., culture, education, religion, etc.)?*

_____
_____
_____
_____

- *What makes for a healthy relationship?*

_____
_____
_____
_____
_____

- *How do problems arise in relationships?*

_____
_____
_____
_____
_____

- *Even when they are "stuck", people often have a pretty good idea about not only what is causing a problem but also what needs to happen for improvement to occur. Do you have a theory of how change is going to happen in your relationship?*

_____
_____
_____
_____
_____

- *Who is responsible for change in your family system? Who is responsible for change in this therapy?*

_____
_____
_____
_____
_____

- *What keeps people from making changes in their lives? What has constrained you in the past?*

_____
_____
_____
_____
_____

- *Clients want different things out of their therapist. Some want a sounding board, some want to problem solve, some want to learn new skills, some want an expert to tell them what to do and, especially in CFT, some want the therapist to tell them that they are "right" and their loved one is "wrong". What do you expect out of me in this therapy?*

_____
_____
_____
_____

- *What are your expectations about how I will balance my time and attention between you and your other family members in this therapy?*

_____
_____
_____
_____

References

Blow, A. J., Davis, S. D., & Sprenkle, D. H. (2012). Therapist–worldview matching: Not as important as matching to clients. *Journal of Marital and Family Therapy, 38*, 13–17.

Blow, A. J., Sprenkle, D. H., & Davis, S. D. (2007). Is who delivers the treatment more important than the treatment itself? The role of the therapist in common factors. *Journal of Marital and Family Therapy, 33*(3), 298–317.

Karam, E. A., Blow, A. J., Sprenkle, D. H., & Davis, S. D. (2015). Strengthening the systemic ties that bind: Integrating common factors into marriage and family therapy curricula. *Journal of Marital and Family Therapy, 41*(2), 136–149.

Norcross, J. C., & Goldfried, M. R. (Eds.). (2005). *Handbook of psychotherapy integration* (2nd ed.). Oxford University Press.

Satir, V. (1988). *The new peoplemaking*. Science & Behavior Books.

Shadish, W. R., & Baldwin, S. A. (2003). Meta-analysis of MFT interventions. *Journal of Marital and Family Therapy, 29*(4), 547–570.

Shadish, W. R., Ragsdale, K., Glaser, R. R., & Montgomery, L. M. (1995). The efficacy and effectiveness of marital and family therapy: A perspective from meta-analysis. *Journal of Marital and Family Therapy, 21*(4), 345–360.

Simon, G. M. (2012). The role of the therapist: What effective therapists do. *Journal of Marital and Family Therapy, 38*, 8–12.

Sprenkle, D. H. (2012). Intervention research in couple and family therapy: A methodological and substantive review and an introduction to the special issue. *Journal of Marital and Family Therapy, 38*(1), 3–29. https://doi.org/10.1111/j.1752-0606.2011.00271x

Sprenkle, D. H., & Blow, A. J. (2004a). Common factors and our sacred models. *Journal of Marital and Family Therapy, 30*(2), 113–129.

Sprenkle, D. H., & Blow, A. J. (2004b). Common factors are not islands—They work through models: A response to Sexton, Ridley, and Kleiner. *Journal of Marital and Family Therapy, 30*(2), 151–157.

Sprenkle, D. H., & Blow, A. J. (2007). The role of the therapist as the bridge between common factors and therapeutic change: More complex than congruency with a worldview. *Journal of Family Therapy, 29*(2), 109–113.

Vargas, H. L., & Wilson, C. M. (2011). Managing worldview influences: Self-awareness and self-supervision in a cross-cultural therapeutic relationship. *Journal of Family Psychotherapy, 22*(2), 97–113.

Whitaker, C. A., & Keith, D. V. (1981). Symbolic-experiential family therapy. *Handbook of Family Therapy, 1,* 187–225.

6
ENHANCING CLIENT AND CONTEXTUAL FACTORS

Introduction

While therapists exert a great deal of influence in therapy, they are not the only change variables by a long shot; client and contextual factors also play a pivotal role in change. Some of these are outside of the influence of the therapist while others can be *enhanced, leveraged and maximized by the therapist* to effect change. When I (AB) was still an intern, I was working with a heterosexual couple who presented complaining of a lack of intimacy in their marriage. Therapy was stuck and "all in the head", with sessions staying on the surface. Out of the blue (and tragically), the husband's brother was killed in a freak accident. The next session was very powerful as the couple dynamic became organized around the loss and the emotions that it brought up. For the first time in a long time the couple were able to share feelings and move toward each other emotionally. This type of event in the life circumstances of clients, although tragic, can also be used as a springboard to change if the therapist is seeking these opportunities (Blow et al., 2009).

The Healing Potential Within Clients and Their Context

In earlier chapters we described how 86% of change can be ascribed to events going on outside of the therapy room (Wampold & Imel, 2015). These are variables that pertain to the client and to the context in which the client lives that all influence change. In this chapter, we detail *how to mobilize client factors* that are related to change – these are factors that are *within clients* as well as factors/events that *exist in the context of the clients*. We work from the assumption that most individuals and family systems have innate healing capacities but get stuck due to a variety of factors, including context, tunnel vision, an oppressive history, avoidance, narrow ways of viewing situations, unaccessed emotions or difficult life circumstances. While these challenges can be overcome without therapy, the skilled therapist is able to help clients come up with new ways to view their situation and make sense of their lives. Even when a therapist is not perfect or operating from the best evidence-based theory, therapy can still be helpful.

DOI: 10.4324/9781315542737-6

Clients use what is offered to them by the therapist to effect change (Tallman & Bohart, 1999). Helmeke and Sprenkle (2000) studied pivotal moments in family therapy and concluded that clients took what therapists' provided and used this information to their own ends in therapy.

Healing is not always accessible to clients because factors in their lives or in their histories get in the way of their healing processes. This would be like an infection in the body preventing a wound from healing. Our goal as therapists is to draw from our own skills but also to "exploit" what the client offers to unlock powerful individual, couple and family-level strengths that will improve therapeutic outcomes. This is even more important when working with systems. In any system there is a capacity for things to go wrong, but there is also tremendous potential when all members are working together to achieve a goal and to bring about healing. There are potent healing capacities in systems, and these capacities are even more pronounced when these shared resources are effectively used and when the whole system is working together toward a common goal.

Clients present in a variety of ways in therapy, and they bring with them their own unique individual characteristics. In addition, when working with systems, we are faced with the task of working with many individuals together who present *a combination of client factors* that work together in systemic ways. As therapists, we start off with what the clients present with, and we work with what we are given at the start of treatment. As we learn about the clients and their unique factors, good therapists seek out ways to fit client variables to the treatment approach to enhance therapy outcomes.

There is no doubt that some clients are easier to work with than others. We have all worked with highly motivated and psychologically minded people who arrive in therapy ready to work and whose change process is quite easy to facilitate. There are other cases that are much more difficult and take more effort, energy and time on the part of the therapist. Each individual client presenting in therapy has factors, including age, genetic predispositions, and ethnic background, that must be considered. Upon meeting these clients, we get to know them based on their unique characteristics and their reporting of their presenting problem. One of the things we assess early on is whether they can accomplish anything in therapy (e.g., whether they have the cognitive abilities) and whether they a good fit for who we are as therapists. There is a "getting to know you" period at the outset of therapy where these factors are assessed overtly and covertly.

Clients not only present in therapy with their unique characteristics but they also present with contextual variables. These are factors that exist in the life context of the client, and these factors can be both a resource for change as well as an impediment. From a systems perspective, the context is always related to the problem in some way, and shifting the context can lead to transformations in many cases. It is critically important to take the full context into consideration as therapy commences and progresses. We will discuss this point more fully later in this chapter, but each level of a context needs to be evaluated and considered in relation to a presenting problem. Clients will struggle more in therapy when they come from very difficult contexts such as those characterized by poverty or neighborhoods filled with violence or when they have scarce resources.

Understanding, Increasing and Sustaining Motivation

Motivation is a key consideration when it comes to change, and it is an important client-related change factor. Ideally clients are not only motivated to change but have the resources to aid their change process (services like therapy) and are able to stick with their change process long enough to reach an effective outcome. We believe that most clients will eventually arrive at a resolution of their issues if they have a motivation to find healing. The resolution may not be what they had in mind when they started, which is rarely the case in life, but most will arrive at a resolution for their issues. There are many factors related to how one defines a resolution of a problem. For many, acceptance of a situation may be a good outcome versus changing the situation. For some couples, a divorce may be the best (and the most painful) outcome. For a few, change is relatively quick, whereas for others it may take time, often years. This may depend on the extent of the issues a client brings into therapy. For example, a client with many past traumatic experiences may need many therapy sessions to work through all of the trauma. We believe that therapy works best when we can help our clients start out in therapy with a strong commitment/motivation to change and the willingness (if resources allow) to put in the required effort and to stick with the process long enough for meaningful change to occur. This is particularly challenging in systemic work in that different members of systems have varying levels of commitment to change and fluctuations in motivations and not everyone wants to stay in therapy for a lengthy period.

Understanding Motivation

There are always different motivations for change among members of a system, and they are rarely equal. Often, some family members are in treatment due to some external leverage such as an ultimatum, a court order or even a bribe, as in the case of teenagers. It is important that the therapist address the different levels of motivation early on. These motivations are also connected to the expectations for therapy and what clients are willing to do or how hard they are willing to work to bring about change. To achieve this, a first question a therapist should ask to individuals presenting for relational therapy is "How do you feel about being here today?" In our experience, the answer to this question reveals a tremendous amount about differing motivations among family members. A therapist can then react to the responses to this question – reactions that serve to enhance motivations. If a husband says, "I don't want to be here tonight, and am only here because my wife threatened divorce," this statement can elicit several responses from the therapist that shift the conversation and hence the motivation of this individual. Sample responses by the therapist include, "Would this be worth your time if I can help make your home life happier?" Or "It is difficult to live with the threat of divorce. What if one result of therapy is that there will be no more threats?" While these are just sample responses, it is readily apparent that an early therapy goal should be to lower his defenses and engage him further as a partner in the therapy.

Other good questions to ask include, "What led to you presenting in therapy at this time?" and "On a scale of 1–10, with 10 been highly motivated and 1 not motivated at all, what would you rate as your motivation to change your problem?" If clients are demotivated, therapists need to be curious and learn about the reasons why they do not want to change. What are their fears about change? Why do they believe their family members are more or less motivated than they are? The lack of motivation is often related to past hurts, mistrust of therapy, fears related to facing problems in therapy or happiness with or acceptance of the status quo. Validation, reassurance and negotiation are key therapist skills at this moment in therapy. In systems, the therapist needs to be able to use differing motivations of family members as early discussion points for resolution. Failure to address these concerns heightens the chances of premature dropout and lowers the odds for success in therapy.

Individuals who are motivated to change and who can see a way to change are more effective at getting through difficult situations such as mental health problems or family difficulties. In general, we will refer to this as *client motivation*. In family/couple systems, motivations can be dampened by pessimistic family members, whereas motivations can be enhanced by members supporting each other, encouraging each other and creating momentum in the direction of change. When family members are working against each other, demoralization is an outcome that can easily occur. In these scenarios, family members pull each other down, undermine each other and harm their progress in therapy (often unintentionally).

Increasing Motivation

Some clients who present in therapy are starting out in a highly demoralized state, and seeing a positive outcome to their situation may not be possible. In these cases, an early therapy goal is to help the client come to a commitment to change and contract for a course of therapy long enough that will allow for change to eventually come about. We find that this is a helpful negotiation to achieve early on in therapy.

> **Case Example 4**
>
> A recent supervisee that I (AB) worked with struggled to motivate a mother and her daughter (age 13) to change (they were working against each other). They had presented for family therapy with numerous problems. The clients had recently lost their husband/father, who had died in surgery; the mom had lost her job; and the daughter was receiving poor grades in school. They were both understandably feeling depressed, overwhelmed and very much alone. The mom had developed an addiction to pain medication (something she did not want to work on in therapy but something the daughter complained about in the first session). This case raised many important issues due to the numerous problems they were facing and the severity of each. Some questions we discussed together were: Which issue was the top priority to address in therapy? What was the goal of each client, and how did this clash or meld with the goal of the therapist? How was the therapist going to address the competing goals of the mom and daughter? What did they feel motivated to work on?
>
> The daughter stated that she wanted to feel happier but mainly wanted to help her mom stop using medications. Mom stated that she did not want to feel pain all the time and she also wanted her daughter to get better grades. When questioned about grades, the daughter was adamant that she was happy with C grades. Both complained that they were completely overwhelmed and liked to sleep a lot. They also stated that the only reason they were in therapy was because the high school principal had threatened to call social service authorities if they did not see a therapist. The reality for this client system was that they were both so sad and had experienced so many losses, and both were unmotivated to change (especially when it came to issues related to their own selves). For example, while their grief reactions to the loss of their husband/father was appropriate, it became clear that even though it had been a year since he died, neither was willing to move on and truly grieve his loss. Mom's growing addiction to pain medication was helping her to numb her feelings to such an extent that she did not wish to give the medication up because of her fears of being overwhelmed by her feelings. As a result, the therapy with the mom spiraled in circles as the aspects of her life that

> she wished to change – her sad feelings – were not immediately accessible because she was not ready to give up her addiction. If she moved through the grief, she was afraid she would dishonor the memory of her husband. If she gave up her addiction, she feared she would completely fall apart. Further, the mom did not feel close to her daughter because they had been arguing with each other a lot for the last 6 months. The daughter was not motivated to change, saying that she did not feel she had very much to live for at this point in time.

Our supervision solution emerged as follows: the key was to find something that the clients could be motivated to work on while slowly raising their consciousness about other areas in their lives that they might want to change. This was not an easy task. The therapist had her first breakthrough when she got both mom and daughter to commit to 12 weeks of conjoint therapy for 1 hour a week. The agreed-on focus of the therapy was on strengthening their relationship. As therapy progressed, both gradually lowered their defenses and were willing to work on issues beyond their relationship, including sadness, depression and addiction. Motivation was not something that came about like a switch being turned on. Rather, it grew over time as each worked on issues they were struggling with.

The willingness and motivations of the client system to work in therapy are vitally important if change is to occur. These include client attitudes of openness and self-exploration (Bachelor & Horvath, 1999). Henry and Strupp (1994) concluded that when clients are willing or able to become involved in and invested in their treatment, outcomes are almost always usually better. This is not a radical finding. Experienced therapists know that it is far easier to form sound therapeutic relationships with clients who are motivated to change and who are engaged in the process. It is interesting to note how this works in the therapy room when there is more than one client present. As will be explored below, this can go both ways. At times, adding family members may enhance client willingness to engage and contribute to the therapeutic process, and at other times, especially when treatment is stalling or negative, adding clients may lead to heightened disengagement. For example, a family working on grief after the loss of a grandparent may all be motivated to work on their emotions related to the loss, whereas in a family with a daughter with anorexia who is highly resistant to change, the level of motivation will vary among family members, and there is likely to be a polarization between the parents, who are pushing for change, and the daughter, who is resisting change. In this case, family polarizations and fears limit the engagement of a powerful system member who is the one family member who is critical to change; that is, the daughter with anorexia. Polarizations in systems directly undermine motivations for change. Think of polarizations as people digging their heels into the ground, which is counter to any movement in the direction of change.

Having multiple individuals in the therapy room allows family members to feed off each other, both with their motivations and with their criticisms. Thus, the therapist can focus on who is motivated in the system, whose motivation is essential to engender change and who to target to engage. This process can work to enhance or weaken the therapeutic relationship. If any individuals are not interested in the process and are merely attending sessions to pacify an important family member, there may not be much the therapist can do to engage these clients and to prevent their influence on each other. On the other hand, if the therapist can engage these clients, wonders in the therapeutic process can result, moving the overall momentum of the therapeutic process in the direction of positive change.

A key early-stage family therapy skill is to change how family members come to see their problems – that is, to change the viewing of the problem – because this is closely connected to motivation. Changing how clients see the problem, the potential outcome and the potential pathway to achieve that outcome raises hope and amplifies motivation (Snyder et al., 1999). Research studies have focused on how to increase motivation and engagement in family therapy, and family therapy models such as functional family therapy devote the entire first stage of therapy to increasing engagement and motivation among members of the family. This is largely achieved through building a secure therapeutic alliance and by providing a view of the problem different to the old through reframing. This new view of the problem provides a vision to the clients – a vision about how things can be different – and it is this vision that motivates them to work for change. Importantly, this new view reduces polarizations between family members, allowing them to shift their polarized positions. It is often the case that family members arrive in therapy pointing fingers at each other and blaming each other for their problems. As soon as they can see the problem (the threat) as something they can agree upon, they can relax and not attack each other directly but shift their focus to solving their problem.

Early therapy sessions are of high importance in setting the stage for subsequent change and enabling momentum in the direction of positive change. Low engagement of a client system early on will result in either early dropout or the wrong players attending therapy. We like to think that therapists need to gain influence early on to springboard therapy in the direction of positive change. Whitaker referred to this as winning the battle for initiative (Neill & Kniskern, 1983).

Sustaining Client Motivation

Not only do we want clients who are motivated to change but we want clients who will give treatment enough time to work – this makes it essential for the therapist to help them to stay motivated. Motivation needs to be more than fleeting. We find it important to ask about motivation on a regular basis. Formalized feedback that is ongoing allows us to inquire regularly about the therapy process and how clients are feeling about therapy, whether things are going well and whether they remain motivated to change (see Chapter 10).

Evidence-based models refer to remaining in therapy long enough for it to have a chance to work as a *dose effect* – meaning that you need to have the correct dosage of an intervention for meaningful healing to occur. We are not talking here about endless, meandering therapy sessions but rather enough sessions that will give change a real chance. Each model of therapy has a recommended number of sessions. In general, for couple and family therapy cases, we like to see weekly 1-hour sessions for 4 to 6 months. This translates to around 15 to 20 sessions. While change can certainly occur in fewer sessions, we encourage our clients to stay longer to give sustained change the best opportunity to occur. This is especially true for clients who are reluctant to look at their problems or hesitant to go deeper into the work of therapy. This is also true for cases with multiple problems – it is simply not possible to solve complex cases in a short period of time. We present clients with these scenarios from the onset of treatment. We let them know what events enhance the likelihood of change. We work to get them to contract to a minimum of 3 months of therapy. Sometimes costs are a barrier, and we assist clients in budgeting the costs of therapy versus the costs of not changing. This cost–benefit analysis often shows that therapy is a bargain.

Dispersion of Motivation in the System

One challenge we run into frequently in systemic family therapy is what we refer to as the *dispersion of motivation* among family members. It is rare that all family members showing up for therapy have the exact same motivation to change. There is always a motivation discrepancy, and this disparity is greater the more members we add to therapy. For couple/family therapy to be successful, we see it as essential to address and combat the dispersion of motivation to attend therapy and to effect change among all members of the system. A couple attending therapy where one member is desperate for change and the other does not see the need for change presents an immediate therapy dilemma. The risk of dropout in this case is high because the less motivated member may simply decide not to return (the less motivated member is instantly more powerful). We see the same dilemma in families presenting with adolescent difficulties. At times it is the adolescent who is demotivated for therapy. At other times it is one of the parents, often the father. In still other cases, we have worked with clients who are mandated by court systems or family members who attended therapy because of an ultimatum from other family members; for example, a spouse threatens divorce or parents threaten an adolescent with loss of driving privileges. The presenting problem can also heighten the urgency with which clients present in treatment, and this often affects motivations to change. For example, couples affected by an affair will often present in treatment soon after discovery of the affair. The presenting motivations may be different once the crisis is peeled back, but the motivations to change will be more urgent early in the process.

Working to Align the Motivation of Key Family Members

It makes sense that one cannot have a cohesive family therapy process if members have different motivations, and especially if their motivations go in different directions. While it is impossible for all members of a system to have the same motivation, treatment will not proceed – or not proceed well – if motivations are vastly different. Less motivated members will undermine the work. Whom one targets for increasing motivation in couple and family therapy depends on the configuration of the system and on the conceptualization of the presenting problem. We will give three scenarios to illustrate aligning of motivation and specific ways in which to work with individuals to increase their motivation.

ALIGNING THE MOTIVATIONS OF THE PARENTAL SUBSYSTEM

When it comes to treating children in therapy, aligning the motivations of the parents to change is a key intervention. In fact, the process of aligning parents will bring about changes in the system, even if nothing else is a target for intervention. When working with children/adolescents, it is important for both parents/all caregivers of influence with the child to attend early therapy sessions. In these early sessions, the therapist assesses the problem and each parental figure's view of the problem and the sense of urgency they have for solving the problem. If one parent is not as motivated to change the problem as the other parent, it is likely that this is an early indication of a system issue that is related to the presenting problem in the child. When both parents/caregivers attend sessions, the therapist should meet with the parental subsystem on their own to dig deeper into reasons why the disparity in motivations exists. Once the therapist gets the parental subsystem on the same page in terms of the motivation (need) for change and the goals the family will be working on as a unit, therapy will progress much more positively. This first step maximizes the system's ability to work together and to draw on their resources in the direction of change.

DEMOTIVATED TEENAGER/CHILD

In a family system where a teenager is the presenting problem, often it is the teenager who has the least motivation to change. In this scenario, the therapist must find a way to engage and motivate the teenager to work in therapy. As long as the members of the parental subsystem are reasonably on the same page (see above), the therapist's attention should move to the adolescent, and early stages of therapy should focus on enhancing adolescent motivation. Reframing is a powerful tool (see Chapter 3) used to enhance motivation. Therapists should use this liberally with all family members present. In addition, the therapist can request brief individual sessions with the adolescent to assess barriers to motivation and build a one-on-one alliance. Questions to be explored include: What is driving the resistance of the adolescent? What is the adolescent afraid of if change occurs? What does the adolescent stand to lose? What would motivate the adolescent to change? At a minimum, the initial goal of the therapist should be to get the adolescent to attend therapy and to participate as much as possible. This may be a negotiation. The right incentive to change may be key to increasing the adolescent's motivation. There are often scenarios where there are multiple children in large family systems and the therapist may need to work with each alone or in child subsystems, especially early in the therapy process.

DISCREPANT MOTIVATIONS IN COUPLES

The third main scenario in which we see discrepancies in motivation is in couple therapy. While it is not unusual for each member in a couple to want something different from treatment, a common early mistake in couples therapy is for the therapist to assume erroneously that both partners have the same or similar levels of interest in maintaining the relationship. Simply because the couple has chosen to show up for an initial session does not equate to high relational commitment. At times, one or both partners might be uncertain about whether they wish to stay in the relationship, and their goal in coming to therapy is to render a decision. Other times, both partners might be unsure about the relationship, though one partner could already be disconnecting from the relationship while the other maintains significant investment.

Bill Doherty and colleagues referred to these couples as "mixed agenda couples" (Doherty et al., 2015). They could also be thought of as discrepant motivation couples. Each party may be uniquely motivated but for very different ends. One party may be motivated to leave the relationship and the other highly motivated to stay. Couples frequently present in therapy with mixed agendas and motivations, and often one party is showing up as the result of an ultimatum of some kind from the other partner. There are different ways to work with these couples. One approach would be joining, reframing and small interventions early on that lead to small changes that increase motivation in the less interested party by providing hope. Another approach would be to do an in-depth assessment of the reasons for low motivation to change and see whether these can be remedied. For example, the least interested party may have tried things to improve the relationship previously and may still have hurt feelings related to these attempts that make stepping up to work on the couple relationship appear very risky (this approach may closely follow emotionally focused therapy). In this sense, discrepancies in motivation are integrally related to the conceptualization of the problem within an attachment-based pursue/distance cycle. Another approach is one used in discernment counseling (Doherty et al., 2015). In discernment counseling, the therapist is specifically targeting mixed agenda couples. In this method, immediate improvement in the relationship is not an early goal; rather, work is done to directly address what is underlying the disparities in motivations and agendas for the relationship. Discernment counselors present the couple with three options: (1) to stay the course in the relationship and not change, (2) dissolution of the relationship and (3) a commitment to 6 months of couples therapy with some conditions. The first condition is that divorce/dissolution is removed from the table during this time of therapy. After the 6 months are up, the couple can reevaluate the relationship. If the couple agrees to option 3, the couple first engages in discernment counseling for one to five sessions. During this time, the therapist has individual sessions with each partner interspersed with joint sessions. The focus of individual sessions is on self-responsibility and self-differentiation, and the goal of these sessions is to create more responsibility in each individual for the well-being of the relationship. In addition, the individual work focuses on a deeper understanding of the couple's interactions and each individual's role in these interactions. The therapist works differently with the "leaning out" partner and the "leaning in" partner and aims to shift how both engage in the relationship. If discernment counseling moves into a therapy phase, each couple comes with their agenda about what they would like from the relationship. This approach does an excellent job of having individuals focus inward on their own issues and individual responsibility in the relationship problems, and then helping them develop an agenda that would lead them to greater happiness in the relationship.

The following screening tool, the Common Factors Couple's Continuum, is a quick and easy way to gauge discrepant motivation. It is designed to be used in an opening session to eliminate confusion around each partner's motivation and help set priorities/direction early in the therapeutic process. Although some partners might not verbally report their true motivation to the therapist in an opening session in front of their partner because they do not want to hurt their significant other or because they have not admitted it to themselves yet, we have found this continuum to be an excellent tool in facilitating this crucial opening session dialogue between the couple and the therapist. The sooner a therapist can identify each client's motivation, the sooner the therapist can act on this information and not waste time with ineffective interventions.

THE COMMON FACTORS COUPLE'S CONTINUUM

C------------A-----------D

The following continuum helps me as your therapist to gauge your current level of motivation for beginning this therapy.

- *The "C" represents commitment. No matter what problems or issues you may be dealing with presently, you are committed to using this venue to save or heal this relationship. Commitment in this therapy involves a very specific skill set that we teach, including (but not limited to) the ability to accept influence from one another, managing conflict, empathetically listening, repairing after relationship tearing and finding mutually beneficial solutions when possible. You are committed to change what is changeable in this relationship or to learn to accept and tolerate those things about your partner and this relationship that might not be as amenable to change.*
- *The "A" represents ambivalence. You are unsure about your commitment to the future of the relationship. The various stressors you encounter undoubtedly make you question the future of this relationship. Some days you are "in" but other days you are "out". In some moments, the answer feels so clear; you cannot live without your partner. And in other moments, you feel a nagging doubt, your partner's flaws seem overwhelming and you know there is something better for you. In some cases you might feel these diametric emotions at the exact same time.*
- *The "D" represents divorce, dissolution or feeling "done" with the current relationship. Continuous tension or conflict in your relationship sets a natural stage for considering healthy ways to end the union without doing further damage to yourself, your partner or the future of the relationship. This is especially important in relationships in which children are involved, necessitating "good enough" cooperation and communication in the co-parenting relationship moving forward. You intend to use this therapy to learn techniques to better manage negative feelings and resolve conflicts associated with ending the relationship. You desire time to address unresolved issues before going your separate ways, giving closure to both of you and providing a positive foundation on which to start the next chapter of your life.*

Each of you has your own perspective; thus, you each have been given your own continuum on a separate piece of paper. Without looking at your partner or overthinking, please mark on the continuum with an "x" how you currently feel about your relationship at the onset of this therapy. Please be as honest as you can but also know that your responses will be shared.

After collecting both continuums, show the markings to the couple. Ask each partner to explain in words what their mark on the continuum means to them. Next, ask the other partner whether they are surprised or not by their partner's response and current motivation for the therapy. Recognizing that partners can identify anywhere along the continuum, even when they are reporting their desire to work on the relationship, can alleviate significant therapeutic pitfalls and lead to better treatment outcomes.

Assess and Then Create "Motivation Carrots" for the Client System

Clients are often reluctant to engage in therapy because they are demoralized and they do not see therapy as a useful way to resolve their problems. It is important to assess clients' motivations early on in therapy and throughout the process as well (see Chapter 10 on formalized feedback). Clients need to be motivated to change, they need to see therapy as an avenue for change and they should trust you (the therapist) as someone who can bring about change. Here are some questions we ask clients when we sense that demotivation is a problem. (Note: it is possible to assess motivation by directly asking clients through formalized feedback and through nonverbal behaviors such as no-shows.) These questions should be asked in systemic ways (circular questioning) because it is often variables such as criticism or confrontation that polarize and demoralize clients. These questions are derived from several sources, including Tomm's work on circular questions (Tomm, 1987a, 1987b, 1988) and solution-focused therapy (de Shazer, 1988). Tomm (1987a, 1987b, 1988) suggested that these questions pose possibilities to clients or get them to anticipate different outcomes in their lives. Systemic circular questions also encourage awareness of the points of view and experiences of others. Reflexive questions are facilitative, opening space for family members to see new possibilities related to their situation. According to Tomm, they are deliberately designed to help clients to look differently at their situation. These types of questions may be good at enhancing the motivation of clients.

EXAMPLES OF QUESTIONS TO ASSESS AND ENHANCE CLIENT MOTIVATION

Individual Questions

How do you feel about being in the session today? [Follow up with prompts depending on the client's response.]

If therapy worked magic and solved all your problems, what would you be feeling or doing? What would therapy look like?

If therapy could help you solve your problem [name problem], would you be more willing to attend?

Systemic Questions

When your mom spoke to you a little while ago, you seemed to recoil. What was going on for you?

When your parents were arguing with each other, it looked like you wanted to run from the room. Did I get that right? (This question could be directed to the parents as well: "When you were arguing, Jason looked like he wanted to run from the room. What do you think was going on for him?)

When your spouse spoke to you in that soft voice with tears in her eyes, I could tell that you moved closer to her. What was going on for you?

Reflexive Questions

When things are going well in your relationship, what would you like to be doing?

What do you think the long-term consequences would be if your father continued to act in this way in the family? [angry father]

What do you think might happen in your relationship if you committed to doing some work in therapy, looking at yourself and speaking out about things that you are not happy about?

What goes through your mind when you hear your mom say that she is not interested in attending therapy each week?

___

___

___

Put yourself in your dad's shoes. What would it be like if you were him and had to come into session and watch his children argue and call each other names?

___

___

___

___

Engagement and Motivation, a Key Early Therapy Task

Santisteban and colleagues (1996) did research on engagement in family therapy and how to improve attendance and motivation to work in therapy. Their approach is implemented strategically by the therapist; that is, the therapist/therapy team decides who to target for engagement in treatment. The therapist, in the assessment process, identifies resistance within the system and then utilizes engagement strategies to overcome this resistance. Therapists reach out to resistant family members and use alliance-building approaches (e.g., joining) to make therapy more palatable and the therapist more human. The therapist uses reframing strategies to help the resistant client see therapy in a different light and see therapy as a mechanism to help solve the problems the family is facing. The therapist works to engage resistant family members through one-on-one calls, and the focus is on both removing barriers to therapy attendance and connecting with the client in a way that they can see therapy as "not so bad". In the brief strategic family therapy (BSFT) model, the basis of Santisteban et al.'s approach, resistance to engagement is viewed as part of the same family dynamics that led to the problem in the first place. That is part of why this approach is effective: when the therapist is reaching out to a disengaged/resistant parent, they are also achieving the goal of engaging the individual in the family. Instead of labeling the client as resistant, the therapist helps the client overcome the resistance through connecting to the client and offering plausible reframes, such as different ways to view the problem situation. The therapist is not focused on changing the individuals early on in treatment. Instead, the focus is on getting them to give therapy a try – to show up and stay in treatment for initial sessions. The BSFT approach comes from the assumption that resistance in treatment is because individuals are reluctant to change the system in which they are embedded. From the first phone call onwards, the therapist is working to engage and motivate clients. The therapist insists that family members attend sessions, and if there are excuses for why members cannot attend, the therapist asks to talk directly to those family members instead of relying on relayed messages.

EXPOSE SYSTEM MEMBERS TO EACH OTHERS' VIEWS

Another way to enhance motivation in couple and family therapy (CFT) is to have family members witness each others' views of the problem; ideally, this witnessing should occur in a safe and authentic context. When family members are interacting outside of therapy, they are often talking to each other in ways that are not helpful. There may be arguing, criticism and hostility. A key goal of early therapy is to have family members see that change is possible and that if it is achieved, it will be something beautiful and beneficial. To achieve this goal of witnessing, the therapist must create a level of safety in the system; that is, ground rules. It would be harmful if clients shared their views and were put down or shamed for their thoughts. When individuals share their points of view, their feelings or their vulnerabilities, they do not want harsh or judgmental reactions from other family members. We have found it very helpful to have families share these vulnerabilities and then to coach other family members to respond with compassion and kindness. Family members often do not listen when they are talking in their home contexts. If the therapist can create a context where family members can listen and be respectful, the chances of change occurring increase substantially.

Meeting Clients Where They Are At: Stages of Change

Clients present in therapy for a wide array of reasons. They come with different views of therapy and a variety of experiences with the therapy process. Some clients have been in therapy many times before, and for others it is their first therapy experience and they come with fears and assumptions about what therapy might be like. Clients also arrive in therapy with differing motivations (as described earlier) and at different places in the change process. In this section we emphasize that the therapist needs to be skilled at meeting clients where they are at in the change process and move with them through this process over time.

Defining the Stages of Change

Prochaska (1999) advocated for an understanding on the part of change-oriented professionals of the unique stages of change in which clients may find themselves. He provided a range of stages of change that should be considered in intervening with clients. Another way to think about stages of change is client readiness for change. Prochaska developed a widely used model for thinking about change. He suggested that change is not linear but is a roller-coaster process that occurs in a somewhat step-by-step manner. A successful outcome in therapy can be conceptualized as moving someone from one stage of change to another. This type of change goes largely unreported in large outcome studies. In some respects, these small changes might not seem to make a huge difference, but in other respects, they might represent a significant shift, even though it is not overtly noticeable.

In his metamodel, Prochaska (1999) described stages that clients navigate as they move through a process of change. Each move between stages represents a significant accomplishment on the part of the client. His six-stage approach consists of the following stages: precontemplation (unaware of or in denial that there is a problem), contemplation (becoming aware that a problem exists), preparation (planning for change), action (taking steps to change), maintenance (keeping the changes made) and termination (moving on). He pointed out that if a client is in a precontemplation stage of change, they may be unaware, uninformed or underinformed about their problem. Such clients we have worked with may include people who are referred by the court for treatment or individuals who are brought to therapy by a family member. An example is an unwilling spouse who is brought to couples counseling at the insistence of their partner. Other clients may present for therapy at the action stage in which they are actively in the process of changing and are highly motivated. In this case, the therapist serves mainly as a resource and a facilitator of the change process in which the client is actively engaged. Clients may cycle through these stages (small outcome) several times before large outcome change is realized.

Prochaska (1999) pointed out that the stage in which the client presents in therapy is closely related to therapeutic outcome and that therapists need to intervene in the lives of clients according to the stage in which they present in therapy. This suggests that therapy is not a 0 to 100 approach but rather is a series of steps that move clients in the desired direction. For an individual who smokes cigarettes, realizing that there is a problem is an enormous positive effect in the long term, even though the overall desired outcome (smoking cessation) may not be reached immediately.

Stages of Change: Matching Client Readiness for Change

The stages of change conceptualization strongly suggests that we should meet clients where they are at and intervene according to what they can handle. A client who is in the precontemplation phase of change needs different therapeutic interventions than a client who is in the action phase. Prochaska (1999) claimed that a mismatch of change processes can result in resistance in therapy. Pressuring clients to change when they are in a precontemplation phase will simply lead to opposition. Instead, Prochaska suggested that clients deemed to be in the precontemplation stage would benefit from consciousness raising about the problem and that this type of intervention will be far more effective. This highlights an important consideration of the stages of change idea – that clients have very different needs depending on their stage of change and ought to be related to very differently depending on where they are at in their lives. For example, clients may respond well to confronting statements in one stage but need more supportive interventions in another stage.

Dealing With Stage of Change Discrepancies Within a Client System

Like motivation, the stages of change conceptualization is further complicated by the fact that quite often different members of a system find themselves in dissimilar stages of change. We contend that it is often different stages of change that lead to discrepancies in motivation and effort in therapy. CFTs will see this a lot in their work in that individuals within a system will see both the problem and the need for change differently. A husband who regularly uses name calling as a communication tactic with his wife may not see this as a problem at all, but his wife may be ready to file for divorce over this matter. This discrepancy in stage of change is quite common when working with systems. The issue arises when the goal of the therapy is to preserve the relationship but one member of the system is taking action steps away from this goal, as would be the case when the wife hires a lawyer to file for divorce. So, when we work with systems, it is important to understand the motivation of each member, how each views the specific problem, whether or not they see the problem as something that needs to change and whether they are willing to take the necessary steps to change. If not, we may end up with a change impasse where things revert to the way they were and some members of the system are forced to live in an unhappy state. In some cases, the change impasse may lead those who were most desirous of change to act, leading to the dissolution of a relationship or escalation of fighting within the system. This escalation on the part of the individual invested in change may lead to a shift in those less invested in change or polarizations that are difficult to resolve.

An individual will not be motivated to change if they do not see the problem as something that needs to be eliminated. This is a critical difference in working with couples and families compared to working with individuals. The therapist is challenged to work with the family members who are most reluctant to change, while at the same time keeping other members who are motivated to change engaged in the process without losing them due to their frustrations with the pace of therapy. In individual therapy, the therapist must manage only the stage of change of one client.

Assessing the Stages of Change

Given the disparities in the change process within a system, we like to integrate stages of change into the assessment of a system. In the first three sessions we want to get a good picture of where clients are at in the change process, their views of the need to change and their willingness to take action to spur along change. We use questions from the University of Rhode Island Change Assessment (URICA) to guide our assessment. This is a widely used measure that can be accessed by a simple internet search. It is a good assessment to provide to clients prior to treatment. The assessment asks questions in four broad areas: precontemplation, contemplation, action and maintenance. We suggest some questions next that can be asked in therapy. Though these questions are informed by the URICA, we have added a systemic lens.

Therapy Questions Tailored to Clients' Stage of Change

Precontemplation Questions

These questions assess the level of awareness that the client has about the specific problem. They include:

- Do you believe you have a problem that needs changing?
- Do you see yourself as having a role in the problem your relationship/family is facing?
- Do you see the need to be in therapy to resolve the problem your relationship/family is facing?
- What are your feelings about the problem your partner/family member keeps bringing up?
- Would you rather keep living with the way things are or try to change?

Contemplation Questions

These types of questions are one step ahead of precontemplation questions. A client in the contemplation stage has begun to realize that there is a problem and is contemplating making changes. Here are some good examples of these questions:

- Have you begun thinking about making some changes? If yes, describe.
- Do you think there will be some benefit to working on the problem your partner/family member has brought up?
- What would you like to change about yourself?
- What do you think your contribution is to the problem that your partner/family member has brought up?

Action Questions

Often clients have made plans to solve their problems before they attend therapy. These clients are in the action stage of change. At times it may be their attempted solution to these problems that has made things worse, and they may need the most help in coming up with effective and efficient action steps. It is important to assess what kinds of plans they have made to change. These questions are like the following:

- What would you like to do to solve your problem?
- What have you tried to do to solve your problem?
- How much do you do each day, week, month to solve your problem?
- What has worked and what has not worked as you have tried to solve your problem?

Maintenance Questions

These types of questions are usually not applicable at intake but are good to ask later on in the therapy process. They are related to how clients can maintain the gains in the changes that they have made in their lives and prevent relapse. Examples of these questions include:

- Describe the gains you have made. Do you have concerns about sliding back?
- Are you able to keep up the change momentum on your own? What kinds of help and support do you still need?
- Do you still struggle with your problem? When is it causing you distress and when is it not?
- What kinds of safeguards do you need to prevent the problem from reemerging?
- How have the changes in your family/relationship helped you with your problem?

Ultimately, with these questions, the therapist is trying to develop a sense of the clients' willingness to change and the disparities in this willingness across the system. Even though all members may not be equally motivated, collectively their motivation to change may result in a motivation override where reluctant family members are swept along by the changing tide. Willingness to acknowledge a problem and change by key family members is infectious. Most clients will engender motivations to change if they are able to see that the changes are in their best interests, that they will not make things worse and that they will not "lose face" in what might be long-time family or couple relationship struggles. Doing a good assessment of stages of change is also important to prevent early dropout.

Stage of Change Specific Interventions in Systems

There is little practical information about how to deal with discrepant stages of change within a system. We provide five key strategies. These work best if they are implemented with all members of the system present and if they are processed in the here and now.

USE PROCESS TO HIGHLIGHT CHANGE DESIRE DISCREPANCIES

Process is a defining feature of family therapy (see Chapter 4). Process consists of the interactions that exist between individuals in a system. Family members have a process around talking about difficult topics. Usually, the needed system change is a topic that brings up strong emotions. Some families can engage around these topics and talk about them (often in unhelpful ways), whereas other families are good at avoiding these topics. Early on in therapy it is useful to have a couple or family talk directly to each other about the need for change. The therapist can use some of the URICA informed questions described earlier to guide this conversation.

TURNING TOWARD QUESTIONS

These types of questions are intended to facilitate a conversation between family members about their views of change. The goal of this is to have system members have the conversations with each other. The therapist learns a great deal about the client interaction in this process and can follow this discussion with reframes, validations or comments that will expand this process. Examples of these questions include:

- Tell your son why change is so important to you currently.
- Tell your spouse about why you do not think change should occur right now.
- Turn to your father and tell him how it makes you feel when he says that he is not interested in changing.

HIGHLIGHTING WHAT IS NOTICED

Another intervention that the therapist can use is simply to highlight what is noticed. This entails reflecting what is heard or witnessed and getting the clients to respond. Highlights can focus on comments, discrepancies or emotions. These comments include:

- I noticed when your mom was talking about her desire to change that you had tears in your eyes. What was going on for you?

- I noticed that your dad sounded critical of you when he was talking about your views of change, and you became quiet. What was happening inside?
- Even though you said you did not want to change, I could also hear you saying that you are not at all happy with how things are going in your life. I wonder whether you also notice this discrepancy?

SET DEFINING A SHARED VIEW OF THE PROBLEM AS A GOAL OF THERAPY

It is not uncommon for clients to get caught up in a polarizing conversation about their diverging views on the need to change. This polarization in and of itself can be what is driving their impasse. The more one family member presses for change, the more others dig in their heels. Systems therapists are familiar with this process and know that it is the process that is the problem rather than the content of the conversation. It is important that the therapist move the family away from this unhelpful dynamic. One strategy that works well is to take the process up a level. We do this by setting up defining a problem as a goal for therapy. In doing this, we are conscious about changing the ways in which system members relate to each other. Using reframing and interrupting unhelpful processes, the therapist slowly moves family members to the same page in coming up with a shared therapy goal.

SPEED UP PRECONTEMPLATORS/CONTEMPLATORS WHILE SLOWING DOWN PLANNERS AND ACTORS

Working within a system is a balancing act. The systems therapist is working to keep all members of the system engaged in treatment. We find that we must speed up the process of those who are still considering change (see earlier questions), and at the same time we want to slow down those who are wanting to rush to action, leaving others behind. Not everyone changes at the same pace. It is important for the therapist to point this out to the clients. Skillfully using assessment questions, the therapist is a negotiator who is working to get clients in a similar place. For precontemplators, the therapist is working to get the person to "give it a try". With members further along, the therapist is working to get them to slow down and bring others along.

BALANCING THE ALLIANCE

In working with entire family systems with discrepancies in desires for change, the therapist should work to reflect this different position in the alliance formed with clients. The alliance will thus be very different for a family member who is quite disinterested in change and is only present in therapy to please a family member, as opposed to the person in the family who initiated therapy and who is eager to change. It is likely that the therapist will need to work to combat resistance with the clients who are least interested in changing. Part of the therapeutic relationship relates to the information that the therapist communicates to clients and how the clients might respond to this information. The therapist says very different things to clients in different stages of change and might hold back more for a precontemplator or be more direct with a person in an action stage of change, or the other way around, depending on the specific needs of the unique client system.

A client who presents in therapy reluctantly at the insistence of a spouse may need far more work in the area of bonds; that is, more safety and comfort with the idea of therapy. Building a connecting relationship may be an excellent first strategy. Establishing goals may not be the ideal focus for this client. For those who are in the action stage, the alliance may be built far more around the goals aspect of the alliance and the therapist might need to stay out of the way to avoid impeding the client's enthusiasm for change with their presence.

Clients react differently to different things and find different things helpful. The therapist's awareness of the different motivations of different clients is a critical component of the therapist's role in the change process. The onus is on the therapist to find and focus on the things that are most helpful to clients (Bachelor & Horvath, 1999). Bachelor and Horvath (1999), in discussing the subject of empathy, concluded that clients may respond differently to empathy-inducing attempts by the therapist and that "clients respond in an idiosyncratic manner to the therapist's attempts to respond facilitatively, depending on their own unique needs" (p. 145). When it comes to families, the therapist needs to become skillful at identifying clients who can move therapy forward in a significant way and connect with them even more than with other family members. In this sense, the therapist leverages the motivated member and uses this leverage to bring along other members of the system.

Working With the Clients' Context

The client context outside of therapy is an essential consideration to what constrains many clients and stands in their way of changing. This context is part of the client, and within the context are both barriers and untapped resources, all of which can be used in the change process.

Client Intersectional Factors

Clients' lives intersect with many things in the world. These include their identities, ethnic origins and socioeconomic status. Diversity is a key consideration in engaging all clients. Many clients have multiple factors that intersect, and some of these create more stress and are barriers to change. A woman who is a person of color, a sexual minority and a single parent will be dealing with multiple identities that are often marginalized in the larger culture. These intersecting identities should be carefully processed as the therapist conceptualizes the relationship of the context to the problem and ways in which the problem can best be resolved. Therapists need to consider this context and how it affects the situation in which clients find themselves. Some live in toxic conditions, whether it be family, neighborhood or other types of abusive situations. Therapists need to actively inquire about the context. This context should begin with the home: Who lives in the household? Who are the key players? What are the living conditions? Where do home resources come from? Who controls these resources? Are the resources sufficient? After the home, we consider the neighborhood: Is it safe? Is it supportive? Then we consider key life aspects beyond the neighborhood. These contexts include schools, places of employment, places for recreation (e.g., parks) and the like. These contexts all suggest places where things may go wrong for an individual. For example, a teenager might be experiencing high degrees of racist bullying in school, suggesting the need for interventions in this context. Contexts that are barriers to change present a lot of challenges for clients. It is not always easy for clients to just rise above these situations. In these cases, therapists may need to engage other resources beyond therapy to help clients. These include social agencies, financial resources, youth supports and the like.

A Context That Is a Barrier to Change

Some contexts are so toxic that they may not be able to be incorporated into the change process. While we like to be optimistic about possibilities for change in every situation, we have too often run across contexts that are toxic and are a major cause of problems and real barriers to change. Example include individuals living in abusive, violent and controlling intimate relationships; adolescents living in families where drugs, crime and neglect prevail; or neighborhoods that are characterized by high levels of gang activity. While working with families always entails assessing and attempting to change the context, there are times when removal from the context may be the best solution for the immediate problem. This decision should come only after (1) careful assessment that the context is too toxic for optimal functioning, (2) careful planning for a new context and considering unintended consequences of leaving a context and (3) planning for backlash from the context the individual is leaving.

Careful Assessment of the Context

We would never recommend removal from a context prior to careful assessment and evaluation of the pros and cons of the context. Some decisions are easy, as in the case of incest – there should be no doubt that an individual needs to be removed and protected from this context immediately. Most considerations of a context are not as straightforward. We have come across many cases where individuals were removed from their families prematurely and the removal created many more problems for the individual than the original concern. Things to consider when making these recommendations include safety (physical, emotional), potential for change, attempts made to change, abuse of drugs and alcohol and the like. We want our clients to be able to live in contexts that are not harmful. Unfortunately, it is not possible to remove clients from all contexts, and it is often only the most extreme situations that clients can be removed from or remove themselves from (such as incest, ongoing violence and profound neglect). Many times, individuals will live in long-term marginally good enough situations that over time will hurt them, wear them down or be a barrier to change. In these cases, we must empower individuals to rise above these unfortunate circumstances.

Consideration of Where an Individual/Family Will Go

Another important consideration is where the person will go and how will they survive once they leave their toxic context. What are their alternatives? What are the unintended consequences of leaving the context? Women in abusive relationships leave to improve their lives and their situations. However, if they do not have the resources to improve their lives, they may end up in a situation where they are as bad or worse off than where they were before. Some may be forced to work jobs that put them at risk. Some may partner with new and more abusive partners, and others may have so little money that they are unable to get on their feet again in the short term. Negative outcomes in these situations are the result of poor planning and impulsive decision making. Therapists can play a key role in slowing down the process, ensuring safety and implementing a sustainable plan as to where the person will go after they leave their context.

Planning for Backlash

Changing a system in a first step move is relatively easy. A woman may say, "He is an abusive person, and I am tired of him hitting me. I am leaving". This is a statement that no family therapy professional would disagree with – all would want this woman to escape this abusive context. However, it is well documented that perpetrators will go out of their way to woo back their victims, and many victims may end up returning to the perpetrator many times before they finally are able to leave for good. There may be other kinds of backlash the individual/family will face depending on their context, and therapists should plan with their clients for all scenarios.

Leveraging the Context for Change

While barriers to change that exist in a context present challenges, there may also be a vast array of untapped resources in a context that are huge facilitators of change. Therapists who truly take clients into consideration in their work are scanning the context of the client for opportunities to support change.

SOCIAL SUPPORT

There is no doubt that social support is one of the most protective factors for mental health and family well-being. Social support is one of the more robust predictors of recovery from a mental health condition. Social support comes in numerous forms. It lies within a relationship, within a family, within an extended family, within a community and within community groups such as religious organizations. A large body of literature points to the utility of social support in helping clients recover or live with mental health difficulties (Sprenkle et al., 1999). In CFT, it can help with family outcomes as well, such as recovery from divorce (Everett & Volgy, 1991). Sprenkle et al. (1999, p. 334) stated:

> No matter their theoretical orientation, wise family therapists use social support as a backbone of their treatment of severely depressed and suicidal clients. Clients' abilities to mobilize social support may, like fortuitous events, have more to do with outcome than we now recognize.

How family members support each other is critical. We assume that at some level, family members or members of an intimate relationship have love for each other. After all, they have a shared history, shared genetics and shared living spaces. But when families present in therapy, love is not always apparent. Instead of hearing support and encouragement, these family members are used to hearing criticism, hostility, barbs and jabs and the like. Other family members' behaviors may be demoralizing. We are looking to enhance positive support within a family, engage extended family, enhance friendship networks and utilize community organizations in providing additional support. These are all very helpful interventions.

COMMUNITY RESOURCES

While communities present some challenges for clients, they also have numerous resources. We encourage all therapists to have comprehensive lists of community resources available to clients. These may range from financial support to babysitting. There are many such supports, such as religious groups, that are ready to help. In some states, organizations such as 211 exist to connect individuals with need to concrete supports.

Maximizing the Opportunity of Extratherapeutic Events

Important events are regularly occurring in the life of the client that all provide opportunities to leverage for change. We are particularly interested in using nodal or emotion-laden events as catalysts for change. These events can be part of the normal life cycle (e.g., a child graduating high school and going to college, death of a parent), they can be completely fortuitous events (such as winning a lottery), they may be events that are expected to occur but occur at random times (e.g., a teenage relationship breakup, a job promotion, a surgery) or they can be life events that bring about great stress (e.g., filing for bankruptcy, loss of a job, a divorce). All of these events stir up emotions in an individual, are often confusing and disruptive and place clients in a difficult space when it comes to life as they knew it. These events are opportunities for change, and some could be leveraged by therapists because of the emotions they bring up and the processes they enact. In one study by Blow and colleagues (2009), extratherapeutic events (some fortuitous) were found to be highly significant in the change process in couple therapy. A therapist who is attuned to these events and who can integrate them into the therapy process can use them to great effect. When these events occur, they should not be treated as content but rather as process. When an aging parent dies, this may become the focus of the work of a couple as they contemplate the meaning of life, the challenges of the loss and their support for each other as they manage emotions. There are four steps in integrating extratherapeutic events into the regular course of therapy.

1. Therapists need to be looking for and need to *highlight/shine a light* on these events when they occur. The therapist starts with the assumption that these events bring up intense thoughts and feelings. Therapists who are tuned in will ask about them. For example, the therapist notices that a mom who has struggled with self-esteem in her marriage and arguing with her children tears up when she mentions her son graduating from high school in 2 weeks and going to college. The therapist shines a light by pointing out that he has noticed this as an event ("I could not help but notice that you teared up when you talked about Larry going to college. What was going on for you?"). Thus, the therapist has highlighted the event and heightened emotions about the event.
2. Therapists *relate the event to the process in the family*. In this family, members have a difficult time talking about their feelings and staying connected to each other around their feelings. In the above example, the therapist asks, "What conversations have you and Larry had about his leaving for college? Have you let him know how difficult it will be for you?" These questions allow the family to reflect on how they engage with each other around difficult events.
3. The therapist moves the extratherapeutic event into a *here-and-now enactment* in the family. For example, the therapist instructs the mom to "tell your son how much you are going to miss him when he goes to college". This makes the feelings around the event real while at the same time shifting dynamics in the family.
4. The therapist *connects the themes of the extratherapeutic event with larger themes* in the family. For example, the therapist states, "I know you have spent a lot of

time arguing in your family. What was it like for all of you to connect around Larry leaving for college? How can you keep this going while he is away?" To the mom, in a one-on-one meeting, the therapist connects this theme to her self-esteem: "I was wondering what your son's leaving for college brought up for you? You have often talked about all the barriers you have encountered in reaching your own dreams. Now that he is headed off to follow his dreams, what is that like for you?"

While there is no perfect formula to talk about these events, they always bring up emotions and thoughts that are invariably helpful in the therapy process. The ways in which families discuss them mirror common processes in their families (see discussions of process in Chapter 4). They provide ideal openings for intensifying connection in families and intervening in common processes.

Augmenting the Innate Healing of Systems

It is important to remember that clients have natural healing tendencies under the right conditions. Many life difficulties will heal on their own with time, but therapists can be instrumental in preventing painful events from occurring and can help in healing when they do occur. Resilience and posttraumatic growth are two popular concepts in the trauma literature. They operate from the premise that individuals can overcome difficulties and that many can grow despite their traumatic experiences, but they need to have certain conditions that allow for this to occur. The therapist is assisting clients to create these conditions for change. For healing mechanisms to occur, we see the following as a good approach to these difficult situations:

1. Clients need help in *facing* and *staying engaged with* the difficult situation to allow healing to take place.
2. Clients need extra support as they move through the healing process.
3. Clients may need psychoeducation to help them understand the processes they need to negotiate in healing.
4. Clients may need other therapeutic interventions as they heal from traumatic events but, at a minimum, the healing relationship with a therapeutic provider and supportive family members is a key.

Resilience

Resilience is defined as "the capacity of a system to adapt successfully to significant challenges that threaten its function, viability, or development" (Masten, 2018, p. 12). For our work as family therapists, this definition is important. It is hopeful and strength based. It assumes that when a system is faced with challenges it can adapt to these challenges and survive the threat the challenge poses. In her work, Masten (2018) suggested that even though systems have the capacity to adapt, they may need help in identifying pathways to resilience and selecting the best pathway. Therapists can be highly instrumental in helping systems identify the pathways that are most protective and will lead to the most positive outcomes. These may be assets or resources in the life of the individual that help combat the negative challenges of the crisis. The therapist can be one of these protective pathways. The list of resilience factors will vary based on the specific situation and system. Support (cohesion) from both the immediate family and extended family is important. One challenge occurs when things go wrong because of the inability of the family to communicate about the stressful situation in helpful ways; that is, the stressful event impedes family healing processes because family dynamics make things worse. In this scenario, family members argue more, and this leads them to be even more stressed out about the situation. As a result, it is helpful for therapists to help family members stand together against the problem and combat it and its effects together. For example, John was held up at gunpoint in a large city. He was beaten by thieves and developed deep anxiety after the event. His spouse wanted him to get over it and berated him for being scared in public when they were perfectly safe. When they presented for couples work due to the tension in their relationship, the therapist made some simple adjustments that helped immediately. She validated John's fears. She helped the spouse only make supportive comments about the trauma anxiety. Through psychoeducation, she helped both partners understand trauma and the conditions for healing from trauma. This shifted the relationship dynamics, allowing John the space to heal from the traumatic event.

Posttraumatic Growth

Another key construct in the literature around client resources is termed *posttraumatic growth*, which means growth or positive change that comes about to an individual or a system after a large traumatic event (Larner & Blow, 2011). For many, a traumatic event completely changes their view of the world. Traumatic events that affect families usually always lead to a permanent change to the way things were. This forces a family to adapt and change. Many families around the world experience large traumas/disruptions that are brought about by wars, famines, drought, crime and the like. These families often become refugees and immigrants to other countries, numbering in the millions each year. There are other events that are not quite as traumatic as war or refugee status but that have a hugely disruptive effect on family life. These can be divorce, death or chronic illness, to name a few. These events change the structure of a family and cause anxiety, pain and distress for all. To grow through these experiences, individuals need to make sense of what has happened to them (meaning making), accept or grieve the losses and work through the distressing memories and emotions related to the traumatic event. We believe that each family faces challenges like these over time, and those who thrive the best are ones who can communicate about their situation together (not avoid), share authentic emotions about their situation and be adaptable, allowing them to grow from the situation. Many see these events as the end of their lives, but with the right kind of processes, these events can be the catalyst for new and more fulfilling life memories. Infidelity is a good example of this process. An affair is usually a very difficult occurrence in any relationship, and it leads to deep pain, lack of trust and, often, to relationship dissolution. However, studies have also shown that helping couples work through the infidelity can lead to them having a deeper and stronger relationship than before (Atkins et al., 2005). The good news is that clients can grow and heal even through difficult circumstances. Part of what therapy can provide is a context where they can commit themselves to a healing process and receive the support that will help them to face their difficulties and grow.

Taking Client Views Into Account

It is of high importance in therapy to consider client views and expectations for therapy. While the therapist is the expert, the clients are experts on their lives, and skillful therapists should incorporate client perspectives as much as possible to create an effective therapy experience.

Considering Client Expectations

When I (AB) was a novice therapist, I worked in a university clinic to complete 500 face-to-face contact hours with individuals, couples and families. One of the early couples (heterosexual) I worked with asked me in the pretherapy phone conversation not to leave them "hanging" after the session was over. By this, she meant that she did not want to leave the session with all of their issues stirred up and instead wanted to leave feeling good about their investment of time and money and about their relationship. As it turned out, this was a couple that were working on several intense and volatile relational issues. In doing the initial assessment, I touched on all of their painful and sensitive issues. At the end of the session, the wife, who had made the request not to leave them hanging, turned to me and exploded angrily, telling me how disappointed she was in the outcome of the session and that things were much worse now that they had been prior to coming in to see me. I was floored and apologized profusely, and they agreed to return; despite this rupture, a productive course of therapy resulted. As I got to know her better, I learned that she was really a kind and caring person but that when she felt let down, she responded with hostile attacks. Helping her talk about her hurt feelings in productive ways was critical in the therapy process. These days, I run my sessions differently. I explain to clients how the initial sessions of therapy work and how I need to take some time to get to know the couple, the issues and their dynamics. I let the couple know that early sessions may stir up issues and to expect to leave with things feeling unresolved. I also do not agree to work with unrealistic expectations; I address expectations from the get-go, and I am honest about how long therapy takes to work and what the first few sessions will look like. I say that I am unable to fix things in the first session and they might in fact leave feeling worse. However, I let them know that this is part of the road to a better relationship in the long run.

Managing expectations is one way to engage clients and to combat demoralization; clients need a *realistic expectation* of what therapy looks like. Treatment involving couples or families is rarely brief and usually takes 15 to 20 sessions to resolve. Sometimes it may be shorter and at other times it may take more sessions. While clients are often looking for a quick fix, explain to them that complex relationship problems are almost impossible to effectively treat within a short amount of time. Clients often worry about what more sessions in treatment may mean in terms of time, discomfort and costs. We suggest that you directly address this investment with the clients. This is also a good opportunity to leverage expectations for change. Explain to clients how therapy works, how you work and how long this takes. Ideally, show them data to this effect. Families are often coming in with problems that have a high cost. For couples on the brink of divorce, saving a marriage is worth tens of thousands of dollars. At times it is helpful to be upfront about these financial costs. For many, knowing what to expect serves to motivate them to work hard and make the most of the opportunity. Even though therapy sounds expensive (e.g., $100 a session), a couple who comes weekly for 15 weeks spends $1,500 to save their relationship. This is a very low cost compared to the price of failure. The reality is that many couples/families are spending far more money on recreational habits, and therapy should be promoted as a good investment of time and resources. Ideally insurance will cover this therapy which makes the investment in therapy a low-cost-high-reward proposition.

Mostly we are interested in creating a therapy context where an open dialogue can occur around the perceptions the clients have about therapy and how those match their expectations. Expectations are closely related to client perceptions of therapy and how it is going. A study on client perceptions of the process of therapy found that asking clients about their perceptions of therapy and allowing them to metacommunicate about the processes of their treatment was very helpful (Bischoff et al., 1996). In their study, clients were asked to comment on whether or not the therapy was addressing their goals and clients were given the opportunity to provide feedback. This supports studies showing the effectiveness of formalized feedback (see Chapter 10).

In another study, Crane et al. (1986) surveyed clients in CFT clinics about treatment outcome. An important finding related to the relationship was the fit of the treatment approach with the client's view (expectations) related to the problem. They concluded that "the therapist's ability to present therapy as consistent and congruent with client expectations is important to the client, at least as assessed retrospectively" (Crane et al., 1986, p. 93). The therapist working with families can address this issue in very simple ways by asking questions such as "What are your expectations of therapy at this time?" "Have you been in therapy before? How was that?" What helped? "What was not helpful?" Or, after the session is over, ask, "We are through with our first session. How did it go for you? Did we talk about things you expected? If not, what can I do differently the next time?" Or prior to therapy even beginning, the therapist can explain to the client how they (the therapist) views therapy and ask whether it works for the client's expectations of therapy. This does not mean that the therapist cannot shape client expectations; it is critical that the therapist do this, especially when the expectations are unrealistic. However, a therapist cannot shape client expectations without first validating and exploring their current perspective.

Learning Client Preferences/Worldview

Clients come to therapy with their own preferences, perceptions and values. These all influence therapy, and if the therapist is not able to align to these important factors, clients are at risk for early dropout. Tallman and Bohart (1999) summarized research on the therapeutic relationship from the perspective of the client. They reported that clients' perceptions of the relationship are far more important than the perceptions held by the therapist or an outside observer and that clients' perceptions are closely related to positive outcomes. It takes a genuinely curious and understanding therapist to explore a client's world and help them to feel understood.

There are many things that a therapist can do to attend to the worldview of the client. It starts with the therapist believing that clients have different worldviews based upon their values, culture and upbringing. Therapists should approach each client system from a stance of curiosity, compassion and collaboration. Therapists ideally spend time learning the clients' views of their problems and their theories about solving the problem. When a therapist tailors treatment to fit with the client's view of the problem, the therapist will end up working on what the client deems to be most important with the methods the clients feel most comfortable with (at least at the outset). The process of therapy is thus a collaborative partnership that involves the dynamic, generative and synergistic work of the therapist and client system. We do not do therapy "to" a client, but we create the process with the client. The therapist needs to learn about where the client wants to go and how therapy and the therapist can best help them get there. Sometimes therapy leads clients into scary or uncomfortable places. Therapy is ideally a partnership, and the therapist should not hold back their expert suggestions; at the same time, regular checking in and allowing for all client points of view is critical. Therapist views are best presented tentatively and as one option for change. It is important that the therapist be tuned in to the perception that all clients in the system have of the therapist and of the process and how these change over the course of treatment. It is common for the alliance to be different and to fluctuate with so many members in the therapy room. How does the therapist make sense of this and process it with the client system? How the therapist relates to the client should be in the client's preferred style and comfort zone. This means that the therapist must be especially attuned and responsive to the large and small things that the client does in the therapy room. Therapists also need to be increasingly flexible in their interactions with clients. We have found that therapists who are more pressured and see too many clients and who are burned out appear to have less time to get to know their clients and to find their unique ways of knowing and experiencing.

Hubble et al. (1999) pointed out that the therapist should learn and accommodate the client's theory of change. They contended that learning and working with the client's theory of change provides for a strong alliance in that the therapist and client can work together in agreement, and together can find interventions that fit in with the clients' interpretation of their problem and hypothesized solutions. Of course, if these do not work, they can discuss why this was the case and come up with a new way of finc-tuning the intervention. The onus is on the therapist to learn, understand and respect the unique viewpoints of clients in the change process.

Tallman and Bohart (1999) wrote extensively about client contributions to the therapeutic relationship. They believed that the client contributes far more to change than does the therapist. They believed that therapy is a context that the client uses for their own best interests regardless of the therapist or theoretical orientation used. The therapist approaches therapy as an expert on therapy processes, but clients are experts on their lives and their views of their problems. Anderson and Goolishian (1992) advocated for therapists to approach each case from a position of not knowing, a position where each unique client system would educate and inform the therapist about their family, problems and dynamics. In this regard, then, the therapist works to put all assumptions aside, especially at the outset of treatment.

Conclusion

Therapists are a key to engaging and motivating most clients in treatment. We want to see therapists establish sound therapy based on their relationships with clients and taking client views into account throughout treatment. This relationship is one of collaboration and respect. This chapter is about finding ways to maximize client factors, how to give clients a voice, how to motivate them and how to utilize the resources and events in their lives for change. Each client and each client system are unique. Skilled therapists can adapt therapy to each unique client systems and each unique situation that arises in the therapy room.

References

Anderson, H., & Goolishian, H. (1992). The client is the expert: A not-knowing approach to therapy. In S. McNamee & K. Gergen (Eds.), *Inquiries in social construction. Therapy as social construction* (pp. 25–39). Sage.

Atkins, D. C., Eldridge, K. A., Baucom, D. H., & Christensen, A. (2005). Infidelity and behavioral couple therapy: Optimism in the face of betrayal. *Journal of Consulting and Clinical Psychology, 73*, 144–150.

Bachelor, A., & Horvath, A. (1999). The therapeutic relationship. In M. A. Hubble, B. L. Duncan, & S. D. Miller (Eds.), *The heart and soul of change: What works in therapy* (pp. 133–178). American Psychological Association.

Bischoff, R., McKeel, A. J., Moon, S., & Sprenkle, D. (1996). Therapist conducted consultation: Using clients as consultants to their own therapy. *Journal of Marital and Family Therapy, 22*, 359–379.

Blow, A., Morrison, N., Tamaren, K., Wright, K., Schaafsma, M., & Nadaud, A. (2009). Change processes in couple therapy: An intensive case analysis of one couple using a common factors lens. *Journal of Marital and Family Therapy, 35*(3), 350–368. doi:10.1111/j.1752-0606.2009.00122.x

Crane, D. R., Griffin, W., & Hill, R. D. (1986). The influence of therapist skills on client perception of marriage and family therapy outcome: Implications for supervision. *Journal of Marital and Family Therapy, 12*, 91–96.

de Shazer, S. (1988). *Clues: Investigating solutions in brief therapy*. Norton.

Doherty, W., Harris, S., & Wilde, J. (2015). Discernment counseling for "mixed-agenda" couples. *Journal of Marital and Family Therapy, 42*. doi:10.1111/jmft.12132

Everett, C. & Volgy, S. (1991). Treating divorce in family therapy practice. In A. S. Gurman & D. P. Kniskern (Eds.), *Handbook of family therapy* (Vol. 2, pp. 508–524). Brunner/Mazel.

Helmeke, K. B., & Sprenkle, D. H. (2000). Clients' perceptions of pivotal moments in couples therapy: A qualitative study of change in therapy. *Journal of Marital and Family Therapy, 26*(4), 469–483. https://doi.org/10.1111/j.1752-0606.2000.tb00317.x

Henry, W. P., & Strupp, H. H. (1994). The therapeutic alliance as interpersonal process. In A. O. Horvath & L. Greenberg (Eds.), *The working alliance: Theory, research, and practice* (pp. 51–85). Wiley.

Hubble, M. A., Duncan, B. L., & Miller, S. (1999). *The heart and soul of change: What works in therapy*. American Psychological Association.

Larner, B. A. & Blow, A. J. (2011). A Model of meaning-making coping and growth in combat veterans. *Review of General Psychology, 15*(3), 187–197.

Masten, A. S. (2018). Resilience theory and research on children and families: Past, present, and promise. *Journal of Family Theory & Review, 10*(1), 12–31. https://doi.org/10.1111/jftr.12255

Neill, J., & Kniskern, D. (1983). *From psyche to system: The evolving therapy of Carl Whitaker.* Guilford.

Prochaska, J. O. (1999). How do people change, and how can we change to help many more people? In M. A. Hubble, B. L. Duncan, & S. Miller (Eds.), *The heart and soul of change: What works in therapy* (pp. 227–255). American Psychological Association.

Santisteban, D. A., Szapocznik, J., Perez-Vidal, A., Kurtines, W. M., Murray, E. J., & LaPerriere, A. (1996). Efficacy of intervention for engaging youth and families into treatment and some variables that may contribute to differential effectiveness. *Journal of Family Psychology, 10*(1), 35–44. http://dx.doi.org/10.1037/0893-3200.10.1.35

Snyder, C., Michael, S., & Cheavens, J. (1999). Hope as a psychotherapeutic foundation of common factors, placebos, and expectancies. In M. Hubble, B. Duncan, & S. Miller (Eds.), *The heart and soul of change: What works in therapy* (pp. 179–200). American Psychological Association.

Sprenkle, D. H., Blow, A. J., & Dickey, M. H. (1999). Common factors and other nontechnique variables in marriage and family therapy. In M. A. Hubble, B. L. Duncan, & S. D. Miller (Eds.), *The heart and soul of change: What works in therapy* (pp. 329–360). American Psychological Association.

Tallman, K., & Bohart, A. C. (1999). The client as a common factor: Clients as self healers. In M. A. Hubble, B. L. Duncan, & S. D. Miller (Eds.), *The heart and soul of change: What works in therapy* (pp. 91–131). American Psychological Association.

Tomm, K. (1987a). Interventive interviewing: Part I. Strategizing as a fourth guideline for the therapist. *Family Process, 26*(1), 3–13. doi:10.1111/j.1545-5300.1987.00003.x

Tomm, K. (1987b). Interventive interviewing: Part II. Reflexive questioning as a means to enable self-healing. *Family Process, 26*(2), 167–183. doi:10.1111/j.1545-5300.1987.00167.x

Tomm, K. (1988). Interventive interviewing: Part III. Intending to ask lineal, circular, strategic, or reflexive questions? *Family Process, 27*(1), 1–15. doi:10.1111/j.1545-5300.1988.00001.x

Wampold, B., & Imel, Z. (2015). *The great psychotherapy debate: The evidence for what makes psychotherapy work* (2nd ed.). Routledge.

7

MOBILIZING HOPE

Overview

This chapter looks to operationalize the construct of hope in couple and family therapy (CFT) so that you can use hope-based interventions with your clients. First, how do we define hope? While it's something you can't touch or see, you can definitely feel it! Hope can exist as a relatively stable personality trait or as a temporary state of mind. It can be both an emotion and a cognition. Snyder (2002) defined hope as a perceived capability to derive pathways to desired goals and motivate oneself by way of agency thinking to activate those pathways. In terms of psychotherapy, the instillation of hope is a mechanism inherent to all successful models. Menninger (1959) and others (e.g., Frank, 1973; Frank & Frank, 1991) consistently have related hope to the presence of positive expectancies for goal attainment, as well as increases in both mental and relational health. A client with high hope possesses the ability to generate many different creative and plausible routes to achieve their goals, whereas a client with low hope is likely to produce few credible routes. According to hope theory, an increase in pathways thinking often leads to an increase in agency thinking, which could result in a client moving from a demoralized state to a remoralized state (Snyder, 1994; Snyder et al., 2000).

Michael Lambert's (1992) work on common factors leading to therapeutic change identified hope as an essential ingredient to positive outcomes in therapy. Specifically, he attributed 15% of positive change to client hopefulness and belief in the treatment and its efficacy. Hope unites expectations of clients and therapists and motivates both to spur on change (O'Hara, 2013). Hope is a construct that can fluctuate throughout therapy, an ebb and flow that occurs bidirectionally between the client system and therapist (Larsen et al., 2007, 2013; O'Hara, 2013). O'Hara (2013) noted that while hope has comparable features to concepts such as optimism, self-efficacy and wish, it also maintains unique features, namely, its capacity to represent both a generalized and a particularized sphere of focus. Generalized hope allows for a positive global outlook, while particularized hope focuses on specific outcomes and expectations and carries a strong action focus.

DOI: 10.4324/9781315542737-7

Research on Hope

The research is clear: hopeful people are more likely to prosper than low-hope people. Hopeful individuals are able to identify productive paths toward reaching their identified goals, while managing life constraints (Chang, 1998; Irving et al., 1998; Ong et al., 2006; Snyder, 2002). Overall, the experience of hope has a positive influence on individual health and well-being (Gallagher & Lopez, 2009; Shorey et al., 2007; Snyder et al., 2000). Hope is linked to more positive and less negative affect (Snyder, 1994; Steffen & Smith, 2013), improved overall life satisfaction (Bailey et al., 2007; Valle et al., 2004), better perceived physical health (Wrobleski & Snyder, 2005) and a greater sense of purpose (Feldman & Snyder, 2005; Michael & Snyder, 2005). Hopeful people have also been found to be less reactive to stressful situations (Chang & DeSimone, 2001; Snyder, 2002). Although these research findings in individual functioning are reassuring, traditionally they have not been operationalized in a relational way so that therapists can incorporate hope research into the practice of CFT.

Hope as Natural Complement to CFT

Couple and family therapists have known for years that instilling hope in client systems plays an important role in galvanizing family members to improve their relationships. When it comes to CFT, hope can be contagious in a system. If hope is ignited in one member of the family system, it may spread like wildfire to motivate other people in the therapy. This system-wide hope can lead to increased collaboration and treatment compliance. Hope is a natural complement to the practice of CFT – a discipline that prioritizes systemic strength and health – as opposed to more individual therapy modalities that are focused on psychopathology and dysfunction. Many classic CFT models have traditionally had a hopeful focus, attempting to highlight positive aspects of clients and relationships. This can be seen in solution-focused therapy with its search for exceptions (de Shazer, 1988), in strategic therapy with reframing (Watzlawick et al., 1974) and in narrative therapy with a focus on unique outcomes and alternative stories (White et al., 1990).

Hope plays an important role during conflict situations by allowing a partner to be resilient and to not catastrophize. More hopeful partners can be less reactive, threatened or rejected in situations when the other partner falters or experiences doubt about the relationship. It can serve as a protective factor or adaptive mechanism to challenging relationship circumstances that couples experience throughout the family life cycle.

We like the concept that Kaethe Weingarten (2010) referred to as "reasonable hope". The first tenet of Weingarten's theory is that hope is relational. In other words, we co-create hope through inspired connection with our client systems. The second tenet focuses on the actual practice of such hope as an "action" verb. We not only talk about hope clients but we "do" hope with them! The next aspect of this construct posits that hope exists in a dialectical relationship with despair, doubt and life constraints. This idea is perhaps the most challenging for CFTs and their clients because it demands that we hold two equal, yet opposing truths. Embracing this contradiction, a person can feel despair and reasonable hope simultaneously.

Reasonable hope contends that an uncertain, unknowable future is not necessarily negative. In dire circumstances – for example, oppression, poverty or illness – it is precisely because we cannot know what the future may bring that reasonable hope helps us work with our client systems toward something better than what they are living now. When we can join with others to galvanize system-wide effort, spontaneous actions deriving from these collective commitments to the therapy may lead to increased hope.

Threats to Hope

When people come to believe that they have no control over what happens to them, they begin to think, feel and act as if they are helpless. Learned helplessness theory posits that people who have been conditioned through experiences learn that they lack behavioral control over environmental events, which, in turn, undermines the motivation to make changes or attempt to alter situations (Seligman, 1972). Helplessness, therefore, can directly threaten hope. Jerome Frank (1973), one of the early pioneers in common factors, asserted that hopelessness can "hasten death" (p. 132), as opposed to its counterpart, hope, which plays a pivotal role in many forms of healing. While hopelessness is not a formal diagnosis found in the *Diagnostic and Statistical Manual of Mental Disorders*, it is highly correlated with mental health issues, including depression, suicide, anxiety, dysthymia, posttraumatic stress disorder and other maladies (Arnau et al., 2007).

Repeated failed attempts to achieve desirable goals can also threaten hope. Low-hope individuals will face goals with a focus on failure and experience negative emotional responses (e.g., anger, sadness, despair). Lack of control over external circumstances (e.g., socioeconomic factors) often impedes hope and clouds clients' abilities to see pathways to change. O'Hara (2013) noted that some clients may indulge in self-defeating internal talk or other strategies that prevent the growth of hope. Situations in which wider societal contexts and circumstances support hopelessness contribute to some of the most difficult work we face as couple and family therapists. These situations range from families who have experienced extraordinary levels of social injustice to client systems that have experienced inordinate amounts of what seems to be just bad luck.

When it comes to intimate or family relationships, client systems face countless threats to their hope, including but not limited to lack of support, financial strain, inability to envision a positive future with a significant other, physical or mental challenges, infidelity and other breaches of trust.

When you spend a significant amount of time with a family member or significant other whose outlook is negative and pessimistic, their maladaptive perceptions and thinking may influence your own such that, over time, you, too, become more vulnerable to feeling hopeless. Therefore, it is ideal if you can be surrounded by people who believe in you and help you to imagine positive possibilities (Adams & Partee, 1998). Social support has been shown to be a critical factor in hope inspiration. Conversely, lack of social connection or loneliness may lead to hopelessness. Loneliness is a risk factor for depression (Green et al., 1992) and other psychiatric disorders (Rotenberg & Flood, 1999), and these findings are consistent with studies showing the lifelong needs for intimacy and attachment.

Helping professionals are often expected to have a ready and limitless supply of hope. Tapping into hope is relatively easy for motivated clients who are making adequate therapeutic progress. However, novice and experienced therapists alike recognize the challenge of maintaining hope when working with difficult presenting problems and demoralized client systems. To hold hope in session while witnessing our clients' hopelessness and experiencing our own can be very difficult. O'Hara (2013) commented on specific threats to the maintenance of therapist hope. Interpersonal factors included a lack of client engagement in the therapeutic process, poor agency by the client, a poor therapeutic alliance or even the transmission of hopelessness from client to therapist. In addition, it was noted that the therapist may feel a sense of hopelessness if the client is bound by restrictive socioeconomic circumstances that cannot be easily changed.

The Hopeful Therapist

It's nearly impossible to engender hope in a difficult client system if you yourself are not a hopeful therapist. Indeed, Snyder (1994) suggested that the therapist's own level of hope is translated into the lives of their clients.

Schwartz (2013) referred to this "buy it to sell it" mentality as becoming a "hope merchant" (p. 4). In addition to owning hope as a personal therapeutic value, we believe that CFTs that want to potentiate this powerful common factor should regularly (1) facilitate shifts in the client system from problem focused to hope focused, (2) use "hope language" and (3) demonstrate nonverbal signs of hope.

In order to facilitate a shift in the client system from problem focused to hope focused, the therapist must communicate hope and optimism in an authentic manner. You should never minimize a client problem or say anything in session that you truly don't believe – your clients will sniff out the insincerity.

Effective therapists acknowledge these client system constraints but continue to communicate hope that each member of the system has the potential to achieve realistic goals with sufficient effort. This hope focus is about both the client (i.e., the client can achieve the goals) and the therapist themself (i.e., "I can work successfully with this couple or family system"). The therapist then mobilizes client strengths and resources to facilitate the system's ability to solve their own problems. Rather than seeing themselves as the most important ingredient for change, the hopeful therapist sees the client as expert. Moreover, the hopeful therapist creates client system attributions such that it is each individual family member, through their work, who is responsible for therapeutic progress, creating a sense of mastery.

Larsen and Stege (2012) found that interventions that invited a client's shift in perspective were identified as being hopeful in therapy. Some central ways of changing perspective were offered through highlighting clients' strengths, reframing difficulties, helping clients become more future focused, recognizing possibilities and making hope intentional using explicit hope-focused questions. Another means of engendering hope, as suggested by O'Hara (2013), explores a more present, "here-and-now" acceptance framework. These types of "mindful" strategies do not use traditional behavioral interventions but instead place emphasis on acceptance and tolerance instead of problem solving (Christensen et al., 2004).

The hopeful therapist is positive, tolerant and intentional in their language toward the client system. Normalizing statements depathologize client thoughts and feelings and can be a pathway to establish or transfer hope between the therapist and other members of the system (Ward & Wampler, 2010). Hopeful language can be subtle and include terms such as "yet", "when" and "I believe" (Edey & Jevne, 2003). For example, a frustrated client laments, "I'll never find a romantic partner who listens". You could respond with "You haven't yet found a partner who listens" or "When you find a partner who listens, I believe it will be easier for you to feel validated and understood". Observe how your words impact the client. As fatalistic language subsides, the client may find themself becoming more positive about their situation and the therapy. Explain to clients that how we talk to ourselves influences our thoughts, feelings and actions. If we speak in hopeful language to ourselves and loved ones, we have an increased likelihood of behaving in a hopeful manner and focusing on opportunities that are available. With this in mind, first, challenge clients to notice when they are thinking or saying these unhopeful statements about their relationships. Next, have members of the family system work together to create a more hopeful version of their original statements or thoughts about their loved ones.

Nonverbal communication demonstrates thoughts, feelings or ideas through physical gestures, posture and facial expressions. A lot of communication in

CFT is nonverbal. With appropriate nods and genuine smiles, you are conveying a sense of hope – showing the clients that you understand, agree and are listening to their opinions. Laughter, when used appropriately, is another great way to lighten the mood within tense, demoralized client systems. Coaching couples how to bring their nonverbals in conjunction with their words may also increase hope in stuck systems. For example, teaching a husband to maintain good eye contact by looking at his wife directly and holding her hand when they are communicating may enhance couple connection, vulnerability and the positive impact of any intervention.

CFT Hope-Building Techniques and Interventions

Remoralizing Rituals of Renewal

Rituals are found across all cultures and have the power to reduce anxiety, alleviate emotional pain, provide opportunities to experience joy and build relationships within communities. Family rituals are special events, such as celebrations, traditions and patterned interactions, with a symbolic meaning shared by the whole family. They tap deeply into a family's shared sense of identity and will tell you a lot about the functioning and health of the system. These rituals can be any organized gathering for some greater purpose, often featuring a ceremonial activity or component.

Therapeutic rituals are different from the abovementioned types of rituals in that therapeutic rituals do not necessarily involve everyday events or historical events accumulated over the years. Therapeutic rituals center more on creating new meanings for clients by either experiencing new situations or reevaluating situations within a different context. Couple and family therapy rituals can activate hope in CFT by helping families recall and celebrate the resilience and strengths within the system (Fiese et al., 2002). The literature indicates that rituals can be useful in the therapeutic process by creating a new perspective, creating a new experience or providing a safe way of communicating thoughts and feelings (Hecker & Schindler, 1994; Imber-Black, 1988; Imber-Black & Roberts, 1992; Laird, 1984). In family therapy literature, there is support for positive associations between participation in rituals and relationship cohesiveness, satisfaction, unity, sense of belonging and clear boundaries (Berg-Cross et al., 1992; Fiese et al., 2002). Rituals provide structure and help define how individuals and families think about their world (Bossard & Boll, 1950; Laird, 1984).

Systemic therapists can help couples and families develop renormalizing rituals by focusing on the following principles:

- *Intention: As you start, set an intention for the ritual. What would you like to practice during this ritual? How will this ritual give hope to counteract previous despair? Set the intention, and then carry that intention throughout the ritual.*

- *Presence and participation: An essential element of ritual creation is to be as fully present as you can, with all potential distractions being eliminated. Each member of the family system should have a part in both creating and enacting the ritual.*
- *Authentic appreciation: When we are hopeless, we often take things for granted – not appreciating important resources and others around us. Ritual is about bringing full appreciation to the act – recognizing both the people and things that give us meaning.*
- *Aspiration: What change do you want to create in your couple or family relationship? How would you like to show up, to shift yourself, to serve others better in your family? Ritual is a way to connect to these aspirations, so that we can be more resolved to live them.*
- *Gracious ending: A ritual has a closing, which might be simply gratitude for whatever you just did or how you practiced or a thanks to the people you are sharing the ritual with.*

The CFT Hope History Interview

In addition to gauging the current level of hope in the system, this interview explores narratives of overcoming both individual and relational obstacles. It is designed to be used either at the beginning of therapy or anytime your client system gets stuck and becomes hopeless. By tapping into previous and existing system-wide resources and significant others in the indirect system, the therapist can "prime the pump" to engender hope.

- *Rate your hope in overcoming the obstacles that you are currently facing in this couple or family relationship on a scale of 0 to 10, with 0 meaning no hope and 10 meaning a lot of hope.*
- *When you think about your current situation, what is it that most threatens your hope?*
- *Who in your life currently diminishes your hope?*
- *Is there anything we've talked about so far in this therapy that has decreased your hope?*
- *Are there other things or experiences in your life that boost your hope?*
- *Can you tell me about a time in this couple or family relationship when you felt particularly hopeful?*
- *What personal qualities in your significant other or family member make you hopeful?*
- *What is the smallest possible change that could increase your hope?*
- *If I wanted to know a hopeful you, where in your personal and relationship history would I need to look?*
- *What changes in your actions would send a message to your family members that you had become more hopeful?*
- *What have we talked about so far in this therapy that has increased your hope?*

In My Control Self-Reflection and Chart

There is nothing that can defeat a client system more than trying to solve a problem that isn't solvable or fix an issue that they have little or no control over.

You can control your own actions, and sometimes thoughts, but that's about it. If you decide that to become successful in couple or family therapy you must change others' behavior or what they think of you, stress and hopelessness will result. Even if your client system is not overtly religious or spiritual, invoking the mantra below may shift the focus of the therapy to something more workable:

> *God, grant me the serenity to accept the things I cannot change,*
> *Courage to change the things I can,*
> *And wisdom to know the difference.*

This is the Serenity Prayer, originally written by the American theologian Reinhold Niebuhr (1943) and commonly used by Alcoholics Anonymous and similar organizations. It is not just a key step toward recovery from addiction – it is a prescription for hope!

The In My Control Self-Reflection operationalizes this prayer and helps clients to focus on realistic tasks, behaviors and decisions that are in their control amidst current relationship and life constraints that are not solvable. With the utility to be implemented in individual, couple or family therapy, the intervention deemphasizes factors out of your clients' control and outcomes based on others' behaviors. The following worksheets may be either completed in session with clients or given as homework.

IN MY CONTROL SELF-REFLECTION

1. In any couple or family relationship, we rarely (if ever) see a situation in which one member of the system is 100% to blame for the problem. Instead of assigning percentages of blame in the current conflict or typical problem cycle with your family member, what is your part in the cycle, and what is theirs?

   _____
   _____
   _____
   _____

2. If you judge the outcome of this therapy based on anyone's actions other than your own, you are potentially setting yourself up for frustration and hopelessness. What can't you control in this situation? What can you control in this situation? Make a list.

   Being honest with yourself, on which of the above items on the list are you spending most of your energy and attention right now?

   _____
   _____
   _____
   _____

3. Instead of trying to change your partner or family member, focus on controlling your own reactions. What can you do to increase your own tolerance and acceptance of their behaviors?

   _____
   _____
   _____
   _____

In My Control Chart – Blank

Problem Situation	Aspects Out of My Control	Aspects in My Control	Tolerance/ Acceptance Skill Needed	Successful/ Hopeful Outcome to Situation

In My Control Chart – Example

Problem Situation	Aspects Out of My Control	Aspects in My Control	Tolerance/ Acceptance Skill Needed	Successful/ Hopeful Outcome to Situation
Argument with my husband because he is not mechanically inclined and cannot complete basic home maintenance and improvement tasks	My husband's handyman skills The age of the house The cost involved to maintain the house	My frustration level with his inability to complete the task The company or person I hire to complete the home improvement task	Understanding that even well-cared for homes need routine maintenance Acceptance that my husband isn't lazy, he just wasn't taught these handyman skills as a younger man	A renewed focus on what my husband does positively to contribute to the marriage/ family instead of dwelling on what he doesn't do well naturally
My teenager is failing chemistry and thinks I am too controlling about her schoolwork	My child's chemistry grade My child's level of motivation for the subject matter The teacher's unwillingness to boost my child's grade	My level of patience with my child Resources (i.e., tutoring) I offer to my child to help	Tolerance that my child is not as naturally talented at chemistry as I was Acceptance that the teacher has 24 other children in the class and gives neither me nor my child special attention	My ability to let my child manage her own academic organization and relationship with the teacher without my unsolicited interference or help A balanced assessment of what my child is doing well at school instead of only measuring the areas she is struggling in

The Hope Mentor

Hope thrives in the right company. When you spend time with hopeful people, they show you the way! Hope is contagious. When activated, it can spread from person to person within a system. Hope mentors are people in the indirect therapy system that the therapist helps clients identify and connect to in order increase hope in their own lives. This relationship may lead to increased positivity and vicarious learning through listening to the mentor's personal inspirational stories. Leading by example, the hope mentor models for the clients how to make interpersonal contacts and introduces them to new opportunities, people, places or ideas. In addition to modeling hopeful behaviors, these mentors express belief and confidence in the clients' abilities and encourage them to take positive actions.

In addition to individuals, hope mentors may take the form of entire couple and family systems. For instance, a couple who is struggling to recover from infidelity may be inspired and motivated by hearing from another couple who has successfully repaired from this type of breach of trust. Similarly, parents dealing with an out-of-control teen can learn coping strategies from other families that have navigated this difficult developmental stage. Sometimes, these mentor systems may have as much (if not more) hope induction ability and credibility as the actual CFT.

In much the same fashion, therapists may also serve in an informal hope mentor role by appropriately self-disclosing about times in their own lives when they were able to connect to hope to improve their important relationships. When clients share vulnerability with a trusted source in a safe environment, they will have a potentially restorative, hopeful experience. Even if their problems aren't solved by contact with this mentor, they will have a positive interaction with a caring individual or system. In addition to combating feelings of isolation and despair, this experience may increase hope in humanity and trusting relationships. Ideally, the mentoring relationship will be a mutually beneficial one, as the mentor learns from the client and the client from the mentor. The following questions help to uncover these hopeful resources in the indirect system:

- *A hope mentor can be any individual, couple or even an entire family that inspires you with their energy, actions or words. Who is a hope mentor in your life?*
- *What made this person(s) a hopeful role model for you?*
- *What did/do you learn from their example?*
- *How can you utilize them now to help you with problems that brought you into this therapy?*
- *What could this person(s) learn from you?*
- *If you don't have a hope mentor, who can you approach to take on this role?*

Keep the Faith: Tapping Into Spiritual Resources

Spirituality, as it pertains to CFT, is a client's personal relationship with a higher form of consciousness and sense of connection to something bigger than themselves. The experience is open to individual interpretation and can include a particular religious affiliation or a more generalized belief system. Spirituality is a critical source of hope for many client systems and should be viewed as a potential resource in therapy rather than as something to be ignored. Usually reserved for the pastoral counseling field, tapping into religious faith or some form of personal spiritual tradition has been removed from both the secular theory and practice of CFT. Even if organized religion does not appeal to your clients, personal spirituality may be a guiding force in their lives. In addition to mobilizing hope, highlighting spiritual values may help certain clients build resilience (Walsh, 2008). Those who are spiritual are more likely to seek involvement in personal growth experiences, creative activities and knowledge-building endeavors (Wink & Dillon, 2003).

Addressing spirituality with couples and families in conjoint therapy may have additional therapeutic value to the extent that incorporation helps you to support your clients connecting to their significant others, moving outside of themselves and contributing to the common good of the family system (Blando, 2006). This spiritual activation is positively correlated with client self-esteem and effective coping in stressful interpersonal situations. (Graham et al., 2001). For those low on faith fuel, religious institutions may serve as "hope filling stations" that clients can visit in times of stress to provide a sense of community and social support. Also identified as potential stress-reducing, hope-inducing activities are prayer and participating in spiritual/religious group activities, which activate the cognitive, behavioral and social aspects of faith (Hathaway & Pargament, 1991).

When mining for hope, you don't need to be clergy or a faith-based therapist to ask clients about their spiritual beliefs. During the assessment process, these questions will help you gauge how spirituality functions in your client system's life:

- *Are you part of an organized religion?*
- *What aspects of your religion are helpful and not so helpful to you?*
- *Do you have personal spiritual beliefs that are independent of organized religion? What are they?*
- *What aspects of your spirituality or spiritual practices do you find most helpful to you personally? (e.g., prayer, meditation, reading scripture, attending religious services, listening to music, hiking, communing with nature) How does it affect how you view your problems and what brought you to this therapy?*
- *How do your religious/spiritual beliefs help you to deal with failure and disappointments in your life and important relationships?*

- *What role might your religion/spirituality play in resolving your problems?*
- *Are you part of a religious or spiritual community? How does it help you to have connection with others who share the same beliefs?*
- *How are your spiritual beliefs similar to or different from those of other members of your family?*
- *How do you use your religious/spiritual beliefs to tap into hope?*

In order to use clients' religious/spiritual resources to mobilize hope, the therapist should first be comfortable answering all of those questions above for themself.

Forgive, Don't Relive

When relationship "tears" occur in a couple or family relationship, they can elicit strong negative feelings and have the potential to reduce or eliminate hope. Forgiveness can be considered a central topic to any modality of therapy where clients have experienced a violation of their sense of fairness, justice or innocence. Hope, in couple and family therapy specifically, may be enhanced after clients forgive their significant others. Forgiveness is accepted as a critical element for healing a relationship damaged by a significant transgression. It is positively correlated with mental and physical health, as well as relationship satisfaction and stability (Fincham et al., 2006; Toussaint et al., 2001).

Without forgiveness, past or ongoing resentment of prior behavior may negatively impact a couple's or family's efforts to resolve later relational issues (Fincham et al., 2004). Many individuals who have been victims in situations where the need for forgiveness arises carry an enormous emotional burden around with them. They continue to be angry with their transgressor and they spend significant amounts of their emotional energy ruminating about the event, harboring grudges and perhaps plotting revenge. They find it difficult to move forward in their lives such is their preoccupation with the wrong done to them. They are still acting out the "victim" or "wronged one" role long after the actual event.

When one partner chooses to forgive, however, the need to blame is removed – allowing for a different, more hopeful interaction with the partner or member of the family system. Forgiveness includes letting go of the need for vengeance and releasing negative thoughts, bitterness and resentment. It might also include a change in perceptions and feelings such that the behavior of the victim indicates that the offender has been forgiven. Forgiving a family member is a potential pathway for providing closure and permanently changing a negative interactional cycle. Specifically, when one partner offers genuine forgiveness, the other partner may be less likely to continue their negative or defensive behavior as well.

How can we help our clients be hopeful about a family member or partner who has failed them? We can normalize the experience in order to help them move toward forgiveness. In actuality, it is a rare person who does not, at some point in their intimate or family relationship, feel hurt, let down, betrayed, disappointed, or wronged by someone they love. In order to facilitate forgiveness within CFT, the therapist must help the injured partner to see the pure intentions underneath their family member's misguided actions that contributed to the relationship transgression or tear. The following questions are designed with that intent:

- *What was the positive intention underneath your family member's misguided action or mistake?*
- *How did your family member's previous life experiences (e.g., in past relationships) influence their behavior?*
- *Write down as many alternative outcomes, both positive and negative, of your family member's actions as you can imagine.*
- *Talk about your family member from the perspective of admiration, including past positive experiences you've had with them.*
- *Develop a list of your family member's strengths that balance out their weaknesses.*
- *What negative emotions are you holding onto from this transgression by your family member? Do you want to release these negative feelings? How do you think holding onto these feelings impacts your other significant relationships?*
- *Reflect on times when you either intentionally or unintentionally hurt someone you cared about and were eventually forgiven by that person. How did that person's forgiveness influence your feelings of hope?*

The goals of these reflective questions are to (a) help one member of the family system experience empathy for another family member who has injured them by developing more hopeful attributions for formerly perceived hurtful or selfish actions and (b) explore how the power of forgiveness could release clients from their own negative feelings that are weighing them down in order to open pathways to hope.

Conclusion

Our point in introducing the questions and interventions in this chapter is not to suggest that these are the only ways to engender hope in CFT. On the contrary, we believe there are unenumerable ways through which to help client systems build their sense of personal efficacy (agency) and collection of strategies (pathways) to instill hope. Hope and hopelessness coexist on a continuum of lived experience. After all, without the emotions of fear, doubt and despair, there would be no need to generate hope. Therapists would do well to remember this dialectical tension when working with hope and loss of hope. In order to be fully present in the room with difficult client systems, CFTs must develop a tolerance for hopelessness and a capacity to hold both despair and hope.

References

Adams, S. M., & Partee, D. J. (1998). Hope: The critical factor in recovery. *Journal of Psychosocial Nursing and Mental Health Services, 36*(4), 29–32.

Arnau, R. C., Rosen, D. H., Finch, J. F., Rhudy, J. L., & Fortunato, V. J. (2007). Longitudinal effects of hope on depression and anxiety: A latent variable analysis. *Journal of Personality, 75*(1), 43–64.

Bailey, T. C., Eng, W., Frisch, M. B., & Snyder, C. R. (2007). Hope and optimism as related to life satisfaction. *The Journal of Positive Psychology, 2*(3), 168–175.

Berg-Cross, L., Daniels, C., & Carr, P. (1992). Marital rituals among divorced and married couples. *Journal of Divorce and Remarriage, 18*, 1–30.

Blando, J. (2006). Spirituality, religion, and counseling. *Counseling and Human Development, 39*(2), 1–14.

Bossard, J., & Boll, E. (1950). *Ritual in family living.* University of Pennsylvania Press.

Chang, E. C. (1998). Hope, problem-solving ability, and coping in a college student population: Some implications for theory and practice. *Journal of Clinical Psychology, 54*, 953–962.

Chang, E. C., & DeSimone, S. L. (2001). The influence of hope on appraisals, coping, and dysphoria: A test of hope theory. *Journal of Social and Clinical Psychology, 20*(2), 117–129.

Christensen, A., Sevier, M., Simpson, L. E., & Gattis, K. S. (2004). Acceptance, mindfulness, and change in couple therapy. In *Mindfulness and acceptance: Expanding the cognitive-behavioral tradition* (pp. 288–309). Guilford.

de Shazer, S. (1988). *Clues: Investigating solutions in brief therapy.* W. W. Norton & Co.

Edey, W., & Jevne, R. F. (2003). Hope, illness, and counselling practice: Making hope visible. *Canadian Journal of Counselling, 37*(1), 44–51.

Feldman, D. B., & Snyder, C. R. (2005). Hope and the meaningful life: Theoretical and empirical associations between goal–directed thinking and life meaning. *Journal of Social and Clinical Psychology, 24*(3), 401–421.

Fiese, B. H., Tomcho, T. J., Douglas, M., Josephs, K., Poltrock, S., & Baker, T. (2002). A review of 50 years of research on naturally occurring family routines and rituals: Cause for celebration? *Journal of Family Psychology, 16*(4), 381–390.

Fincham, F. D., Beach, S. R., & Davila, J. (2004). Forgiveness and conflict resolution in marriage. *Journal of Family Psychology, 18*(1), 72.-81.

Fincham, F. D., Hall, J., & Beach, S. R. (2006). Forgiveness in marriage: Current status and future directions. *Family Relations, 55*(4), 415–427.

Frank, J. D. (1973). *Persuasion and healing: A comparative study of psychotherapy* (Rev. ed.). Johns Hopkins University Press.

Frank, J. D., & Frank, J. B. (1991). *Persuasion and healing: A comparative study of psychotherapy* (3rd ed.). Johns Hopkins University Press.

Gallagher, M. W., & Lopez, S. J. (2009). Positive expectancies and mental health: Identifying the unique contributions of hope and optimism. *Journal of Positive Psychology, 4*, 548–556.

Graham, S., Furr, S., Flowers, C., & Burke, M. T. (2001). Research and theory religion and spirituality in coping with stress. *Counseling and Values, 46*(1), 2–13.

Green, B. H., Copeland, J. R. M., Dewey, M. E., Sharma, V., Saunders, P. A., Davidson, I. A., Sullivan, C., & McWilliam, C. (1992). Risk factors for depression in elderly people: A prospective study. *Acta Psychiatrica Scandinavica, 86*(3), 213–217.

Hathaway, W. L., & Pargament, K. I. (1991). The religious dimensions of coping: Implications for prevention and promotion. *Prevention in Human Services, 9*(2), 65–92.

Hecker, L. L., & Schindler, M. (1994). The use of rituals in family therapy. *Journal of Family Psychotherapy, 5*(3), 1–24.

Imber-Black, E. (1988). Normative and therapeutic rituals in couples therapy. In *Rituals in families and family therapy* (pp. 113–134). W. W. Norton & Co.

Imber-Black, E., & Roberts, J. (1992). *Rituals for our times: Celebrating, healing, and changing our lives and relationships.* Harper Perennial.

Irving, L. M., Snyder, C. R., & Crowson, J. J., Jr. (1998). Hope and the negotiation of cancer facts by college women. *Journal of Personality, 66*, 195–214.

Laird, J. (1984). Sorcerers, shamans, and social workers: The use of ritual in social work practice. *Social Work, 29*(2), 123–129.

Lambert, M. J. (1992). Psychotherapy outcome research: Implications for integrative and eclectical therapists. In J. C. Norcross & M. R. Goldfried (Eds.), *Handbook of psychotherapy integration* (pp. 94–129). Basic Books.

Larsen, D. J., Edey, W., & Lemay, L. (2007). Understanding the role of hope in counselling: Exploring the intentional uses of hope. *Counselling Psychology Quarterly, 20*(4), 401–416.

Larsen, D. J., & Stege, R. (2012). Client accounts of hope in early counseling sessions: A qualitative study. *Journal of Counseling & Development, 90*(1), 45–54.

Larsen, D. J., Stege, R., & Flesaker, K. (2013). "It's important for me not to let go of hope": Psychologists' in-session experiences of hope. *Reflective Practice, 14*(4), 472–486.

Menninger, K. (1959). The academic lecture: Hope. *American Journal of Psychiatry, 116*(6), 481–491.

Michael, S. T., & Snyder, C. R. (2005). Getting unstuck: The roles of hope, finding meaning, and rumination in the adjustment to bereavement among college students. *Death Studies, 29*(5), 435–458.

Niebuhr, R. (1943). The serenity prayer. *Bulletin of the Federal Council of Churches.*

O'Hara, D. (2013). *Hope in counselling and psychotherapy.* Sage.

Ong, A. D., Edwards, L. M., & Bergeman, C. S. (2006). Hope as a source of resilience in later adulthood. *Personality and Individual Differences, 41*(7), 1263–1273.

Rotenberg, K. J., & Flood, D. (1999). Loneliness, dysphoria, dietary restraint, and eating behavior. *International Journal of Eating Disorders, 25*(1), 55–64.

Schwartz, R. C. (2013). The therapist client relationship and the transformative power of self. In M. Sweezy & E. L. Ziskind (Eds.), *Internal family systems therapy: New dimensions* (pp. 1–23). Routledge.

Seligman, M. E. (1972). Learned helplessness. *Annual Review of Medicine, 23*(1), 407–412.

Shorey, H. S., Little, T. D., Snyder, C. R., Kluck, B., Robitschek, C. (2007). Hope and personal growth initiative: A comparison of positive, future-oriented constructs. *Personality and Individual Differences, 43*, 1917–1926.

Snyder, C. R. (1994). *The psychology of hope: You can get there from here.* Free Press.

Snyder, C. R. (2002). Hope theory: Rainbows in the mind. *Psychological Inquiry, 13*(4), 249–275.

Snyder, C. R., Ilardi, S., Michael, S. T., & Cheavens, J. (2000). Hope theory: Updating a common process for psychological change. In C. R. Snyder & R. E. Ingram (Eds.), *Handbook of psychological change: Psychotherapy processes and practices for the 21st century* (pp. 128–153). John Wiley & Sons.

Steffen, L. E., & Smith, B. W. (2013). The influence of between and within-person hope among emergency responders on daily affect in a stress and coping model. *Journal of Research in Personality, 47*(6), 738–747.

Toussaint, L. L., Williams, D. R., Musick, M. A., & Everson, S. A. (2001). Forgiveness and health: Age differences in a US probability sample. *Journal of Adult Development, 8*(4), 249–257.

Valle, M. F., Huebner, E. S., & Suldo, S. M. (2004). Further evaluation of the Children's Hope Scale. *Journal of Psychoeducational Assessment, 22*(4), 320–337.

Walsh, F. (2008). Integrating spirituality in family therapy. *Spiritual Resources in Family Therapy, 31,* 495–501.

Ward, D. B., & Wampler, K. S. (2010). Moving up the continuum of hope: Developing a theory of hope and understanding its influence in couples therapy. *Journal of Marital and Family Therapy, 36*(2), 212–228.

Watzlawick, P., Weakland, J. H., & Fisch, R. (1974). *Change: Principles of problem formation and problem resolution.* Norton.

Weingarten, K. (2010). Reasonable hope: Construct, clinical applications, and supports. *Family Process, 49*(1), 5–25.

White, M., White, M. K., Wijaya, M., & Epston, D. (1990). *Narrative means to therapeutic ends.* W. W. Norton & Company.

Wink, P., & Dillon, M. (2003). Religiousness, spirituality, and psychosocial functioning in late adulthood: Findings from a longitudinal study. *Psychology and Aging, 18*(4), 916–924.

Wrobleski, K. K., & Snyder, C. R. (2005). Hopeful thinking in older adults: Back to the future. *Experimental Aging Research, 31*(2), 217–233.

8
THE TALENTED AND SKILLED THERAPIST

Introduction

As therapists, we are often approached by family members, students or friends asking for a referral to a mental health provider for problems such as child acting-out behaviors or marital difficulties. In coming up with referrals for these requests, we are mindful of many things, but at the forefront is that we want a therapist who would be a *good fit* and *effective* in helping them with their problems. Most of the time, we echo what Blow et al. (2007) said in their article on the topic: "When most of us consider referring a close friend or relative to a therapist, we are more likely to consider the competence and expertise of the therapist more than his or her theoretical allegiance" (p. 298). There are variables we never consider when making these referrals – therapist GRE scores, grades on class papers or grade point average – while there are other variables we may consider, such as professional ethics and reputation. Unavoidably, subjective variables creep into the process of therapist selection, even though these variables may have no relationship with therapist's skills, fit or effectiveness; these are items related to branding and status, including promotional photographs, website layout, office location, reputation of school they graduated from, number of publications, espoused theoretical orientation – and even though some of these may be connected to therapist effectiveness in general, on the specific level, these are not connected to therapy outcomes. If you refer a couple to a therapist because they have some training in emotionally focused therapy (EFT), you may think that is a good referral. However, the therapist may not have a good understanding of EFT, may not operationalize it correctly and may be a terrible fit with the couple relationally or culturally. These are considerations that may not be considered in therapist selection.

Our referrals may also vary depending on the presenting problem and other characteristics of a client. We are not likely to refer a client with an alcohol use disorder to a therapist with limited experience with this type of problem. Those of us who have in-depth training in couple therapy are not quick to refer clients with interpersonal difficulties to therapists without training and a good reputation for working with relationship systems. However, for the larger therapy world, it is quite common for therapists with limited training or expertise in working with couples to regularly work with these types of relationships or presenting problems. We are living in a *Psychology Today*–driven referral system where decisions about which therapist to choose are related to variables such as therapist internet branding (e.g., picture, website), therapist availability, and a therapist's ability to bill client insurance. We strongly advocate for a move away from these variables to one of evidence-based therapists where referrals are made based on data showing therapist effectiveness and skills in working with specific presenting problems (Blow & Karam, 2017). While the ability to pay for services is a real issue for many people, we continue to be disturbed by how referrals are made to therapists and how therapists may be doing work with problems for which they have little training and for which they are unable to show evidence for their effectiveness. We are particularly concerned about this in cases pertaining to couple therapy or family therapy, both highly specialized and difficult lines of work, yet we continue to witness therapists untrained in these areas advertising for these services. While help for couples and families can come from many sources and providers, we feel strongly that those who are best trained to work with these presenting problems should be the first-line treatment providers.

As you move ahead in this chapter, the questions we want you to consider about therapists are the following:

1. What would you want in a therapist if you had a problem in your marriage/intimate relationship? What qualifications would you seek? What interpersonal qualities would be most useful? What would you like their track record to be in working with couples? What theoretical orientation should they have? How much would you be willing to pay for effective treatment for your relationship difficulties?
2. Now change the presenting issue. Would your choice of a therapist differ if you were suffering from depression? How would your criteria for choice of therapist change?
3. Or consider what kind of therapist you would desire if your adolescent son was abusing substances and having difficulties at school.

Would the therapist you selected in (1) still be the same therapist you would want to treat your depression or adolescent's difficulties?

These are all important questions to consider. Most clients say that a good relationship with their therapist is the most important element of successful therapy (Friedlander et al., 2006), and in our view this one variable is an essential criterion in any therapy. But is this relationship sufficient? Evidence would suggest not (see Sprenkle & Blow, 2004a, for a review). In this chapter, we consider variables beyond the relationship, and we discuss things that you can do to increase your effectiveness with your clients and ways that you can market your effectiveness.

What We Know About Good Therapists (General)

The Central Role of the Therapist

Just as many common factors work through models, models in turn work through therapists (Blow et al., 2007; Sprenkle & Blow, 2004b). There is consistent evidence that therapists are key to change, and they can work with a range of clients and presenting problems because they can adapt to client preferences, expectations and characteristics (Blow et al., 2007; Sprenkle & Blow, 2007). We contend that most key changes in therapy are either initiated by the therapist or influenced by the therapist and that a therapist's ability to identify and maximize these change opportunities largely determines the therapist's – and hence the therapy's – effectiveness. It is the therapist who decides the structure of therapy, which family members are included in the therapy, if any, and what interventions are used and when. In this sense, the therapist has considerable influence over treatment outcomes. There is no doubt in our minds that a competent therapist (separate from theoretical orientation) is a core component of effective therapy.

The Main Players in the Therapeutic Relationship; the Therapist Leads

We have a whole chapter devoted to the therapeutic relationship (see Chapter 9). This is one of the most well-studied issues in therapy, and findings across many studies show that this is one of the most robust predictors of positive therapeutic change. Most researchers conclude that even though this is an important variable, it is not sufficient on its own to bring about change. There also needs to be therapeutic content added to this relationship, and the responses to this content are channeled directly through the therapist. The therapist is the key player in this therapeutic relationship. Therapists must be able to connect with each member of the system (bonds) and set collaborative goals with each member in a way that each therapy participant believes their goals will be potentially achieved in the therapy process (goals), and the therapist must be able to walk with each member on this journey in a way that each is engaged and comfortable (tasks). The therapist is undoubtably influenced by theory in this process, and the theoretical components that arise out of the alliance are initiated by the therapist. For example, take a family who comes to therapy because a 12-year-old boy is misbehaving at school. After further assessment, the therapist learns that the parents are conflictual with each other and that they also have considerable financial strain. There are also very few rules in the family and no consequences to breaking of rules. The therapist builds a strong relationship with the mother, the father and the boy. Having this strong relationship is the platform from where change springs. Using a systemic theoretical lens, the therapist decides to intervene in the couple relationship (interventions include communication, emotional bonding, problem solving around finances, parenting skills and cohesion around the approach to parenting) and in the parent–child relationship (interventions include strengthening the positive bonds between parents and child, working on boundaries/rules in the family and appropriate parental responses when boundaries are violated). The therapist is a hub in this work, and their relationship with each client, conceptualization of the case in systemic terms and interventions based on this conceptualization are all crucial in how the therapy plays out. The therapist is making many decisions based on their training, their experience, their relationship with this *specific family*, the assessment of the problems of this *specific family* and the therapist's recalibrations in response to the *specific family's* responses to initial treatment. This process requires therapist engagement and active decision making and adaptation throughout the course of therapy.

Alexander et al. (1976), found that *therapists' abilities* in terms of structuring sessions and in forming relationships were related to therapeutic outcome. They concluded that 59% of therapy outcomes could be attributed to the therapeutic relationship and structuring skills and that therapists' relationship skills "may be crucial determinants of therapy success" (Alexander et al., 1976, p. 656). Therapists' relationship skills were defined in the study as the ability of the therapist to use humor, warmth, directiveness, self-confidence and structuring skills in sessions. The study has some methodological weaknesses to it, but it does point to the importance of global relational skills and their relation to good outcomes. Further, these relationship skills are enhanced by a well-structured therapeutic agenda and operational framework.

It seems clear from the literature on therapist factors and change that different therapists form different relationships with their clients (Gelso & Carter, 1985). In this regard, one must consider how much of this is due to personality differences, relationship-building differences, experience and learned skills. Empathy on the part of the therapist is key to forming solid therapeutic relationships. In Bohart and Greenberg's (1997) definition of empathy, they see it as the "making of deep and sustained psychological contact with another in which one is highly attentive to, and aware of, the experience of the other as a unique other" (p. 5). They further stated that it includes the "deep sustained empathic inquiry or immersing of oneself in the experience of the other" (Bohart & Greenberg, 1997, p. 5). They concluded that empathy helps individuals to make sense of their experiences and to understand themselves in new and deeper ways. It also helps an individual move from a negative view of self to one of self-empathy. It is important to consider how this might play out in couple and family therapy. The therapist's empathy in a family context not only allows for deeper levels of self-empathy to occur within an individual in a family but further allows for family members who witness to possibly view their own situations more empathically and, more important, to view the situation of their family member more empathically. Orlinsky et al. (1994) referred to *empathy* as careful communicative attunement. Bohart and Greenberg stated that "the therapist attempts to imaginatively enter the client's experience of struggling to articulate, share, and dialogue with the therapist, as well as to try to grasp the content of what the client is striving to communicate" (p. 7). In this regard, when one thinks of families, the therapist is not only trying to be attuned to the individual family members but is also trying to be attuned to the experience of the couple or family collectively.

The Therapist System

Client systems benefit from a well-established therapist system. This involves having a clear line of authority and minimization of interferences in this process. We have become aware over the years that the power of the therapist system is often diluted by factors such as other therapists/therapeutic influences outside of the primary therapist, along with things in the life of the therapist that may get in the way of effective treatment. The therapist system consists of everything in the therapeutic system that influences the outcome of treatment in either a positive or a negative direction. The therapist is the primary instrument in contacting a client system. However, the therapist is influenced by many things in their life that in essence could have a significant impact on the client. These include supervisors, friends and family, life crises, new knowledge and other similar factors that may be imparted to the client system in both conscious and unconscious ways. Further, there are other treatment providers frequently involved in the life of clients, including psychiatrists, individual therapists, group therapists, nutritionists, religious leaders, extended family, schoolteachers and other support systems (Pinsof, 1994). The therapist system consists of the *direct system*, which includes the primary treatment providers who are directly involved with the client, and the *indirect therapist system*, which includes those who have an input into treatment but are never directly involved. It is important that there be alignment across these systems. For example, if an influential religious leader is undermining the work of the primary therapist, treatment may fail. Often, we find it is other therapists (e.g., psychiatrists, school counselors) who are undermining the therapist. So, starting out, we encourage therapists to find out who else is involved in treatment and then either bring everyone on the same page regarding treatment or eliminate other therapists as a condition of treatment. The second author (AB) has done extensive work treating couples with infidelity occurring in their relationship. It is not uncommon that one or both parties have an individual therapist in addition to the couple therapist. In these scenarios I often find that the individual therapists are working against the goals of the couples work. They may inadvertently be encouraging the affair to continue by validating the feelings the person is experiencing from the affair (e.g., loved, cared for, noticed, excited). These may be contrary to the couple therapist, who is encouraging a rigid boundary with the affair. When therapy begins, the effective systemic therapist is aware of threats to the therapist system and is setting up processes to maximize the impact of the therapist system in the process of change.

The Position of the Therapist

The role of the therapist is different in varying couple and family therapy (CFT) approaches. In some models, the therapist is viewed as active and a primary instrument of change. In other models, such as Bowen's, the therapist is more of a coach who operates from a detached, differentiated position. For Bowen (1978), the goal of the therapist is to stay out of the emotional reactivity offered by the couple or family. In the view of Satir (1988), the therapist operates from a position of warmth and empathy and works in the therapy room as an equal collaborator with clients. She validates both positive and painful family feelings and demonstrates respect for all family members. The Milan approach (Selvini-Palazolli et al., 1978) refers a lot to the team and, in this way, provides the therapist with additional leverage. Unfortunately, the team approach is neither pragmatic nor cost-effective. Whitaker (Whitaker & Bumberry, 1988) advocated for the use of cotherapy in managing the therapy relationship. In this regard, one co-therapist would be more controversial and perturb the family toward change, while the other would be in a more good cop role and process with the family what had been stirred up. In this model, therapists could support and complement each other. They would also have time to think about what to say next instead of having to come up with an answer, a question or a response in the moment. Again, a co-therapy approach is not cost-effective, and it is more complex than it seems on the surface. Minuchin (1974) advocated for the therapist who joins with a family to be flexible and accommodate the unique styles of unique family members. Postmodern approaches have emphasized collaboration, genuineness, respect and curiosity. The central role of the therapist in these approaches is to create therapeutic space in which therapeutic conversations can occur. They advocate for an egalitarian relationship between the therapist and client systems.

In this book, we see the therapist as an active part of change who needs to act with authority but also in collaboration with clients, especially in establishing the alliance. The therapist needs to be highly engaged in the therapy process but should be creating a space where members in the room can work together; that is, the dialogue should be among family members and not through the therapist. We like to think of the systemic therapist as the conductor of the therapy process. The conductor, while in charge, is not playing each instrument but rather is facilitating how the instruments play together to create a harmonious sound.

It is important to think about the qualities that the therapist brings to the therapeutic relationship. Not everyone is cut out to be a good therapist, especially a good couple and family therapist. In fact, many of the criteria that are used by training programs to accept new therapists in training are not related to abilities, talents and skills in forming therapeutic relationships with clients or in managing systemic therapy sessions. Rather, they are based on qualities such as sound grade point averages, high GRE scores and solid letters of recommendation. However, these studious and intellectualized qualities are often the very things that stand in the way of building sound relationships with clients.

Through a process of engagement and alliance building, the therapist gains a position of influence within a system. The active therapist gains trust, respect and, ultimately, leadership within the family. The family comes to trust the therapist and believe that the therapist can help bring about change and that the therapist will protect and help them. Within reason, each family member believes that the therapist understands and supports their values, positions and beliefs and that the therapist is on their side and will help them. This is the position of leadership in the system that each therapist should strive to attain.

There are many things that therapists must deal with in the therapy room. Information is continually presenting itself to the therapist, who must take in the information, assess its meaning in the context of the problem and then decide on what questions to ask next and what interventions to design. For example, the therapist asks, "What are the presenting issues this client is describing to me? Where are these clients in the process of change? What considerations do I need to make in terms of client learning style, internal world, culture and life experiences? What theoretical principles are a good initial fit? How will these need to change as therapy progresses? How do I relate with all members of the system? How do I get ongoing feedback from all members of the system as to how things are going? What is the best time to intervene, and in what way? What needs to be prioritized in sessions?"

The Role of the Therapist in Change

What do we know about effective therapists in general? The bottom line is that therapy is effective for most who partake and that the therapist is a key part of this effectiveness. The research on good therapists is summarized in a couple of excellent publications (Beutler et al., 2004; Blow et al., 2007; Wampold, 2001;

Wampold & Imel, 2015). We are extremely impressed with the work of Bruce Wampold (Wampold, 2001; Wampold & Brown, 2005; Wampold & Imel, 2015), who used scientific reasoning and meta-analysis to estimate the effects of psychotherapy and then what parts of psychotherapy are important contributors to meaningful change. We also discuss this in other parts of the book. While his work may be confusing for non-researchers to read, he arrives at some critical conclusions. First, he concludes that psychotherapy is efficacious and that people who participate in psychotherapy are better off than those who do not: "... the average client receiving therapy would be better off than 79 percent of untreated clients, that psychotherapy accounts for about 14 percent of the variance in outcomes . . ." (Wampold & Imel, 2015, p. 94). This strong conclusion indicates that psychotherapy is highly effective. However, it also shines a light on how much of client improvement can be explained by psychotherapy, and in their conclusion, Wampold and Imel (2015) attributed 14% of change to the ingredients of psychotherapy. This means that 86% of treatment is explained by factors other than therapy. This does not mean that psychotherapy is not important; rather that there are other factors at work outside of the control of the therapist or the realm of therapy. Wampold also concluded that among bona fide treatments for specific conditions, one treatment is not superior to another (Wampold & Imel, 2015). This provides strong support for the dodo bird verdict, which concluded that all bona fide treatments produce comparable outcomes (Rosenzweig, 1936; Sprenkle & Blow, 2004a). This does not mean that treatments (models) are not of value (Sprenkle & Blow, 2004b) but rather that when models are designed to be efficacious, they are.

Second, it is important to note that of the 14% of change attributable to psychotherapy, the therapist (separate from theoretical model used) is a critical part of the change. Wampold concluded that the therapist's contributions to change in therapy are large and are between 3% and 7% of therapy change:

> ... the preponderance of the evidence indicates that there are important therapist effects (in the range of 3 percent to 7 percent of the variability in outcomes accounted for by the therapists, with substantial variability around these estimates). Therapist effects generally exceed treatment effects, which at most account for one percent of the variability in outcomes. . . . (Wampold & Imel, 2015, p. 176)

The therapist is a true common factor in that there is always a human therapist assigned in traditional therapy. However, as Wampold and Imel (2015) highlighted, even though the therapist is crucially important, *there is widespread variability between therapists and their contributions to therapy*. No matter which model is used or the theoretical orientation, therapists are not equally effective, and the effectiveness of even the best therapist varies depending on the client and the presenting problem. It should be noted that most therapists in clinical trials are well trained and receive a great deal of structure (e.g., supervision, monitoring) in these studies. There are fewer studies of therapists' effectiveness in less controlled settings, such as in community practice, but we believe that therapist variables are even more important in these "real-life" contexts, outside of the intensive structure of clinical trials.

As highlighted above, a growing body of literature has pointed to differences in therapists' effectiveness. This suggests that if the same couple or family were assigned to different therapists, results would be different: some therapists would help a lot, others only a little and still others somewhere in the middle. A small percentage of therapists may cause harm. These findings would likely differ across cases and presenting problems. This also means that some therapists are better working with certain types of family configurations and presenting problems than are other therapists. Some therapists are more effective working with more difficult cases. Some of these differences between therapists are related to superior talent, a poor fit with the therapy profession or unchangeable personal characteristics that are a part of who the therapist is (see Beutler et al., 2004, for a detailed discussion of these variables).

These findings raise several issues when it comes to working with couples and families. First, what does the research as a whole say about the importance of CFT therapists in the change process? Remember that the Wampold and Imel's (2015) review is of psychotherapy as a whole and not CFT specifically. Second, what kinds of skills are needed when it comes to working with complex cases such as those seen by couple and family therapists? Third, how much of the variance between therapists is attributable to inherent talent, and how much can be taught by good training? Can a therapist who is largely ineffective or ineffective with certain types of cases or presenting problems receive training, supervision or something different that would improve outcomes across cases? What can you do as a therapist to increase your skill set in working with complex couple and family therapy cases? Fourth, what kinds of systems are needed to increase the accountability of therapists in relation to the outcomes of their clients? Fifth, theory is important in change, but how do therapists best integrate core theories into who they are as people and how they practice as therapists? As you will see below, we advocate for an emphasis on evidence-based therapists (as opposed to models), but this does have implications for how therapists integrate theory into their work. All of these issues will be discussed below. Before you go on to read those sections, answer the following questions about your work:

1. Are you a good couple and family therapist? How do you know? Is this just your opinion, or do you collect credible outcome data from your clients?

2. What presenting problems or family configurations are you most effective in treating? Why are you more effective with these cases/configurations?
3. What would your clients say are your strengths? What would you say are your strengths?
4. Over the course of your career, what have you done to improve your effectiveness as a therapist? Have these been the best strategies to improve?
5. Are you open to feedback about your effectiveness as a therapist? Who are you willing to get this feedback from?
6. Looking back, what has most contributed to your effectiveness as a therapist?
7. What types of couple or family configurations are you good at working with? What types of presenting issues are you good at resolving? What is it about these configurations or presenting issues that makes you effective?

The Effectiveness of Therapists Who Practice Couple and Family Therapy

Unfortunately, to date, not a lot of research has explored the specific contributions of CFT therapists in therapeutic change. Most of the conclusions on the topic (e.g., Blow et al., 2007; Sprenkle & Blow, 2007) are arrived at from reviews of the work of individual psychotherapy such as the work of Wampold and Beutler. These works emphasize that a competent therapist is a central ingredient in effective therapy and that many key changes in therapy are either initiated by the therapist or influenced by the therapist. But what exactly makes someone competent or effective as a systemic therapist? We can conclude that not all therapists are equally talented or equally effective, but we don't know much more than that at this point in time. In our recent article (Blow & Karam, 2017), we made the case for evidence-based couple and family therapists, and we argued that CFTs require significantly more skills than those working solely with individuals and that systemic therapy requires a great deal of talent when it comes to working with multiple entities in the therapy room at one time. Even though these therapist competencies seem important in CFT work, we don't have studies demonstrating their importance or studies that show how therapists acquire or develop these skills. In this chapter, we assume that the CFT therapist is at least as important as the therapists are in individual psychotherapy and likely much more important. Here we expand on this work and suggest that competent/effective systemic therapists need four key skills. We note that some of these skills are also talents in that some individuals may have a difficult time learning and acquiring these skills. This is an important consideration we expound on below. Some of these can be learned, and some are inherent to the personality of the individual (although they can be honed with practice).

Management Skills

At the core, the couple and family therapist is a manager of people in a space for a period of time. The ability of the therapist to effectively manage these individuals sets the tone for therapy and provides a space where work can occur. The challenge of this work is that the individuals the therapist is working with are often in conflict and have strong feelings toward each other. They may be hostile at times toward the therapist. Management skills cannot simply be learned, memorized and applied. They need work and nurturing.

Even though the therapist is ultimately aiming to get members in the room to work together on their issues, the therapist must be able to manage the dynamics in the room while keeping in check their own issues related to their own personal relationships in their family of origin and their current family/intimate relationships. CFT presenting problems are often complex and prolonged, problems that may have spanned multiple months, years or even generations. These complex cases may involve numerous intertwined issues, and the therapist must be able manage the individuals and the issues and then make the right decisions about to how best to intervene, absorb feedback about initial interventions and then alter the work based upon this feedback. In this process, the therapist needs to be able to sit with intense emotions, present interventions with the right timing and step back from the content to shift the processes of how system members relate to each other.

Couple and family therapists need to be able to take charge of meetings and establish themselves as leaders of the system, with the ability to influence all or key members of the system. This takes impeccable timing – knowing when to pursue for more information and when to wait. It can be a delicate dance. Working with large systems is a complex process, and it takes a therapist who can think on their feet and manage multiple complexities, including diverse people and conflicting personalities, all in a short space of time. In an interview with José Szapocznik, one of the founders of brief strategic family therapy (an evidence-based systemic therapy), he described the complexities of the skills of the systemic therapist (Distelberg, 2008). He emphasized that systemic therapists need to be highly active in therapy, must be able to take charge of sessions and are, at a basic level, session managers.

Facilitative Interpersonal Skills

Timothy Anderson and colleagues (T. Anderson et al., 1999, 2020) came up with the term "facilitative interpersonal skills". These can be defined as "the ability to effectively understand and send interpersonal messages as well as the ability to communicate a rationale for another's problems and to propose new and effective solutions" (T. Anderson et al., 2016, p. 513) and as "... sociability, empathy, and an ability to perceive, decode, and send a wide range of interpersonal communications" (T. Anderson et al., 1999, p. 314). These skills involve a therapist's capacity to deal with interpersonal situations in the moment, situations that are often challenging in CFT. Therapists working with families must have excellent relationship-building skills and the ability to process what is occurring interpersonally in the moment. The therapist engages in a process of establishing a collaborative relationship with a client system, one in which the client has a voice in how things play out but also one in which the therapist can accommodate other voices as well as their own voice. T. Anderson et al. (2016) made the important conclusion in their study that relationship factors are continually modified as treatment plays out and are informed by the treatment process. This is a critically important point as therapists adapt and mold their responses to how treatment plays out in the moment. It is important to note that the therapist uses these skills to bring together all of the competing voices in systemic therapy and to come up with collaborative processes that keep everyone engaged and pleased. Facilitative interpersonal skills focus on how the therapist can communicate qualities like empathy to clients, manage expectations and keep them engaged. This is not one skill or operation per se but is an ongoing negotiation-type process where the therapist is constantly reacting and responding to statements and cues put out by clients. In the group setting such as in CFT, there are numerous pieces of information to respond to all the time. Systemic therapists need to be able to relate to all members of the system, who are often very different in terms of age, gender and presenting problem. Szapocznik emphasized that the best therapists have excellent interpersonal skills, and these skills are broad enough to relate to different family members. These family members can include parents, adolescents and grandparents, all in the same session, and each of these individuals is likely at a very different place in the therapy process (Distelberg, 2008).

Thinking Skills

Another skill therapists need is the ability to think on their feet, in terms of conceptualization of the case theoretically but also in terms of decision making related to how to intervene and when. Therapists need to decide what questions to ask, who to engage and who to temporarily silence. Szapocznik suggested that these therapists need to be able to quickly engage in abstract thinking. He stated,

> The therapist has to be able to observe the interactions in the family, conceptualize what's going on in the family, conceptualize what the appropriate intervention would be and then behave with great attention to family and individual sensibilities. The therapist must be able to do this in a very

short period of time (with high speed of information processing). Individuals who are concrete or slow thinkers are unable to do [this] well. (p. 177)

In addition, thinking skills pertain to conceptualization of the case in terms of what is creating the problems in the system and how to best intervene with the problems. CFTs must be able to conceptualize presenting problems within a systemic framework, build and sustain alliances with all members of a system and manage the ins and outs of therapy sessions that differ in content, focus and intensity. Couple and family therapists who are effective need to be able to be strong in conceptualizing problems within their systemic context and in coming up with ways in which the system can resolve these problems. In this regard, the therapist draws from theory, their own personal family and relational experiences and previous experiences in working with systems. It is important that therapists have their own personal issues under control so that they do not unknowingly influence the therapy process in a negative way (Timm & Blow, 1999). Blow and Karam (2017) stated: "Successful family therapists are influential, persuasive, and convincing; they provide an acceptable and adaptive explanation for the client's distress and frame the problem skillfully for all the members of the system to buy into" (p. 719).

Process Skills

Critical to working with systems is the ability to work with process within these systems. Therapists need to understand process and be able to intervene in the process at the right time and then be able to respond appropriately to the systems responses to the process intervention. Szapocznik suggested that these therapists also need to have the ability to conceptualize problems and to quickly assimilate a great deal of information, often presented in an emotional climate that is intense. They also need to be able to quickly change as new information and processes emerge. Szapocznik referred to this as the ability to "think on one's feet". Szapocznik went on to describe the therapist as

> ...a choreographer or a director of a play.... We want the therapy to focus on the family, the interactions to stay within the family, for the therapist to be choreographing new and more functional interactions within the family. Thus, the therapist is active but not central. (Distelberg, 2008, p. 177)

As the therapist intervenes in the system process, they work to get the system members to interact with each other. In this way, the therapist is a facilitator of the systems process (see Chapter 4). It involves the therapist stepping forward, intervening with a question or a comment or a reflection and then stepping back out of the central role to allow the system members to process with each other. This is a multifaceted dance, and it may involve complexities such as using silence, punctuating certain emotions, giving individuals or topics a voice, validating perspectives/emotions, or choosing not to validate in some cases, and many more.

Blow et al. (2007) described the therapeutic process with a quote from Gurman and Kniskern (1978):

> The ability of the therapist to establish a positive relationship with his or her clients, long a central issue of individual therapy, receives the most consistent support as an important outcome-related therapist factor in marital-family therapy. Therapist empathy, warmth, and genuineness, "the client-centered triad," appear to be very important in keeping families in treatment beyond the first interview. . . . Apparently *it is important for the marital-family therapist to be active and to provide some structure to early interviews, but not to assault family defenses too quickly*. . . . *[A] reasonable mastery of technical skills may be sufficient to prevent worsening or maintain pretreatment functioning, but more refined therapist relationship skills seem necessary to yield truly positive outcomes in marital-family therapy.* (p. 875; italics in original)

This quote does an excellent job of capturing the chess-like approach to working with systems. The therapist has to move and then react based on how the family reacts to the therapist. This recursive process is unique to each family, and it truly captures the ability of therapists to think on their feet.

Therapist Competence: Inherent Talent Versus Learned Skills

As stated earlier, we believe that good CFTs have unique skills that equip them to be effective in the complexities of their work. In this book we focus especially on therapists who work with large systems – couples, families and systems that extend beyond the family. In Blow and Karam (2017), we argued that CFTs require unique skills. These therapists work with multifaceted systems, and they need a base level of therapist talent; they also need to be highly relational, building and maintaining relationships with multiple voices; able to think on their feet; capable of both tolerating and facilitating intense emotions; and they ideally can manage in-the-moment meeting dynamics with several people. They need to be able to clearly conceptualize cases in systemic contexts, and they need to display attunement, empathy and validation to each family member. The therapist must be able to successfully create a minimal level of safety for all in the therapy space so that work can occur and progress. These therapists need to be able to use silence effectively at times and amplify emotions at others. The bottom line is that in CFT, an active and involved therapist is a key part of change.

The question of therapist talent is controversial, but it is worthy of consideration. Some therapists naturally possess strong interpersonal skills and can think on their feet, and these two skills alone are fundamental qualities found in effective family therapists. The opposing question to the issue of talent is whether these skills can be developed and enhanced through instruction, practice and hard work. We strongly believe that effective CFTs need a solid basic level of talent that facilitates their effective learning and practice. Not everyone is cut out to be a therapist, and among those who are therapists, not everyone is able to work with couples and families. Even among those who do work with couples and families, not all are equally effective, and some may do more harm than good. In this chapter, we are not going to attempt to resolve the talent question. We are assuming that you are reading this because you are in the field and along the way someone deemed that you have enough talent to work with couples and families. We will, however, highlight the idea that there are many things that can be done to enhance your talent. Just like a marathon runner can attain better times through a well-designed training regimen and a good diet, a therapist can be more effective in their work through proper skill enhancement. In the next section, we will highlight several key things therapists can do to improve their skill set and their effectiveness with their clients.

Questions include: Can a therapist who is largely ineffective receive training, supervision or something different that would improve outcomes across cases? What can you do as a therapist to increase your skill set in working with complex couple and family therapy cases? How can you maximize your potential?

Steps to Becoming a Good Therapist (Maximizing Your Potential)

In the following pages, we will provide five core strategies that therapists can use to improve their skills. There may be others, but we believe that these five approaches will help even the worst therapist to improve their effectiveness with clients.

Deliberate Practice to Enhance Core skills

In recent years, deliberate practice (DP) has emerged as a key approach to enhancing the skills of therapists. We discuss DP related to therapist development here and again in Chapter 11 related to using DP in supervision. Deliberate practice has been around for some time, and in the last decade there has been greater application of these skill-enhancing methods to psychotherapy (Chow et al., 2015; Goldberg et al., 2016; Rousmaniere, 2016; Rousmaniere et al., 2017). This work is only recently beginning to be mentioned in CFT literature (e.g., Karam & Blow, 2020), even though skills needed in CFT are well suited to deliberate practice because of the complexities involved in working with couples and families.

Deliberate practice is based on the notion that there is a high level of variability in the effectiveness of therapists and that DP is a way for therapists to enhance their skills (assuming that there is a base level of talent for the individual to be a competent therapist). DP is used in non-psychotherapy disciplines such as music, business, sports, chess and medicine to improve the performance of practitioners (Chow et al., 2015). In DP, a person engages in intentional and individualized training focused on the acquisition of specific skills. This ongoing rehearsal allows the individual to become increasingly competent at the skill until a minimum level of mastery is achieved. DP is a focused activity where the individual hones in on a specific skill thought to be just beyond the individual's current level of expertise. The individual measures their outcomes in the skill over time, routinely practices and observes the skill (through video) and obtains honest, authentic feedback from others (such as a colleague or supervisor). The individual then takes this feedback and inserts it into the practice routine; over time, the individual becomes more adept at the skill. In short, DP involves the identification of a skill to be acquired, behavioral rehearsal of the skill, refinement of the skill through feedback mechanisms and then more rehearsal of the skill. This process is recommended both for skill acquisition and for skill maintenance (Hill et al., 2019).

In CFT, there are many skills that are important for therapists to acquire, ranging from fundamental skills such as building the therapeutic alliance with several people at one time and reframing to more complex skills such as enactments and creating safety in therapy. Starting out in DP, the therapist needs to operationalize the skill they are going to learn. This operationalization begins with a thorough understanding of the skill – why it is used (the theoretical rationale behind the skill), when it is used, complete steps that encompass the skill from beginning to end, actions to implementing the skill and ways to assess whether the skill has been successfully implemented and whether the therapist is able to maintain the skill over time. The therapist would also need a way of obtaining feedback on the skill both from a video recording and from a supervisor/colleague. The therapist begins rehearsing the skill in a nontherapeutic setting, alone and with peers. Ideally, the peers would provide feedback. The therapist also rehearses the skill by using video recordings of these skill rehearsals; the therapist critically watches these videos with a view to weaknesses and areas for improvement. When the therapist has achieved a sufficient level of competency in the skill, they implement the skill with real clients in therapy and ideally record a video of this real-life process. After this session, the therapist views the video alone and also seeks out honest feedback from supervisors and peers. The therapist practices parts of the skill not quite mastered and implements it again, both in role plays and in the therapy room. Over time, the therapist reaches a point where they have achieved competency in the skill.

Rousmaniere (2016) emphasized that for this to be effective, therapists must be in a good habit of reviewing their work and must be open to feedback. They also need to have an expert coach, consultant or supervisor who is also an expert on the skill and who is willing to provide honest feedback. Ideally, therapists should focus on small and incremental learning goals so that they can track their mastery of the skill over time. Therapists then need to repeat their skill over time, continually assessing their performance through client feedback and supervisor feedback mechanisms.

> **Deliberate Practice Example, Reframing**
>
> There are several core CFT skills. One we consider particularly important, and that we write about elsewhere in the book, is reframing. This is a key skill used widely in the majority of CFT training models. If we are to consider doing DP with reframing, we need to answer the questions we posed earlier.
>
> **Why is it used** (the theoretical rationale behind the skill)? Reframing aims to shift a system by changing the ways in which individuals come to think about or view their problems (Sprenkle & Blow, 2004a). Reframing, if successful, leads to a reattribution of the problems the clients are facing, and these reattributions allow individuals to engage with each other in new ways. For example, a couple who experiences low connection in their relationship is able to move closer to each other after the therapist successfully frames their problem within the fears and insecurities of their attachment cycle (Johnson, 2004). No longer is the couple in conflict with each other and they can respond and move closer to each other because of the new way of looking at their problem.
>
> **When is it used?** Reframing is used throughout the therapy process. It is especially important that it be used liberally early on in therapy, especially as the therapeutic system (clients and therapist) is working to define the problem that brought them to therapy, the goals of therapy and the steps necessary to resolve these problems. Reframes in this sense serve to keep the members of the system engaged in therapy; they also help them not to feel blamed or attacked. The frame provided is more palatable, allowing the members of the system to engage with each other in new ways.
>
> **Complete Steps That Encompass the Reframing Skill From Beginning to End**
>
> It must be emphasized that some parts of a reframe arise out of a specific context based on key factual considerations based on the client system

the therapist is working with at the time. It should be noted that reframes would look different if a couple presented with an affair as the problem versus only communication difficulties. The reframes may sound the same, but the emotional climate in the room affects how they play out. Reframing has three essential steps (Alexander & Parsons, 1982). First, the therapist needs to *understand* and *validate* the individual members of a family's existing views of the problem. This is an individual-level understanding and validation. For a couple who presented because they "argue all the time", the therapist seeks to connect with each individual's view of why they argue, and the therapist validates this viewpoint. It is essential that the understanding of the problem be validated by the therapist. Second, after the therapist has understood and provided validation, the therapist provides an alternative frame/way of looking at the problem. For couples, common reframes exist around the attachment cycle – fears and insecurities about the relationship. Depending on the context, frames could also be about stress at work, difficulties with young children or financial concerns that spill over into the relationship. Third, it is critical that the therapist check with each member of the system about the fit of the frame and, ideally, there would be a conversation that would occur about this new frame. This conversation would lead to the adoption of the frame or would lead to an alternative new frame. This process is ongoing until there is a shared understanding between all members of the therapeutic system.

What Are the Required Actions Related to Implementing the Skill of Reframing?

It is essential for the success of reframing that the therapist have a level of credibility or trust with the client system. While it cannot be instantly achieved, from the outset, the therapist is attempting to achieve a position of influence with the family. In order to implement reframing, the therapist needs to consider the timing of the new frame. This cannot occur without the therapist first understanding and validating each member of the system's view of the problem under consideration. Failure to understand and validate each member's view of the problem prior to providing a new frame could be premature and could lead to a weakening of the alliance. It is also important for the therapist to know the system well enough so that the frame provided is *plausible* and *relatable* to the issues that the family is facing. It is also important that the therapist have a working list of examples of good reframes. While every system is different, we find that core frames come up again and again depending on the family/couple and their situation. Finally, it is important that the therapist consider that the frame provided is not a rigid application but rather is a beginning attempt to create a collaborative and shared frame of the situation. The therapist is not attempting to win points by coming up with the perfect frame but rather to initiate a conversation about different ways of thinking about the problem. Even if the initial proposed frame is inaccurate, the resulting conversation should allow the system to come up with a new frame that fits all.

What Are Ways to Assess Whether the Skill Has Been Successfully Implemented?

There are immediate ways for a therapist to assess the success of a reframe. The first way is in-the-moment, here-and-now assessment. The therapist can simply ask, "Does this new frame fit your experience?" or "Tell me more about why this does not fit your experience. What would be a better way to view the situation?" In addition to the immediate in-the-moment check of the frame, the therapist can use formalized feedback mechanisms to assess how things are going. One formalized question that can be asked is related to a new view of a situation (see Chapter 10 on formalized feedback) provided by the specific reframe. In this case, the therapist can simply ask a question such as:

> In the last session, I framed the fighting in your relationship as fears you both have related to closeness. When your Jim [husband] gets too close to Mary [wife], Mary ends up feeling vulnerable because it reminds her of her first marriage when she was hurt when her husband left her for another woman. This leads her to lash out. When she lashes out, Jim feels wounded and it brings up past criticisms and related hurts he experienced as a child when he felt like he could never be good enough for his father.

Please rate your views on the accuracy of this description. What changes would you make?

Deliberate Practice in Action Based on Reframing Operationalization

The above is an example of how the operationalization of a key CFT skill should occur. Therapists should write this up for themselves and have a colleague review this description. Then the therapist begins rehearsing these skills, first alone and then with peers and, finally, with clients. It is not good enough just to be able to memorize these skills. They need to be rehearsed by saying the words out loud. The reframes should also be rehearsed depending on the specific clients and their presenting problems. While the global features of the reframe are good to consider – for example, (1) understand and validate each member of the family's view of the problem, (2) provide a new frame for the problem and (3) check the fit of the frame with each member of the system – it is also essential that the therapist can adapt these problems to a unique family context. Reframes are different for an arguing couple versus a family who has a rebellious adolescent who is also creating tensions in the couple relationship. As the therapist moves through implementing these skills, rehearsing, obtaining feedback and rehearsing them again, it is useful for the therapist to consider some questions:

1. What am I doing well? How do I know what I am doing is going well?
2. What am I not doing well? What are my ongoing challenges, blind spots and stumbles in learning this skill?
3. What emotions are coming up for me as I implement this skill? Are these emotions related to the cases I am working with implementing this skill or some more personal issue I am dealing with in my life currently or in the past?

Managing Self-of-the-Therapist Reactions

The self-of-the-therapist is an important topic related to who the therapist is in the therapy room. Blow et al. (2007) described therapists' awareness of their worldview and relevant personal issues as an important component of therapist training, development and effectiveness. There are many aspects to this work, much of what can be addressed if a therapist is genuinely interested in getting these issues under control.

Overall Self-of-the-Therapist Importance

Working with couples and families can be a challenge because therapists bring their own issues to the therapy room that can both help and hurt therapy (Timm & Blow, 1999). Every therapist brings baggage to therapy related to their own families and relationships. This baggage is not always negative, but it still influences therapy, the questions asked, the issues avoided, the ability to sit with emotions and the like. A therapist who grew up in a violent household will bring both insights and barriers related to this upbringing when it comes to therapy, especially when working with angry clients. A therapist who is going through a divorce will unavoidably be affected by this experience when working with couples. This does not have to be an impediment, but it surely can be if the therapist has heightened hurts and sensitivities and unresolved issues related to these personal experiences. Self-of-the-therapist work allows therapists to face and deal with unhelpful (although changeable) therapist qualities.

It is important that therapists at least be aware of these limitations and how they may be playing out in the therapy room. We believe that personal growth related to self-of-the-therapist is a key part of therapist effectiveness. This is something that all therapists can work on in order to improve their effectiveness and the outcomes for their clients. There are numerous ways in which therapists can work on their self-of-the-therapist issues (see Timm & Blow, 1999, for a greater discussion of this topic). Not all therapists receive good self-of-the-therapist preparation in their training programs. In fact, for many this is completely absent. We are biased and believe that this work is essential. But working through self-of-the-therapist in the training program is just the first step. Therapists benefit from personal therapy tremendously, and this includes individual, couple and family therapy. While it is not possible for therapists to receive all of these modes of therapy, the more they can experience firsthand, the more insight they will have into the therapy process. We also know therapists who belong to support groups where they can focus on the personal issues they bring to the table. These groups are often unstructured but need to have safety built into them so that therapists can be vulnerable with each other. While the data on self-of-the-therapist and client outcomes are still not as strong as we would like to see, we have no doubt that this internal work has an impact on clients and their outcomes. We encourage all therapists who work with couples and families to commit themselves to a career of internal exploration and personal growth.

Resisting the Pull of the System

At the heart of our understanding of self-of-the-therapist is the ability of the therapist to avoid getting pulled into issues of the system. This usually would occur when a therapist has unresolved issues or overidentifies with a client or problem. According to Rait (2000), the family therapist is always subject to the pull of the system. This is particularly important as the therapist works with families in which there is high tension or a wide range of emotional intensity. There will always be an emotional pull on the therapist to take sides, intervene in conflict, rescue a family member or diffuse tension. The couple or family can place a lot of pressure on the therapist to bring about their preferred change in the system by having the therapist take their side. We believe it to be most helpful if the therapist can be informed by the pull of the system and become a part of the system but not be overwhelmed by the system (Timm & Blow, 1999).

Novice therapists will struggle with this as there will always be an attempt by the family to return to a homeostatic state. The therapist will usually be pulled into a system when they do not have their own issues under control. For example, the therapist who likes to please people will experience difficulties in establishing firm boundaries. The family may "gang up" on the therapist in multiple ways, including undermining their leadership, sabotaging interventions and the like. It is always essential for therapists to step back and evaluate whether they are being pulled into the family's ways of interacting with each other.

Personal Self-of-the-Therapist Work

One way in which therapists can grow is by doing self-of-the-therapist work. Many have written about this topic (see Aponte & Kissil, 2014; Aponte et al., 2009; Timm & Blow, 1999). Timm and Blow (1999) suggested that this work goes well when therapists can achieve a balance in their work; that is, when they can be aware of and unimpeded by negative or traumatic past experiences and, at the same time, can draw on the resources from these experiences to inform their work in positive ways. Timm and Blow suggested three key aspects to self-of-the-therapist work.

DO YOUR OWN WORK

Therapists' personal growth that deals with facing and dealing with personal experiences can significantly help in the therapy room especially with systems. Many systemic therapists are drawn to the work because of difficulties they faced in their own families of origin or relationships. These motivations may become hazards in therapy, especially when they are either unresolved or raw. A therapist who is a survivor of abuse in their childhood will be informed by this in their work with families. There are cases where therapists are still raw or triggered by these past events, and this can contaminate the work in unhelpful ways. We believe that all therapists should attend therapy to experience what it is like as a client and to work through their own painful issues. These experiences are invaluable for times when the therapist is doing this work with clients. Therapists learn from both the helpful aspects of this work but also from the mistakes their own therapists make. Therapists should dedicate themselves to a lifetime of personal growth. This may not always involve therapy, but there are many other ways therapists can grow. This growth leads to heightened awareness and maturity that help the therapist negotiate the emotion-laden work of CFT.

THERAPIST SUPPORT GROUPS

We have grown in our own work by being a part of therapist support groups. These groups can be helpful in providing additional supervision or insight into cases and, from that standpoint, can be an intellectually helpful exercise.

However, these groups can also be a place for personal growth, and they should be set up in that way. Timm and Blow (1999) went into great detail about these groups, including carefully selecting who else is in the group and setting up clear rules and expectations such as frequency of meeting, purpose, confidentiality, content and the like. Four members is an ideal size. We find in our work that these groups can be very helpful if each member takes a turn in presenting information that will lead to great effectiveness as a therapist. It is important that what is presented be circled back to things that come up in the therapy room. Useful ideas include presenting genogram information, a timeline that highlights past and recent nodal events, or a presentation revolving around certain client themes and how they trigger the therapist. These groups should be real and authentic, and group members should respond with supportive comments and suggestions for growth. This work not only can increase the awareness of therapists in relation to therapy triggers but can also alert them to resources that they have based on their lived experiences that will help them in their work. For example, a therapist who has been through two contentious divorces in their personal life may run into issues in working with conflictual couples, being drawn to take the side of the individual who may be most aligned with their issues. However, after some work on these sensitivities, the therapist can draw upon these experiences and become an expert in divorce, knowing the legal issues, what works best for children and how to set good boundaries. In this regard, the therapist who is willing to do this work will be more effective.

GROWTH THROUGH INCREASING SELF-AWARENESS

Another area we challenge therapists to grow is in their self-awareness. This includes awareness of themselves and their own issues as well as cultural awareness so that therapists are aware of and sensitive to cultural issues. This includes an awareness of their own privileged position in society, gender biases and understanding of clients and their unique cultural situations. Every therapist exists within a cultural context, including a political context. Therapists should be continually working on their awareness of their worldviews, biases and values. Blow et al. (2007) suggested that the ability of therapists to match treatment to unique client systems is really important, but therapists are simply not able to do this without being in touch with what they are bringing to the table. In short, therapists who learn about and are sensitive to the unique cultures in which they work and who match their interventions to these contexts are more successful in engaging families in treatment and affecting change. For example, every therapist has unique values, attitudes and beliefs, and it is rare that these ever align with those of their clients. If the Christian therapist does not have insight into their values and their blind spots, they will have challenge helping a Muslim family or a family without any religious beliefs. Blow et al. (2007)

contended that CFTs are faced with a multitude of value-related issues. This is because the problems that families present with are frequently at the very heart of our value systems – topics like sexuality, parenting, beliefs and substance use.

One of the ways in which therapists can be more attuned to their clients is by becoming more aware of and sensitive toward other cultural groups and what they might be experiencing. Baker (1999) suggested that the therapeutic relationship is influenced by the extent to which therapists and clients know themselves, the openness of therapists to know clients as they are (separate from societal norms and prejudices) and the willingness of therapists to learn the unique intricacies of the cultural contexts of their clients, including their social norms and social systems. Baker talked about the second-order cybernetic idea that the therapist is influenced by the system with which they interact as well as influencing the system by their presence. Baker stated: "Therapists must remember that their own cultural history comprises a lens that will influence their perceptions of clients outside of their culture" (p. 58). It is suggested that the therapist becomes more aware of their own background, including culture, gender, socioeconomic status, race, age and the like, and, through this process, identifies possible prejudices toward other groups.

Two Additional Personal Growth Activities for Therapists

Increasing Reflective Functioning (Mentalization)

A recent study focused on the variable of reflective functioning (mentalization) and therapists. We believe that this is an extremely important topic for therapists to focus on as it represents something that they can do to grow and be more effective (Cologon et al., 2017). This group of scholars assessed therapists for reflective functioning and concluded that reflective functioning predicted therapists' effectiveness. Therapists who were able to engage in higher levels of reflective functioning were more effective compared to therapists who did not have this ability. This finding was true regardless of the theoretical orientation of the therapist. The definition of reflective functioning provided by the study was "the ability to conceptualize, identify, and understand mental states in the self and others" and the ability to hold "in mind multiple, concurrent points of view" (Cologon et al., 2017, p. 615). This is a quality that is highly applicable to CFTs. In the parenting literature, interventions focused on increased reflective functioning have helped parents increase this capacity, which in turn improves child outcomes (e.g., Bammens et al., 2015; Sadler et al., 2013). One of the things we were concerned about is that increasing reflective functioning/mentalization is a vague concept. Below we provide a step-by-step activity you can engage in to increase your reflective functioning. These ideas are taken from a study by Bateman and Fonagy (2010). These authors focused on a mentalization-based treatment. They defined *mentalization* as the process by which individuals make sense of themselves and others and said this process is both overt and covert. When we engage with others in interactions, we need to make sense of this experience, and this is always subjective. They suggested that therapists develop a mentalizing therapeutic stance that includes:

> a) humility deriving from a sense of "not-knowing"; b) patience in taking time to identify differences in perspectives; c) legitimizing and accepting different perspectives; d) actively questioning the patient about his/her experience – asking for detailed descriptions of experience ("what questions") rather than explanations ("why questions"); e) careful eschewing of the need to understand what makes no sense (i.e., saying explicitly that something is unclear). An important component of this stance is monitoring one's own mentalizing failures as a therapist. In this context, it is important to be aware that the therapist is constantly at risk of losing his/her capacity to mentalize in the face of a nonmentalizing patient. . . . As with other instances of breaks in mentalizing, such incidents require that the process is "rewound and the incident explored". Hence, in this collaborative patient-therapist relationship, the two partners involved have a joint responsibility to understand mental processes underpinning events both within and without therapy. (Bateman & Fonagy, 2010, p. 13)

Essentially, an individual high in mentalization can think and contemplate before reacting to their own feelings or perceptions of the feelings of others. As you move toward high reflective functioning/mentalization, we suggest that you work with yourself (and maybe also with your supervisor or therapist) to increase your mentalization. These are also the steps you would use as you worked with your clients.

1. Adopt a humble, not-knowing stance in your work. This is particularly important as you work with systems where you need to be able to hold multiple realities at one time and not judge these realities. This reminds us of the collaborative language systems approach of Harlene Anderson and colleagues that was popular in the 1990s (H. Anderson & Goolishian, 1992).
2. Work on beginning your interaction with all members of systems from the standpoint that there are different views and perspectives to situations. This is very important in CFT as there are always different perspectives, feelings and experiences around an issue.

3. The therapist must train themselves to legitimize and accept different perspectives. This is akin to validation in reframing. It does not imply agreement with the perspective, which is important to realize, especially during polarizing times when politics and related views dominate many parts of the culture. The therapist needs to be able to validate that the beliefs of clients are legitimate to the client, even if the therapist personally strongly disagrees with them.
4. Therapists approach the client problem with an open curiosity, questioning and learning about the issue from multiple sides and perspectives. This is a useful stance in a family therapy context where the therapist invites different voices to provide their perspective of the situation. In this regard, the therapist asks for detailed descriptions of the experience.
5. When an impasse in understanding occurs, it is not the end of the quest. Rather, mentalizing results through having an ongoing dialogue about the differences and, through this process, arriving at a deepening of understanding.

The Use of Mindfulness to Increase Therapist Effectiveness

In another study of therapists effectiveness, Pereira and colleagues (2017) examined how therapist mindfulness is related to clinical effectiveness. They concluded that practitioners who were more effective had higher levels of mindfulness when compared to less effective therapists. These therapists were intentional in their mindfulness practice, and they applied this with deliberation and consistency over time. Based on the results of this study, therapists should be more aware of themselves, their bodies and their surroundings. They should have time to focus on what is going on internally and externally in the present moment. We encourage therapists to get into a practice of mindfulness. This does not have to be for hours a day. Rather, this works better if therapists can do this at least once a day but during key times, including before a difficult session, between sessions or at the start of the day. We encourage therapists to be intentional in scheduling these times; for example, scheduling a longer break between two sessions (e.g., 15 extra minutes). During this time, you should slow down and reflect and focus on your breathing and the internal sensations of your body. Ask yourself the following questions.

1. How am I feeling today? What am I thinking about? (notice feelings and thoughts)
2. What am I anxious about? (focus on understanding anxiety and breathing it out)
3. What do I need to do to feel centered? (focus on grounding and centering self)

We find that therapists who are seeing clients may not find the time to pay attention to what is going on inside of them. They may get pulled into back-to-back sessions, case notes, time to eat, phone time and computer time and not take time to stop to reflect.

Therapists Knowing Theory With the Best Evidence

Effective therapists operate from a strong knowledge base. One study reported that master therapists are voracious learners (Jennings & Skovholt, 1999). This means that these therapists have a strong desire for knowledge, along with a will to learn more and become more proficient in their work. Not only do therapists need this desire for knowledge but the more they have, the better. This knowledge acquisition should be so that they are truly able to understand the reason for theories and their application.

There is strong evidence that a therapist's belief in therapy and allegiance to positive outcomes affects therapy in a positive way. Blow et al. (2007) discussed how a therapist's belief in a treatment and in its potential to bring about positive change is an important therapist quality, and a wavering in these beliefs will negatively jeopardize therapy outcomes. In the early sessions with client(s), therapists develop hypotheses/maps/hunches about what is going on in the system and how the client may be helped. These are based on the therapist's reading of theory, personal experiences and knowledge of the client. All of this gets integrated through the person of the therapist, who takes in information from the client, runs it through their internal therapy filters and through the therapeutic relationship and then shares interventions with the client. In this sense, the therapist knows theory and know what brings about change but is also free to "forget" these in therapy as they engage with clients. As Piercy and Nelson (1999) suggested, having a solid grasp on change ideas from many different models allows therapists to follow their intuition on the one hand and be informed by theory on the other. All therapists use models or theories to guide their work. Therapists tend to lean toward specific models, and we advocate for therapists to privilege evidence-based approaches. We want therapists to know as many evidence-based models as possible (as opposed to picking a favorite; see Blow et al., 2007, for an in-depth discussion). The question we ask is, even though theory is important in change, how do therapists best integrate core theories into who they are as people and how they practice as therapists? Whereas the evidence-based movement has focused in on models and which models (as depicted in treatment manuals) are better than other models, these models are nothing when they are not operationalized through the human therapist. It is the therapist who learns theories and understands how they are relevant to clients and their situations, but therapists still must implement interventions drawing from theory through the relationships they build with clients. In large research studies, therapists are viewed as variables to be controlled. In fact, to test whether treatments are being followed as written, therapists are carefully trained and then are monitored with close supervision to ensure that they are delivering the treatment with fidelity (i.e., as it was intended by the model developer).

Maximizing Your Use of Theory

We have several suggestions to help you in maximizing your use of theory. First, know evidence-based models and the foundational models on which they are based (Blow et al., 2007). Realize that theory is important in change, but it should not be rigidly applied in the same way across all cases. Therapy is not applying theory in a cookie-cutter way. It requires nimbleness, flexibility and adaptability on the part of the therapist. We encourage you to read as much as possible. Finally, we encourage you to learn more about your own work by studying your own therapy. It is easy these days to videotape sessions. Videotape 5% of your cases and then review them to see what you are doing well, what you are not doing well and steps you can take to improve.

Increasing Accountability

Staying focused on outcomes is not something that is built into our current practice models. Currently there are systemic therapists in active practice who have limited accountability. As detailed in Blow and Karam (2017), therapists graduate with degrees, get licensed and enter into practice with little to no data showing their effectiveness with clients. In fact, there are many therapists claiming effectiveness with specialty populations, but there is little showing why they can be called specialists in these issues. We would like to see many more systems of accountability built into mental health care for couple and family therapists. We envision a time in the future where honest and accurate data on therapists' effectiveness will be available to consumers. We encourage you not to wait for this time but work to display aggregated data about your effectiveness on your website. We have seen some share effectiveness data that are greatly exaggerated. An honest and authentic display of data will be highly appealing to clients, who can enter therapy treatment with the correct expectations on what treatment will look like.

Integrate Longitudinal Outcome Data Into Your Clinical Practice

Reliable data showing therapists' effectiveness over time should be highly important to therapy consumers. We encourage you to collect data on your cases, showing progress toward solving the presenting problem or other identified problems along the way and also data showing overall client satisfaction with therapy/the therapist (see Chapter 10 on feedback).

Measures you can use are session-by-session progress (e.g., the Session Rating Form and the Outcome Rating Form are widely used), overall outcomes (e.g., the Outcome Questionnaire), measures of family and couple change or measures you develop yourself. A useful measure at the outset of therapy may involve a rigorous description of the presenting problem (e.g., adolescent curfew, infidelity in marriage) and then collecting data on this specific outcome in addition to others, not only during but also immediately after therapy. It would be even better if you could collect the same data at 6-, 12-, and 24-month follow-up points to show the success of your work over time. In this regard, you will be able to see general progress on measures such as the The Outcome Questionnaire 45 (OQ45) and specific progress on the issue that brought them into treatment. We believe it is important for CFTs to collect data on couple and family outcomes. This in and of itself will distinguish your work from other practitioners in your community. There are some good examples on the internet of this type of data collection; for example, the work of Tony Rousmaniere details a way to collect data on client outcomes over time (https://drtonyr.com/outcome-data). At a minimum, we would like to see therapists report on a trajectory of change through therapy. Setting this up will take work on the part of the therapist to ensure that clients are on board with data collection. Clients will need to give their permission, knowing that the data will be reported in aggregate and that their names would never be associated with any data. It will also take some effort to collect post-therapy data, but this can occur if the therapist is organized. Finally, it is important that the measures can be quickly completed and can be filled out on a device such as a cell phone. There are several online platforms including Google, Qualtrics, and Survey Monkey that allow for short surveys that are easy to complete.

Report Data on Work With Your Specialty Areas

As mentioned earlier, there is little data to show therapist effectiveness in specialty areas. For CFTs, this would include outcomes for couples; for example, increased satisfaction, resolution of conflict, forgiveness after an affair. Even if a couple divorces, a therapist can report data on a successful resolution of divorce issues; for example, a joint parenting contract established, low attorney costs and the like. For families, there are numerous outcomes to report, including child behavior, family routines and less conflict, to name a few. These outcomes over time will help to identify therapists' strengths and expertise and help therapists figure out what clients and client configurations are most suited to their talents. While therapists may know this intuitively, having data to support this is invaluable.

Publish Your Data on Your Website

Most therapists have a website, but very few publish their outcome data. For some this is because it takes too much time; others don't know good ways to collect or interpret data, and some do not like what the data are reporting in terms of their overall effectiveness. There may be little incentive to report data on one's effectiveness. Publishing one's data takes a great deal of transparency, something that is lacking in current therapy practice. The following categories of data are important: general therapy outcomes, outcomes related to specific presenting problems, different outcomes for individual members within a family, the average number of sessions to achieve outcomes and total number of clients in the data set. Different types of outcomes can be discussed, including large, moderate and small improvements.

Be Willing to Change Based on the Data

If you are willing to collect and post your data, you should have a plan for how you want to use your data. First, it is marketing tool for your practice. Second, therapists should use these data for personal growth. For example, if over time one notices that certain clients do not improve and another category of clients drops out early, this is a signal that change on the part of the therapist is needed. The therapist can then do a closer analysis of these cases, ideally discuss them with a supervisor and then decide how to change things up, learn new ways of practicing or shift the focus of the practice to clients where successes are more constant.

Supervision as a Venue to Grow Your Skills as a Therapist

Can supervision enhance the effectiveness of therapists? This question is unanswered in the empirical literature, although intuitively it would seem that a good supervisor would improve the skills and therefore the client outcomes of therapists in the same way as coaches improve the performance of athletes with whom they work (see also Chapter 11 on self-supervision). CFTs have long been recognized as having one of the most robust supervision systems available. The American Association for Marriage and Family Therapy (AAMFT) Approved Supervisor designation is a credential that organizes and provides credibility to the supervisory process. While we believe that some supervisors, similar to therapists, are more effective than are others, there remains a lack of knowledge about this variable. One issue we will now discuss is the orienting of supervision around client outcomes and therapists' personal growth in terms of becoming more effective. These two variables should be central to the supervisory process, but often supervision shifts in focus to updating the supervisor about cases, focusing on regulations related to therapy or a superficial and intellectual discussion about cases. We challenge readers of this book to seek out supervisors who are willing to help you to grow as a therapist – not necessarily personal growth but rather growth in terms of efficacy as measured by improved outcomes in clients. It is time that subjectivity be removed from the supervision process. Therapists are not competent because they are kind or easy to get along with but rather because they are able to bring about sustained changes in the clients they work with. Not all supervisors are willing to enter into this kind of work with therapists because it is not easy work and entails a more challenging relationship. However, the best athletic coaches, by comparison, are willing to engage in challenging relationships with the athletes they coach, which leads to improved performances and improved outcomes in game results. We suggest two additions in the supervisory process (beyond the traditional relationship) that will lead to improved therapist development outcomes.

A Supervisory Relationship Where Discussions Are Driven by Short- and Long-Term Client Outcomes

In this regard we are essentially advocating for data to be used to a greater degree in supervision. While data are used in supervision such as video, live or process data, these data are not connected to client outcomes, and they are not sufficiently incorporated into supervision. This is because there is not enough time to process all of these data, and there is inherent subjectivity in this process. The supervisory relationship is time limited to approximately 1 hour a week in many cases, and this is insufficient time to do all of the necessary work required. Often this time includes an updating of cases and possibly a more intellectual exploration of one or two cases. Often therapists can hide cases that are not going well or topics where they feel more vulnerable from their supervisors. We would like to see therapists work more to collect written session-by-session feedback data from clients as well as pre/post/follow-up data on client outcomes and therapy experiences. When these types of data are then folded into supervision, the supervisor has the real opportunity to explore with the client how the therapist is doing in their development. However, this kind of work creates a much more challenging climate for supervision and means that the supervisor–therapist relationship and its expectations should be clearly developed and laid out at the onset of the supervisor–supervisee relationship. The supervisor can review these data each week and explore with the therapist where things are not going well and for what reasons.

A Supervisory Relationship That Incorporates Deliberate Practice Into Supervisory Activities

Deliberate practice, as discussed earlier, is an excellent growth tool for therapists. See Chapter 11 for an in-depth discussion of the utilization of DP in supervision.

A Supervision Context That Works on Self-of-the-Therapist Issues

There is no doubt that self-of-the-therapist issues affect therapy. We incorporate self-of-the-therapist into all individual and group supervision of students. This is key, especially when supervising beginning therapists who are quickly going to be working with intense cases involving couples and families (see earlier discussion on self-of-the-therapist). The supervision arena is one place where it is natural to focus on these personal issues and their influence on the therapy process.

Conclusion

We hope that this chapter will inspire you to improve your work as a therapist. In every profession, one can become stale and bored. Airplane pilots regularly perform additional trainings in simulators to stay on top of their ability to fly. Musicians and athletes practice every day for their performances. We encourage therapists to develop a hunger for learning and improving their work and showing their effectiveness with real data.

References

Alexander, J., & Parsons, B. (1982). *Functional family therapy: Principles and procedures.* Brooks/Cole.

Alexander, J. F., Barton, C., Schiavo, R. S., & Parsons, B. V. (1976). Systems-behavioral intervention with families of delinquents: Therapist characteristics, family behavior, and outcome. *Journal of Consulting and Clinical Psychology, 44,* 656–664.

Anderson, H., & Goolishian, H. (1992). The client is the expert: A not-knowing approach to therapy. In S. McNamee & K. Gergen (Eds.), *Inquiries in social construction. Therapy as social construction* (pp. 25–39). Sage.

Anderson, T., Crowley, M. E. J., Himawan, L., Holmberg, J. K., & Uhlin, B. D. (2016). Therapist facilitative interpersonal skills and training status: A randomized clinical trial on alliance and outcome. *Psychotherapy Research, 26*(5), 511–529. https://doi.org/10.1080/10503307.2015.1049671

Anderson, T., Finkelstein, J. D., & Horvath, S. A. (2020). The facilitative interpersonal skills method: Difficult psychotherapy moments and appropriate therapist responsiveness. *Counselling and Psychotherapy Research, 20*(3), 463–469. https://doi.org/10.1002/capr.12302

Anderson, T., Ogles, B., & Weis, A. (1999). Creative use of interpersonal skills in building a therapeutic alliance. *Journal of Constructivist Psychology, 12*(4), 313–330. https://doi.org/10.1080/107205399266037

Aponte, H. J., & Kissil, K. (2014). "If I can grapple with this I can truly be of use in the therapy room": Using the therapist's own emotional struggles to facilitate effective therapy. *Journal of Marital and Family Therapy, 40*(2), 152–164. https://doi.org/10.1111/jmft.12011

Aponte, H. J., Powell, F. D., Brooks, S., Watson, M. F., Litzke, C., Lawless, J., & Johnson, E. (2009). Training the person of the therapist in an academic setting. *Journal of Marital and Family Therapy, 35*(4), 381–394. https://doi.org/10.1111/j.1752-0606.2009.00123.x

Baker, K. A. (1999). The importance of cultural sensitivity and therapist self-awareness when working with mandatory clients. *Family Process, 38,* 55–67.

Bammens, A.-S., Adkins, T., & Badger, J. (2015). Psycho-educational intervention increases reflective functioning in foster and adoptive parents. *Adoption & Fostering, 39*(1), 38–50. doi:10.1177/0308575914565069

Bateman, A., & Fonagy, P. (2010). Mentalization based treatment for borderline personality disorder. *World Psychiatry, 9*(1), 11–15. https://doi.org/10.1002/j.2051-5545.2010.tb00255.x

Beutler, L., Malik, M., Alimohamed, S., Harwood, M., Talebi, H., Noble, S., & Wong, E. (2004). Therapist variables. In M. J. Lambert (Ed.), *Bergin and Garfields handbook of psychotherapy and behavioral change* (pp. 227–306). John Wiley & Sons.

Blow, A., & Karam, E. (2017). The therapist's role in effective marriage and family therapy practice: The case for evidence based therapists. *Administration and Policy in Mental Health and Mental Health Services Research, 44*(5), 716–723. https://doi.org/10.1007/s10488-016-0768-8

Blow, A., Sprenkle, D., & Davis, S. (2007). Is who delivers the treatment more important than the treatment itself? The role of the therapist in common factors. *Journal of Marital and Family Therapy, 33*, 298–318.

Bohart, A. C., & Greenberg, L. S. (1997). *Empathy reconsidered: New directions in psychotherapy.* American Psychological Association.

Bowen, M. (1978). *Family therapy in clinical practice.* Jason Aronson.

Chow, D. L., Miller, S. D., Seidel, J. A., Kane, R. T., Thornton, J. A., & Andrews, W. P. (2015). The role of deliberate practice in the development of highly effective psychotherapists. *Psychotherapy, 52*(3), 337–345. https://doi.org/10.1037/pst0000015

Cologon, J., Schweitzer, R. D., King, R., & Nolte, T. (2017). Therapist reflective functioning, therapist attachment style and therapist effectiveness. *Administration and Policy in Mental Health and Mental Health Services Research, 44*, 614–625. doi:10.1007/s10488-017-0790-5

Distelberg, B. J. (2008). History of evidence-based practices: An interview with José Szapocznik. *The Family Journal, 16*(2), 173–179. https://doi.org/10.1177/1066480707313823

Friedlander, M., Escudero, V., & Heatherington, L. (2006). *Therapeutic alliances in couple and family therapy: An empirically informed guide to practice.* American Psychological Association.

Gelso, C. J., & Carter, J. A. (1985). The relationship in counseling and psychotherapy: Components, consequences, and theoretical antecedents. *The Counseling Psychologist, 13*, 155–243.

Goldberg, S. B., Babins-Wagner, R., Rousmaniere, T., Berzins, S., Hoyt, W. T., Whipple, J. L., Miller, S. D., & Wampold, B. E. (2016). Creating a climate for therapist improvement: A case study of an agency focused on outcomes and deliberate practice. *Psychotherapy, 53*(3), 367–375. https://doi.org/10.1037/pst0000060

Gurman, A. S., & Kniskern, D. P. (1978). Research on marital and family therapy: Progress, perspective, and prospect. In S. Garfield & A. Bergin (Eds.), *Handbook of psychotherapy and behavior change: An empirical analysis* (2nd ed., pp. 817–902). Wiley.

Hill, C., Kivlighan, D., Rousmaniere, T., Kivlighan, D., Gerstenblith, J., & Hillman, J. (2019). Deliberate practice for the skill of immediacy: A multiple case study of doctoral student therapists and clients. *Psychotherapy.* Advance online publication. https://doi.org/10.1037/pst0000247

Jennings, L., & Skovholt, T. M. (1999). The cognitive, emotional, and relational characteristics of master therapists. *Journal of Counseling Psychology, 46*(1), 3–11. https://doi.org/10.1037/0022-0167.46.1.3

Johnson, S. (2004). *The practice of emotionally focused couple therapy: Creating connection* (2nd ed.). Brunner-Routledge.

Karam, E., & Blow, A. (2020). Common factors underlying systemic family therapy. In R. Miller, R. Seedall, & K. Wampler (Eds.), *Handbook of systemic family therapy* (Vol. 2, pp. 147–169). John Wiley & Sons.

Minuchin, S. (1974). *Families and family therapy.* Harvard University Press.

Orlinsky, D. E., Grawe, K., & Parks, B. K. (1994). Process and outcome in psychotherapy—Noch einmal. In A. E. Bergin & S. L. Garfield (Eds.), *Handbook of psychotherapy and behavior change* (4th ed., pp. 270–378). Wiley.

Pereira, J.-A., Barkham, M., Kellett, S., & Saxon, D. (2017). The role of practitioner resilience and mindfulness in effective practice: A practice-based feasibility study. *Administration and Policy in Mental Health and Mental Health Services Research, 44*(5), 691–704. https://doi.org/10.1007/s10488-016-0747-0

Piercy, F. P., & Nelson, T. (1999, January/February). Flow in the consultation room. *Family Therapy Networker,* 46–47.

Pinsof, W. M. (1994). An integrative systems perspective on the therapeutic alliance: Theoretical, clinical, and research implications. In A. O. Horvath & L. Greenberg (Eds.), *The working alliance: Theory, research, and practice* (pp. 173–195). Wiley.

Rait, D. (2000). The therapeutic alliance in couples and family therapy. *Journal of Clinical Psychology, 56,* 211–224. https://doi.org/10.1002/(SICI)1097-4679(200002)56:23.0.CO;2-H

Rosenzweig, S. (1936). Some implicit common factors in diverse methods of psychotherapy: "At last the Dodo said, 'Everybody has won and all must have prizes'." *American Journal of Orthopsychiatry, 6,* 412–415.

Rousmaniere, T. (2016). *Deliberative practice for psychotherapists.* Routledge.

Rousmaniere, T., Goodyear, R., Miller, S., & Wampold, B. (2017). *The cycle of excellence: Using deliberate practice to improve supervision and training.* Wiley.

Sadler, L. S., Slade, A., Close, N., Webb, D. L., Simpson, T., Fennie, K., & Mayes, L. C. (2013). Minding the baby: Enhancing reflectiveness to improve early health and relationship outcomes in an interdisciplinary home visiting program. *Infant Mental Health Journal, 34*(5), 391–405. https://doi.org/10.1002/imhj.21406

Satir, V. (1988). *The new peoplemaking.* Science and Behavior Books.

Selvini-Palazzoli, M., Boscolo, L., Cecchin, G., & Prata, G. (1978). *Paradox and counterparadox.* Jason Aronson.

Sprenkle, D., & Blow, A. (2004a). Common factors and our sacred models. *Journal of Marital and Family Therapy, 30,* 113–129.

Sprenkle, D., & Blow, A. (2004b). Common factors are not islands—They work through models: A response to Sexton, Ridley, and Kleiner. *Journal of Marital and Family Therapy, 30,* 151–158.

Sprenkle, D., & Blow, A. (2007). The role of the therapist as the bridge between common factors and therapeutic change: More complex than congruency with a worldview. *Journal of Family Therapy, 29,* 109–113.

Timm, T. M., & Blow, A. J. (1999). Self-of-the-therapist work: A balance between removing restraints and identifying resources. *Contemporary Family Therapy, 21*(3), 331–351. https://doi.org/10.1023/a:1021960315503

Wampold, B. (2001). *The great psychotherapy debate.* Lawrence Erlbaum.

Wampold, B., & Brown, G. (2005). Estimating variability in outcomes attributable to therapists: A naturalistic study of outcomes in managed care. *Journal of Consulting and Clinical Psychology, 73,* 914–923.

Wampold, B., & Imel, Z. (2015). *The great psychotherapy debate: The evidence for what makes psychotherapy work* (2nd ed.). Routledge.

Whitaker, C. A., & Bumberry, W. A. (1988). *Dancing with the family: A symbolic-experiential approach.* Brunner/Mazel.

9
NURTURING THE THERAPEUTIC ALLIANCE

Overview: The Importance of Focusing on the Therapeutic Alliance

It's hard to imagine having a successful therapy experience without first having a strong relationship between the therapist and client system. Most close relationships have problems, difficulties or misunderstandings at some point in time, and the relationship between the therapist and client system is no exception. The manner in which the therapist and client system handle these difficulties together, however, is a crucial component of the success of the relationship. This relationship, known as the *therapeutic alliance*, has been deemed by most as a necessary but not sufficient ingredient in all effective therapies (Sprenkle & Blow, 2004).

Recall a time you have been in a therapy room, and it feels as though you could cut the tension with a knife – it is a palpable and potentially anxiety provoking situation for a couple and family therapist (CFT). As the stress goes up in a family system, there might be far more pressure on the therapist to form and maintain certain relationships with family members. If the therapist fails to resolve or lessen the stress, they might be the first and easiest person for the family members to turn on, for failing to lessen the stress and for failing to curb the out-of-control family member.

Simply meeting with a couple or family can be an overwhelming experience. It is no doubt easier to do therapy when one only has one individual's pressures to deal with. Furthermore, it is common for a couple or family to collectively gang up on a therapist in ways that put the therapist on the spot. If the therapist is not adept at dealing with these situations, they can place an incredible amount of pressure on the therapist. Further, conjoint sessions may be noisier and have higher levels of open conflict between family members. Another major difficulty in dealing with multiple alliances is that not every family member presents in therapy in the same way. Each family member possesses unique motivations, agendas, goals and visions of change.

DOI: 10.4324/9781315542737-9

I (AB) recently began to work with a family that was referred to me from a colleague. The family had refused to continue to work with her, even though she is an excellent therapist, because the son had launched into a tirade in session in which he had used all kinds of profanities. This had offended the parents and they had blamed the therapist for not being able to effectively control the son in the session. To be honest, very few therapists would have been able to control him. I addressed this issue overtly in the first session, telling them that I was not sure if I could prevent him from exploding but my goal was to help him to share his concerns with his parents in ways in which he could be heard. Luckily, he did not go into one of his tirades in the first two sessions. In the third session, he did, but I had already formed a good relationship with the parents. I immediately challenged this tirade and asked him to speak in ways he could be heard. The parents seemed to like and feel supported by this therapeutic gesture. The point of the above illustration is that in dealing with multiple family members, there is a lot of pressure on the therapist to perform, especially early in the process. Mismanagement of the alliance can lead to premature dropout.

Every family member is different in their goals, expectations for therapy and beliefs about how therapy could help them to change. Further, not all family members believe that there is a problem, family members are at different levels of development and each family member has a different relationship to the problem or the family member with the problem. In dealing with these multiple relationships, it is completely unrealistic to think that the therapist will have an identical relationship with each family member. To the contrary. Because family members are different, the relationship between the therapist and individual family members will always be different. Further, some family members are easy to connect with. This might be accomplished by simply asking them a question or remembering their name. Other family members are impossible to connect with, even after many sessions. The therapist needs to have a good enough relationship with these family members.

So many questions arise when trying to qualify or describe this multifaceted relationship. Do the therapist and client system trust that the other is working hard to contribute to the therapy's success? Is there an empathic connection between the people in the room? Is there agreement on the goals of therapy between all members of the system? Do the therapist and client system collaborate on decisions that need to be made about how the therapy is being conducted and what intervention strategies are used? When difficulties arise, do clients feel comfortable enough to share any negative feelings, hurt or anger that may have resulted? And how can the therapist and client system work together to resolve any problems that may have occurred? In this chapter we seek to give context to these questions by operationalizing the construct of the therapeutic alliance in CFT and articulating practical strategies to build, balance and repair these systemic relationships.

Therapeutic Alliance Defined

Although *therapeutic alliance* has been described in a variety of different ways, we will focus on Edward Bordin's (1979) pantheoretical conceptualization of it as composed of three distinct content dimensions: tasks, goals and bonds. The tasks component of alliance describes agreement between therapist and client about how the therapy will be structured and the actual events that occur within the sessions. The goals component of alliance consists of agreement between therapist and clients on the preferred outcomes of therapy. The bonds component of alliance refers to the degree to which the clients and therapist feel connected interpersonally and hold empathetic, positive regard for each other. Generally speaking, according to Bordin's model, alignment on each of these three aspects of alliance must be present for therapy to be successful.

The therapeutic alliance has been clearly established through meta-analyses as a strong predictor of outcome in psychotherapy across diverse treatment orientations and modalities (Horvath & Bedi, 2002). These studies, which used diverse client groups (children and adults, inpatients and outpatients) treated for all types of problems (i.e., depression, anxiety, drug abuse, work and social problems), all showed the important role of the therapeutic relationship in treatment success (Horvath & Symonds, 1991; Martin et al., 2000). Most of the studies involved client self-reports or therapist and trainer observer checklists/reports (Horvath & Bedi, 2002).

An important nuance in these overall findings is that the client's view of the alliance is consistently found to be a better predictor of outcome than the therapist's view. Similarly, therapist views of the alliance frequently do not correlate well with the views of the client system. Consequently, a model for collecting continuous alliance feedback from the client system is needed in CFT both to help therapists check their assumptions and to privilege the clients' voices in building, maintaining and potentially repairing the therapeutic relationship.

While clients may know best when it comes to accurately assessing the strength of the alliance, therapists make important contributions to the establishment of a good therapeutic relationship. The therapist's ability to communicate empathy and understanding to the client system is very important. Another essential component is the therapist's openness, flexibility and willingness to adapt the treatment to the client system's needs. Skilled therapists actively solicit clients' input about the goals and methods of treatment to facilitate collaboration (Horvath, 2001). Research shows that the ability to form good relationships with clients is not simply a function of therapist training or experience level. Many beginning therapists are as skilled as their more experienced counterparts at forming good therapeutic relationships (Horvath, 2001). However, we believe that common factors–informed therapists who are more intentional in their monitoring and nurturing of the alliance may be better at forming relationships with difficult couple and family systems. In addition, alliance-sensitive CFTs are better at identifying and resolving problems in the therapeutic relationship before it is too late (Karam & Sprenkle, 2010; Karam et al., 2015).

The Complexity of the Alliance in the Practice of Couple and Family Therapy

In individual therapy, the alliance has been defined almost exclusively as the relationship between the client and therapist. A more systemic conceptualization that considers the relational complexities inherent to having more than one client present in the therapy room, however, is necessary to better understand the therapeutic alliance in the practice of CFT. For instance, when working with a traditional married couple, you are contending with at least four different alliance relationships (therapist–husband, therapist–wife, therapist–husband and wife together, husband and wife together without therapist).

Pinsof and Catherall (1986) devised therapeutic alliance scales that have been revised specifically for couples, the Couple Therapeutic Alliance Scale–Revised, and families, the Family Therapy Alliance Scale–Revised (Pinsof, 1994). To account for the systemic nature of the alliance in CFT, Pinsof (1995) articulated several interpersonal dimensions of the therapeutic relationship. The interpersonal system of the integrative psychotherapy alliance includes the following four domains: (a) self-therapist ("the therapist and me"), (b) other–therapist ("the therapist and my significant other or another family member"), (c) group–therapist ("the therapist and my partner/family and myself") and (d) within-system ("my partner/family members and I together without the therapist"). Therapists must be able to identify and track these interpersonal subsystems with all of their cases in order to understand the full range of the therapeutic alliance.

Family members entering and exiting the direct therapeutic system at different points in the therapeutic process, at varying developmental levels and with contrasting motivations for being in therapy make the building and maintenance of the therapeutic alliance in conjoint therapies a more complex process compared to individual therapy (Escudero et al., 2012). Individual therapists do not have to worry about caught in a tug-of-war between family members. This scenario in CFT, known as the *split alliance* (Pinsof, 1995), occurs when system members' feelings and reactions toward therapy and the therapist differ notably. A split alliance can be a result of system members in the couple or family trying to manipulate the therapeutic relationship to have the therapist side with them and to determine who is right and who needs to make changes. If a client experiences the therapist taking sides, a split alliance may exist where one client has aligned with the therapist and the other has not. If the relationship becomes too unbalanced, the family member who feels sided against or estranged by the therapist may not return to therapy. Therapy is more productive for all family members when they all feel heard and valued; that is, when a split alliance is avoided.

It is not at all uncommon for family members to engage in therapy only because of the pressure of another family member. *Noncompliant* is a difficult word to define and can mean several different things. We define it as an individual who would not normally seek out therapy for themself and who remains skeptical about the benefits of therapy. This individual only attends therapy meetings at the urging or pressure of loved ones or family members. In this regard, because there are more members present in CFT and it is a group effort, it is feasible that the CFT therapist has to deal with more noncompliant clients than the individually oriented therapist.

Often as therapists we may work with these involuntary or reluctant participants, affectionately referred to as "hostage clients". These people do not initially want your help, as they have been required or mandated by agencies or outside stakeholders (e.g., schools, courts, child protection services, employers). In the couple and family therapy modalities, hostage clients potentially become even more problematic because it's your job to develop a good therapeutic alliance with each individual, subsystem and the whole family. Within a family system, some members may be willing participants while others are anything but open to the therapeutic process; for example, adolescents who attend family therapy only after extreme coercion by their parents or a spouse who receives the ultimatum "that it's either couples therapy or divorce". Sometimes these clients may actually be self-aware enough to realize that they need to improve some aspect of themselves or their relationship but they did not initialize the search for professional help. Conversely, other members are not aware of a personal issue because they think their family member is the one who needs to change.

Alliance Skill Building in CFT

Nurturing Bonds

The bond dimension of the alliance forms more easily in CFT when you naturally connect to likeable elements of a clients' personalities, motivation and other strengths in and between members of the system. Some clients enter therapy more motivated to change and are inherently more likeable than others. Alternatively, each member of the system may be likeable on an individual basis but when put together in couples or family therapy, the conflict and acrimony may make it harder to develop a bond with the client system as a whole. To tap into this bond dimension, ask yourself the following questions:

- *What do I like or appreciate about each member of the client system?*
- *What do I like about the couple or family system as a whole?*
- *What bothers me or constrains my ability to like each member of the client system?*
- *What keeps me from liking the family system as a whole?*
- *In the past, what have I tried to do to increase my bond with the client system?*

DEFINE THE THERAPEUTIC ROLE

In order to strengthen and nurture the bond, therapists must define their role by explicitly reminding the couple or family that their alliance is with entire system, not just the individual (Pinsof, 1995). While it may be unavoidable to be inducted into the chaos of the family system, CFTs may diminish their ability to form bonds if they begin to function in the role of judge or jury. Therapists should assert that they are not there to be swayed or join with one spouse or family member against the other. This does not mean, however, that therapists should not advocate for someone in the system when another member is clearly wrong or out of line. Practice your role statement with clients (to be used both at the beginning of therapy and at times of potential triangulation between client system and therapist). The following is an example of how a therapist may define their role with a couple or family system:

> *Let me stop all of you for a moment, please. I sense that each of you are trying very hard to get me to see things from your point of view or for me to tell your loved one that you are "right" and they are "wrong" in this dispute. I'm attempting to validate your perspective and want everyone to feel valued and heard in this therapy. Although it may appear that I am taking sides momentarily with one of you, my intent is to honor both my alliance to the family as well as my alliance to specific family members. I'm trying to understand your cycle that stops you all from moving forward in your relationship and in this therapy. In order to build our bond in this work, do not think of me as a judge or jury who renders a verdict against one of you; rather, think of me as advocate for this family who partners with each of you to increase understanding and acceptance in this relationship.*

DEVELOP CURIOSITY FOR MEMBERS OF THE CLIENT SYSTEM

How do you foster the bond dimension in CFT, however, when the client system is not inherently likeable? Therapists should also explore personal constraints that inhibit the ability to form bonds. We believe that if you do not automatically "like" your clients, you must at least learn to be curious about them. It is helpful to keep the following questions in mind as you attempt to nurture bonds with less likable clients:

- *How did the client get to be this way? How has their family of origin impacted their way of relating? Where did they learn this response that is triggering to you or their family member?*
- *What keeps the client or system stuck in the same pattern or engaging in repeated behaviors that they know are not beneficial to their individual or relational health?*
- *What is the primary emotion (e.g., fear, insecurity, shame) that underlies your client's presentation that makes them unlikable both to you and their family member?*
- *Is this pattern or cycle specific to only this relationship that you are currently working with, or is it present for your client in other relationships, both past and present?*
- *Despite their triggering presentation, what underlying abilities or strengths do each individual client and whole system exhibit?*
- *How does the individual client or entire system remind you of any difficult person, relationship or interface issue from your own personal life or background?*

A client's emotional distance and lack of strong bond may not be correlated with your skills but may reflect the system member's longstanding personal difficulties and family-of-origin issues. Even though we as CFTs tend to be "therapist centric" in our viewpoint, remember that this emotional chilliness may also result from something that happened outside of the therapy room between system members that has nothing to do with you. Engage your own curiosity about this dynamic without implicitly viewing clients as being resistant or sabotaging. Explore clients' behaviors with questions about their origins. Is the discomfort more related to issues of trust, feelings of vulnerability, rejection or a need to be independent and in control? What does this say about their upbringing, previous relationships or prior therapy? Your tone should be casual, respectful and curious. To foster the bond dimension of the alliance, therapists must learn to share genuine feelings of hope and strength within the system without minimizing client deficits or constraints.

Creating Credible Tasks

The tasks dimension of the therapeutic alliance refers to the degree to which clients find both the structure and activities of therapy helpful and consistent with their expectations (Bordin, 1979). Johnson and Talitman (1997) reported that this tasks component was the most important alliance dimension in predicting a successful response to emotionally focused therapy (EFT). Whereas clients should take the lead in initiating goals, it is the therapist's responsibility to develop appropriate tasks that fit the client system. For those clients who enter treatment lacking some type of order in their personal lives or without previous therapy experience, the structure provided by a therapist may be a stabilizing influence. Therapists must be careful to match appropriate tasks with the proper developmental and cognitive level of each client. In devising appropriate therapeutic tasks, however, the therapist should not only use clinical wisdom but must also pay close attention to client system values, preferences, ethnicity and culture to ensure goodness-of-fit (Blow et al., 2007). For instance, if a couple enters therapy expecting to learn fair-fighting skills with an action-oriented approach but the therapist devises a structure that is more self-reflective and insight oriented, the overall fit and agreement on this tasks dimension will probably be very low. It is helpful to keep the following questions in mind as you create credible tasks:

- *What about this client system's values and preferences have informed the way I structure this therapy?*
- *What type of structure is ideal for this system? Is this system seeking more of an action-oriented, skills approach or an insight-oriented, reflective approach?*
- *How do I seek collaboration from this client system in obtaining homework tasks?*
- *How do I create enough space for clients to ask questions about the homework I assign?*
- *Does this client system routinely complete the homework? If no, why not?*
- *What questions have I asked my clients to assess fit with the tasks of this therapy?*
- *What feedback have I received from this client system that has helped me modify the way I structure this therapy?*
- *In what other ways do we collaborate on decisions that need to be made about the way the treatment is being conducted and what intervention strategies are used?*
- *Are the tasks utilized in this therapy a good fit for the clients' culture, belief systems, worldview? How do I know?*

Operationalizing and Collaborating on Goals

In order to have a strong goals dimension of the therapeutic alliance, clients must experience the therapist as collaborating with them on the problems for which they are seeking help. Ideally, goals should originate from the client and then be clarified or refined by the therapist. Each member of the family system should have a say in this goal-setting phase. If therapists prematurely focus the therapy on what they deem important rather than addressing client concerns, the alliance may never solidify. There are risks involved in not clearly defining treatment goals at the onset of therapy (within the first one to three sessions). The ambiguity involved in not knowing exactly what you are working toward could lead to confusion and frustration, from both the client's and the therapist's perspectives. These feelings may prevent engagement or lead to early dropout (Lambert et al., 2001).

The miracle question (de Shazer, 1988) can be used to help clients visualize goals and articulate what their problems would be like if suddenly they were solved. A variant on this question to highlight potential goals is, "If I were to wave a magic wand and whisk your problems away, what would you be doing?" Rather than a distinct phase of therapy that only occurs once and is never revisited, goal setting should be part of an ongoing dialogue between client system and therapist – one that is frequently addressed and modified, if necessary, throughout the course of treatment.

Develop S.M.A.R.T.E.R. Goal Statements

To avoid uncertainty and establish a benchmark for progress, therapists must lead clients in the discussion and subsequent operationalization of treatment goals. Some clients may easily be able to identify general areas of their relationship they want to work on in therapy (i.e., communication, trust, respect) but need assistance in refining therapy goals to move from the abstract to the concrete. Goals should be S.M.A.R.T.E.R. – specific, measurable, attainable, relevant, timebound, equitable and relational.

A *specific* goal has a clear focus to it. It isn't saying, "I want better communication in this relationship"; it's saying, "I want to learning fair-fighting and problem-solving skills to improve our communication in this relationship". Specificity is important so that you know exactly what needs to be done in order for the goal to be deemed a success.

A *measurable* goal is one that is based on some sort of metric. Instead of saying "I want to have more help with housework", a measurable goal would be "I would like your help to do the dishes/laundry/vacuuming at least three times a week".

A goal that is *attainable* is one that can be accomplished. Clients may tend to get overzealous with their goals when they first enter therapy. It's more important to be realistic than too aspirational here. Help the client system break down larger goals into pieces if necessary to accomplish them. For example, some ambitious families with young kids seem determined to have an immaculate home. That's not impossible, but it's not necessarily realistic or achievable for most couples balancing a busy work and home life. As clients attain certain goals and get better at something, new goals may become attainable. During this dialogue about goal attainability, therapists should also explore with clients the potential constraints to achieving their goal(s).

Relevant goals are goals that are directly related to helping the client system make progress in their areas tied to the presenting problem. Clients sometimes make the mistake of chasing goals that are not really connected with what their therapeutic focus is all about, and they waste time and energy that could be better spent in their target area. For example, if you're dealing with an emotionally disconnected couple that is already good at co-parenting, creating goals that include spending more time together as family doing kid-related activities may not be the most relevant to the couple's overall needs and demands.

The best goals are also *timebound*. Adding this parameter is important so that you can keep the client system accountable. Setting goals is sort of like creating a to-do list. Clients have on their list what they want to do today, what they want to do tomorrow, etc. Be very careful in helping clients with the time frame they choose, ensuring that they would also be able to complete the goal without unreasonable stress. It may also benefit clients to condense larger goals into smaller, more time-limited subgoals. By helping the client modify their goals in this way, the seemingly insurmountable outcome becomes more possible. As an example of this, a therapist might ask the client system what is feasible to begin making progress on the goal between the current time and the subsequent session or help them divide the big goal into three or four smaller steps or subgoals along the way.

Goals should be *equitable*, prioritizing the betterment of the whole system over any individual member. According to Friedlander and colleagues (2006), therapists must limit therapeutic ultimatums and the tendency for clients in relational therapies to define the outcome of a goal in "win/lose" terms. If there is disagreement within the client system on goals, CFTs should take an active and unifying stance in reframing the resistance by finding shared meaning and a sense of equity.

Even when goals have been grouped into individual and couple/family levels, it is important for the therapist to help the system frame the goal in *relational* terms. In conjoint sessions, CFTs must avoid accepting only one member's conceptualization of what direction the therapy should take, as couples or families do not always have the same initial motivations or reasons for attending.

In order to develop competency within this dimension of the alliance for each of your cases, we recommend you complete a S.M.A.R.T.E.R Goal Statement from the template below.

S.M.A.R.T.E.R. GOAL STATEMENT

Crafting S.M.A.R.T.E.R. goals is designed to help you collaborate with the client system to identify whether what they want to achieve is realistic and determine a deadline. When writing S.M.A.R.T.E.R. goals, use concise language but include relevant information.

Initial Goal	Write the goal that the client system has stated. Which member(s) of the system set the goal?	
Specific	Is the goal too broad? How can this goal be more focused and narrower?	
Measurable	How will you operationalize progress and know whether your clients have successfully met this goal?	
Achievable	What are the constraints in the system that may prevent the goal? Does the client system have the skills and resources required to achieve the goal? What is each member of the system's motivation for this goal? On a 1–10 scale, how confident is everyone in the system that they will achieve the goal? Does the goal need to be broken down into smaller steps to promote success?	
Relevant	Why is the client system setting this goal now? How does it fit with the presenting problem and why they are coming to see you?	
Timebound	What's the deadline, and is it realistic?	
Equitable	How is the goal framed fairly to promote buy-in and equity for each member of the family system, so that there is no one member's wants or desires prioritized over another member's wishes?	
Relational	Is this an individual- or couple/family-level goal? How is the goal connected to the couple/family cycle and related to collective functioning of the system?	
S.M.A.R.T.E.R. Goal	Review what you have written and collaborate with the system members to craft a new goal statement based on what the answers to the questions above have revealed	

Explicitly Linking Tasks, Goals and Bonds

To promote a healthy, integrated alliance, therapeutic tasks, goals and bonds should be explicitly linked together by systemic therapists for their clients. In a qualitative inquiry, Sells and colleagues (1996) reported that treatment effectiveness for both therapists and clients was linked to the perceived clarity of goals and their relationship to therapeutic tasks. Bordin (1979) believed it was the synergy between goals and tasks that gave rise to strong emotional bonds. Therapists should not take it for granted that clients automatically understand why they are being asked to practice a skill or complete a homework assignment. Engagement may be threatened if a therapist does not make their rationale transparent and if the clients do not "buy" their rationale (Davis & Piercy, 2007).

For example, a wife is pursuing couples therapy because she wants her husband to communicate and share more vulnerable emotions with her. She will measure progress on this goal by the number of times he approaches her in the evenings to vent about his work frustrations after their two small children go to bed. The husband, on the other hand, only wants to participate in the therapy if it will improve his sex life. He states that his individual goal is to make love to his wife two to three times per week. To achieve consensus amidst such different surface motivations, the CFT must skillfully reframe these individual goals to address the underlying needs for connection of both partners. In this instance, the therapist clarifies that the couple goal is to increase intimacy in the marriage. By framing the goal within the broader context of intimacy, the therapist connects with the wife around her need for emotional closeness without ignoring the husband's concern for increased physical connection in the marriage. When thinking of constraints that could prevent them from reaching this goal, both agree that having young children reduces the ability to spend as much quality time together currently as they did when they were first married. To increase the bond, the therapist reminds each spouse about their dedication and commitment to each other, while encouraging them to obtain childcare so that they will have more time to themselves. Taking their values and preferences into consideration to devise appropriate therapeutic tasks, the therapist explains how an emotionally focused structure to therapy will both increase the bond and move the couple forward toward their therapeutic goal.

Thinking Systemically About Your Alliance With the Indirect System

In systemic therapy, many times key members of the family system are not present in the room. For example, a young couple is constantly arguing over the level of involvement their parents have in their relationship. While they are important to the treatment, these in-laws reside in the indirect system (Pinsof, 1995). When building an alliance in systemic therapy, the therapist must remember that they are intervening in a system that is larger than the people with whom they are interacting directly. Even if the client is motivated and fully engaged in therapy, members of the indirect system who either do not adequately understand or believe in the treatment may negate therapeutic gains and momentum. Conversely, a client system may need family and friends to support the tasks, goals and bonds of therapy in order to succeed. A therapist may be able to monitor the client's alliance with the indirect system by asking some of the following questions:

- *How does your relationship with important people outside of this therapy room impact your progress in therapy?*
- *Do you feel that I as the therapist appreciate how important some of your relationships are to you?*
- *What would the people who are important to you think about the way your therapy is being conducted?*
- *Do you feel that the people who are important to you would trust that this therapy is good for your relationships with them?*
- *How do you feel about what important people in your life think about your therapy?*

If the therapist feels like therapeutic progress is being jeopardized by involvement from someone in the indirect system after this assessment, they could either engage in boundary-making work with that client or intentionally reach out to the person(s) of interest, in essence moving the client from the indirect system into the direct system to address the conflict.

Alliance "Tear and Repair"

The therapeutic relationship, much like the important couple and family relationships we deal with, is rarely static in nature – it develops and changes over time. One such type of change, called *tear and repair*, occurs when an alliance undergoes damage (tear), before the therapist and client system take action to restore, or repair, it to a healthy state (Safran & Muran, 1996, 2000; Stiles & Goldsmith, 2010). Therapeutic tears, also known as *ruptures*, can occur for a multitude of reasons, especially in a systemically oriented couple or family therapy when multiple relationships must be managed, balanced and maintained. Unresolved tears are associated with deterioration in the alliance and may lead to poor outcome or system dropout (Safran & Kraus, 2014). There are several common psychotherapeutic constructs that are related to these tears in the alliance, including resistance, transference, countertransference, empathic failure, therapeutic impasse and misunderstanding events (Safran & Muran, 1996,

2000). In the face of a tear, therapy cannot continue without a successful repair, but often clients are reluctant to bring up concerns about how the therapy is going or negative feelings they have about their therapists (see Chapter 10 on feedback for ways to overcome this problem). Even more troubling is the finding that therapists often fail to either notice or know what to do when there are ruptures in the therapeutic alliance (Safran & Muran, 1996). The upside to this potential "therapy killer" is that when systemic therapists are good at detecting tears with various system members and develop the skills to work with them therapeutically, it can end up being one of the most valuable thing to happen to the alliance!

This tear and repair cycle should be thought of as normal of part of the CFT process (Karam et al., 2015). Often as couple and family therapists we must help our clients break the homeostatic, gravitational pull of their problem cycle by "pushing the system" with brutally honest and powerful but potentially alienating interventions and feedback. In these pivotal moments, tears are highly possible when engaging with the clients' defenses and challenging core beliefs. It is helpful to remind clients of the net benefit of working through the tear and repair cycle. These events present an opportunity for clients to practice new relational behaviors. They are moments when the therapist may teach or model alternative ways of handling conflict and a chance for clients to practice implementing new conflict resolution skills in a safe and supportive environment. They also serve as evidence for the client that, even in the face of difficulty, relationships may continue and thrive or that addressing difficult topics can lead to successful outcomes. Pinsof (1995) also argued that after completing the successful process of repair, the relationship between client and therapist is fortified in such a way that facilitates not only greater transparency into the therapeutic process but also deeper or more intense relational work.

Common Therapeutic Alliance Tears in CFT

The same reasons that make rupture–repair events so important in couple and family therapy also make it difficult for some clients to address ruptures with their therapists. A particular challenge for CFT practitioners involves balancing the often conflicting needs and relational styles of family members at odds with each other (Pinsof, 1995; Pinsof & Catherall, 1986). Compared to individual therapy, therefore, the tear and repair cycle is predicted to occur with great frequency in couple and family treatment (Pinsof, 1995). Tears in the therapeutic alliance in CFT can be triggered by the following systemic events.

There is a disagreement about goals or tasks of therapy. When a client disagrees, questions or rejects the treatment strategy employed by the therapist, a tear in the alliance is likely to occur, especially if the individual is unable to voice their concern. All family members may not agree with each other about the goals for therapy, they may have different responses to the tasks that the therapist chooses and the therapist's attempts to join with one member of the system may inadvertently alienate another family member (Pinsof, 1995). Also related to the tasks, the therapist may err by either not providing enough direction with the tasks of the therapy or not creating enough space for clients to collaborate on the therapeutic structure.

The tear is related to lack of perceived fairness by the therapist from other members of the system. Traditionally, the suggested stance of a family therapist was one of neutrality, where the therapist actively avoids siding with any member of the family over the others (Butler et al., 2011). Both Cecchin (1987) and Butler and colleagues (2011) recognized, however, that this detached neutrality can lead to the therapist being perceived as uninvolved, cold and aloof. Ruptures in the relationship therefore may occur when one client in the system perceives the therapist as being overly aligned with another or to be taking sides or when therapy overall is not seen as fair and balanced to all members present in the room (Friedlander, Escudero, & Heatherington, 2006).

The therapist misuses sensitive information from an individual session in a couple or family meeting. Unlike what happens in individual therapy, what is revealed or discussed inside of couple/family sessions (secrets, conflicts, feelings) – confidential information – may lead to fallout or repercussions in the room or at home. If individuals in the family system feel betrayed by what was revealed, their sense of safety and trust in the therapist may be jeopardized. Similarly, as family members get more comfortable within the therapeutic context, greater risks may be taken, secrets may emerge and new areas may be explored, which may contribute to a tear for any of the members present in therapy (Friedlander et al., 2011). We suggest that therapists avoid at all costs positions where they would inadvertently breach client individual confidentiality.

The therapist forgets to follow-up on a homework assignment after clients took time outside of session to complete the therapeutic task. Many CFTs include homework assignments as a way to engage the family system actively in the process of therapy between sessions. In addition to extending the clients' work beyond the therapy room, homework assignments can provide practice for couple/family communication and other skill development, increasing generalization of behavior change from therapy to the clients' everyday life. Therapists who either entirely forget or do not consistently follow up on homework assignments, however, may tear their alliance with frustrated system members. Due to this therapist oversight, these clients may also be less likely to complete future out-of-session assignments.

Steps to Repairing the Tear

When a rupture in the relationship occurs, it is not the end of therapy. Rather, it is an opportunity for therapists to "right the ship" and strengthen the alliance through appropriate repair. Here are steps we suggest in repairing these relationship breakdowns.

1. *Detect the tear.* Sometimes the tear in the alliance is blatantly obvious, as someone in the client system will directly tell you that you upset or offended them. If the alienated client is not comfortable alerting the CFT to the tear, perhaps another family member will speak up on their loved one's behalf. In other instances, a client's nonverbal reaction will demonstrate that there is something amiss in the alliance. There are also instances where a member of the system will withdraw during a session, potentially signaling a tear in the therapeutic relationship. Repeated no-shows or cancellations without proper explanation may also indicate trouble. Another way to detect a tear in the alliance is using an assessment or feedback measure, as many clients will find it safer to voice their displeasure with the therapist or the therapy in this more indirect manner (see Chapter 10).

2. *Determine the type of tear.* Some tears in systemic therapy can be relatively minor and temporarily disrupt the therapeutic process, but others can be much more severe and jeopardize the entire future of the work. Safran and Muran (2000) identified two variations of alliance tears in therapy: withdrawal and confrontation. In the withdrawal type, a member of the client system may disengage from the therapist and certain aspects of the therapeutic process. A withdrawal tear may take the form of nonresponsiveness to an intervention or an avoidance maneuver, like when a client avoids interventions presented by the therapist by changing the subject, refuses to explore topics at greater depth or completely ignores the therapist. Another type of withdrawal tear is demonstrated by indirect communication of negative sentiments or hostility, exemplified by a client indirectly using sarcasm, nonverbal cues or passive-aggressive behavior. Conversely, in confrontations, the client directly expresses anger or dissatisfaction about the therapist or certain aspects of the therapy. These overt expressions of negative sentiment toward the therapist through means of accusations, attacks or ill will are impossible for the therapist to miss. When a confrontation occurs, an unprepared therapist may respond defensively to the client's opinions or criticisms. These may be more challenging to deal with in CFT as other members may become involved in (join in) the confrontation against the therapist or they may confront each other about their different experiences of the therapist.

3. *Acknowledge the tear.* As research indicates, continuing with "therapy as usual" in the context of a tear may further erode the alliance and, if possible, it is important for the therapist to acknowledge the tear in real time (Piper et al., 1999). This is more feasible (although not necessarily easier if the therapist reacts defensively) if the clients address the issue directly with overt confrontations compared to more subtle withdrawal tears. The face-to-face encounter is always the preferred method of acknowledgment. For tears that cannot be caught immediately, however, the likelihood of dropout could increase. In these situations, deal with the rupture as soon as it comes to your awareness, even if this means placing a phone call to the injured member of the client system. Do not wait or carry on with a specific couple or family intervention that you have been planning when you determine that a tear has occurred. Remember that alliance repair takes precedence over all other therapeutic game planning! Acknowledgment of a confrontation in CFT may look something like this: "I can tell by your reaction and what you are saying that I have upset you". On the other hand, a withdrawal acknowledgment may be more tentative in nature on behalf of the therapist: "I am not sure, but I believe your lack of reaction to me trying to be helpful may mean that I have missed something or made you feel unsupported in our therapy. Is this the case?"

4. *Create space/safety to express feelings.* Restoration of safety to the client system is another essential element of an alliance repair (Friedlander et al., 2006). In order to create the proper therapeutic environment for a member of the client system to express their true feelings after a tear, the CFT must create space by normalizing, remaining curious and staying nonreactive with both their verbal and nonverbal reactions. Following the mantra that "client knows best" when it comes to alliance appraisals, humble therapists don't dismiss clients' perceptions of a tear and should always privilege clients' experiences of the therapeutic relationship. There is preliminary evidence that therapists' abilities to regulate their emotions after an alliance tear predict improved treatment outcomes (Kaplowitz et al., 2011). Therapists must be able to tolerate the uncomfortable emotions, both their own and their clients', that arise from an alliance tear. Therefore, effective affect regulation is essential for responding empathically and resisting the urge to answer client hostility with therapist defensiveness or to use avoidance behaviors to reduce one's own anxiety. After client confirmation of the tear, first express a genuine desire to hear the client experience of what exactly happened. Avoid being defensive at all costs. Praise the clients for having the courage to speak up, before reassuring them that it is impossible to offend you in this therapeutic setting and what they disclose will never be used against them. Next,

explain the importance of vocalizing their experience of the tear for both the health and longevity of the therapy. Normalize that this type of conflict is potentially part of every important interpersonal relationship, even therapeutic ones. While still maintaining appropriate curiosity, pay careful attention to your own nonverbal signals by making eye contact and maintaining an open posture.

5. *Validate feelings underneath the tear.* Tears involve some type of invalidation by the therapist to a member of the family system. Invalidation communicates that a client response is not understandable or is trivial (Linehan, 1997). Invalidation in the therapy room delegitimizes the client's experience, generally leading to negative emotional arousal (Fruzzetti & Worrall, 2010) and an increase in emotional reactivity that can hinder participation and engagement (Shenk & Fruzzetti, 2011). These experiences thought to be associated with invalidation might impede progress in treatment goals and increase the likelihood of dropping out. The antidote to the invalidation that causes the alliance tear therefore is an acknowledgment or validating exchange that promotes understanding and repair by the therapist. Validation involves communicating with acceptance that another's behaviors, thoughts or feelings make sense and are understandable given the current situation or personal history (Linehan, 1997). Validation does not mean that the therapist agrees with everything that the client is upset about, and there may be things the client has wrong or misunderstood. Validation aims to highlight, rather than change, the other's emotional experience, which encourages acceptance and experiencing of emotions (Shenk & Fruzzetti, 2011). To validate in the therapeutic context, the therapist must find and acknowledge the kernel of truth in the client's experience and, similarly, not validate the components that are invalid or out of line with the client's goals. Remember that you can validate without necessarily agreeing. Find the more primary, vulnerable emotions (sadness, hurt, insecurity, inadequacy, etc.) beneath secondary anger and frustration with confrontation tears and validate passivity and avoidance that often lie beneath withdrawal tears. Also, validate the dialectical tension around alliance tears – that it can be both equally freeing and upsetting to express emotion around the event. When practicing this validation step, CFTs are actively modeling and reinforcing couple/family reflective listening skills taught previously in the therapy. For some ruptures it may be necessary to apologize for what you did that led to hurt feelings. For example, if the therapist fails to follow up on homework given and the clients are unhappy, the therapist can say that they simply forgot, they are sorry, and they will work hard to not allow it to happen again.

6. *Ask questions to promote understanding and explore potential parallel processes.* Once a tear is acknowledged and validated, you should feel liberated enough to

inquire about other relational aspects that could be related to this strain in alliance. Linking the alliance tear to common patterns in a client's relationship history may be helpful in increasing the insight necessary to facilitate the repair. For example, some clients may experience you judging them unfairly, like another member of their family system has done in the past. Perhaps your client has difficulty working with a specific gender, therapists in general or authority figures, etc. Being somewhat isomorphic in nature, repairing a tear can involve explicitly generalizing the link between the tear that occurs in the session and some situation in the client's life. If a therapist can successfully help the clients generalize what happened in the therapy room to what typically occurs outside of it, clients may develop a fuller understanding of their problematic interpersonal interactions. Ideally, this corrective relational experience in conjunction with increased insight will aid clients in becoming more comfortable with their own emotional states and needs and to develop greater flexibility in expressing those feelings and needs to their family, friends and other significant relationship partners. These questions could include, but should not be limited to, the following:

- *Does this dynamic/feeling remind of you of any other disappointments or wounds you've experienced in other relationships?*
- *How has your confidence in my ability to help you and your loved ones changed due to this tear in our alliance?*
- *What was it like for you to share you feeling about this event with me?*
- *How have you handled misunderstandings/disappointments with others like this in the past?*

7. *Make modifications based on client feedback.* Humble therapists also have the necessary self-awareness to realize that they are imperfect and acknowledge their mistakes and errors in the therapeutic process. While modeling a spirit of nondefensive collaboration, accept responsibility for your part by talking about your own contribution (intended or unintended) to the tear and making an apology. Dialogue around how the tear will impact future of the therapy, reframing the event as a positive ongoing discussion about progress instead of a one-time conversation. By normalizing the idea of regular check-ins, clients should never feel hesitant or embarrassed to bring up their concerns in the future. Welcome feedback from the entire family system, not just the injured client, to facilitate the repair and rebalance with other members. This system-wide attention ensures that you can repair with one member of the system without damaging alliances with other family members. This feedback may result in clarifying and modifying tasks or goals to make the intervention strategies more accessible and meaningful

for the individual client or system as a whole. If it jeopardizes the repair, respect the client's wishes not to complete a task. Taking in the client's suggestions about moving forward should restore the client's sense of power and safety within the relationship by promoting the therapeutic relationship as a partnership.

Conclusion

Clinical wisdom and empirical research suggest that paying close attention to the multifaceted therapeutic alliance is not only necessary in the systemic practice of couple and family therapy but is also an essential mechanism of change in itself. The alliance with one family member affects the alliances with other family members in a circular, reciprocal manner. In this regard, it is impossible to look at alliances in CFT in isolation from each other, as they all impact each other in multiple ways. By explicitly practicing these alliance-building skills, therapists may detect and repair tears, prevent dropout and avoid splits throughout the couple or family system in their relationships with the therapist.

References

Blow, A. J., Sprenkle, D. H., & Davis, S. D. (2007). Is who delivers the treatment more important than the treatment itself? The role of the therapist in common factors. *Journal of Marital and Family Therapy, 33*, 298–317.

Bordin, E. S. (1979). The generalizability of the psychoanalytic concept of the working alliance. *Psychotherapy: Theory, Research, and Practice, 16*, 252–260.

Butler, M. H., Brimhall, A. S., & Harper, J. M. (2011). A primer on the evolution of therapeutic engagement in MFT: Understanding and resolving the dialectic tension of alliance and neutrality. Part 2—Recommendations: Dynamic neutrality through multipartiality and enactments. *The American Journal of Family Therapy, 39*(3), 193–213.

Cecchin, G. (1987). Hypothesizing, circularity, and neutrality revisited: An invitation to curiosity. *Family Process, 26*(4), 405–413.

Davis, S. D. & Piercy, F. P. (2007). What clients of MFT model developers and their former students say about change, Part I: Model dependent common factors across three models. *Journal of Marital and Family Therapy, 33*, 318–343.

de Shazer, S. (1988). *Clues: Investigating solutions in brief therapy.* Norton.

Escudero, V., Boogmans, E., Loots, G., & Friedlander, M. L. (2012). Alliance rupture and repair in conjoint family therapy: An exploratory study. *Psychotherapy, 49*(1), 26–37.

Friedlander, M. L., Escudero, V., & Heatherington, L. (2006). *Therapeutic alliances in couple and family therapy: An empirically informed guide to practice.* American Psychological Association.

Friedlander, M. L., Escudero, V., Heatherington, L., & Diamond, G. M. (2011). Alliance in couple and family therapy. *Psychotherapy, 48*(1), 25–33.

Friedlander, M. L., Escudero, V., Horvath, S., Heatherington, L., Cabero, A., & Martens, M. P. (2006). System for observing family therapy alliances: A tool for research and practice. *Journal of Counseling Psychology, 53*, 214–224.

Fruzzetti, A. E., & Worrall, J. M. (2010). Accurate expression and validating responses: A transactional model for understanding individual and relationship distress. In K. T. Sullivan & J. Davila (Eds.), *Support processes in intimate relationships* (pp. 121–150). Oxford University Press.

Horvath, A. O. (2001). The alliance. *Psychotherapy: Theory, Research, Practice, Training, 38*(4), 365–372.

Horvath, A. O., & Bedi, R. P. (2002). The alliance. In J. C. Norcross (Ed.), *Psychotherapy relationships that work: Therapists contributions and responsiveness to patients* (pp. 37–69). Oxford University Press.

Horvath, A. O., & Symonds, B. D. (1991). Relation between working alliance and outcome in psychotherapy: A meta-analysis. *Journal of Consulting and Clinical Psychology, 38*, 139–149.

Johnson, S. M., & Talitman, E. (1997). Predictors of success in emotionally focused marital therapy. *Journal of Marital and Family Therapy, 23*, 135–152.

Kaplowitz, M. J., Safran, J. D., & Muran, C. J. (2011). Impact of therapist emotional intelligence on psychotherapy. *The Journal of Nervous and Mental Disease, 199*(2), 74–84.

Karam, E. A., & Sprenkle, D. H. (2010). The research-informed clinician: A guide to training the next-generation MFT. *Journal of Marital and Family Therapy, 36*(3), 307–319.

Karam, E. A., Sprenkle, D. H., & Davis, S. D. (2015). Targeting threats to the therapeutic alliance: A primer for marriage and family therapy training. *Journal of Marital and Family Therapy, 41*(4), 389–400.

Lambert, M. J., Hansen, N. B., & Finch, A. E. (2001). Patient-focused research: Using patient outcome data to enhance treatment effects. *Journal of Consulting and Clinical Psychology, 69*, 159–172.

Linehan, M. M. (1997). Validation and psychotherapy. In A. C. Bohart & L. S. Greenberg (Eds.), *Empathy reconsidered: New directions* (pp. 353–392). American Psychological Association.

Martin, D. J., Garske, J. P., & Davis, M. K. (2000). Relation of the therapeutic alliance with outcome and other variables: A meta-analytic review. *Journal of Consulting and Clinical Psychology, 68*, 438–450.

Pinsof, W. M. (1994). An integrative systems perspective on the therapeutic alliance: Theoretical, clinical, and research implications. In A. O. Horvath & L. S. Greenberg (Eds.), *The working alliance: Theory, research, and practice* (pp. 173–195). Wiley.

Pinsof, W. M. (1995). *Integrative problem centered therapy: A synthesis of biological, individual and family therapies.* Basic Books.

Pinsof, W. M., & Catherall, D. R. (1986). The integrative psychotherapy alliance: Family, couple, and individual therapy scales. *Journal of Marital and Family Therapy, 12,* 132–151.

Piper, W. E., Ogrodniczuk, J. S., Joyce, A. S., McCallum, M., Rosie, J. S., O'Kelly, J. G., & Steinberg, P. I. (1999). Prediction of dropping out in time-limited, interpretive individual psychotherapy. *Psychotherapy: Theory, Research, Practice, Training, 36*(2), 114–122.

Safran, J. D., & Kraus, J. (2014). Alliance ruptures, impasses, and enactments: A relational perspective. *Psychotherapy, 51*(3), 381–387.

Safran, J. D., & Muran, J. C. (1996). The resolution of ruptures in the therapeutic alliance. *Journal of Consulting and Clinical Psychology, 64,* 447–458.

Safran, J. D., & Muran, J. C. (2000). *Negotiating the therapeutic alliance in brief psychotherapy.* Guilford.

Sells, S. P., Smith, T. E., & Moon, S. (1996). An ethnographic study of client and therapist perceptions of therapy effectiveness in a university-based training clinic. *Journal of Marital and Family Therapy, 22*(3), 321–342.

Shenk, C. E., & Fruzzetti, A. E. (2011). The impact of validating and invalidating responses on emotional reactivity. *Journal of Social and Clinical Psychology, 30,* 163–183.

Sprenkle, D. H., & Blow, A. J. (2004). Common factors and our sacred models. *Journal of Marital and Family Therapy, 30,* 113–129.

Stiles, W. B., & Goldsmith, J. Z. (2010). The alliance over time. In J. C. Muran & J. P. Barber (Eds.), *The therapeutic alliance: An evidence-based guide to practice* (pp. 44–62). Guilford.

10
UTILIZING FEEDBACK IN CFT

Overview

How do you measure your level of effectiveness in your work with individuals, couples and families? In everyday practice, couple and family therapists (CFTs) typically only rely on their own clinical intuitions and assumptions about the therapeutic progress in their work with different client systems. Few would argue against the importance of good clinical expertise, but there is persistent evidence that therapists' views of the alliance and client outcomes are often out of synch with the views of their clients (Lambert & Hawkins, 2001).

Using outcome data in the form of client feedback to monitor and drive the progress of treatment, also known as *progress research* (Pinsof & Wynne, 2000), *feedback-informed treatment* (FIT; Miller et al., 2015), *patient-focused research* (Lambert et al., 2001) and *routine outcome monitoring* (ROM; Boswell et al., 2015), has yielded impressive results in psychotherapy as a way to enhance psychotherapy as usual.

Common factors feedback in CFT, as we will present in this chapter, is a systematic and regular monitoring procedure wherein members of the client system both complete questionnaires and respond to therapist verbal inquires targeting therapy process (e.g., alliance) and progress (e.g., measures on individual/couple/family functioning and well-being) on a frequent basis. This information is processed into a format that therapists can utilize as guidance for treatment decisions and to stimulate important dialogue between all members of the client system. Unfortunately, most couple and family therapists do not utilize this type of client feedback, despite the demonstrable evidence in favor of the practice (e.g., Lappan et al., 2018; Miller et al., 2006).

Why Should I Incorporate a Feedback Routine Into My CFT Practice?

By studying your own practice and clients through a feedback routine, undocumented therapeutic experiences once considered subjective and abstract may become more objective and concrete. Many clinicians, especially those in private practice, are looking for ways to validate that what they do is actually effective. Others, striving to compete in a competitive mental health marketplace, are looking for concrete numbers that accurately represent their practice in order to answer the questions of discriminating consumers and potential clients. You cannot speak intelligently about your services, however, if you cannot somehow quantify your practice patterns and client outcomes. In an era of managed care, some third-party reimbursement may indeed depend on documenting exactly what happens in therapy. For example, recently some clinicians became eligible to take part in the Centers for Medicare & Medicaid Services (2016) Merit-Based Incentive Payment System (MIPS). The system rewards providers with larger payments when they track and show patient improvement on process and outcome measures, including depression, anxiety and social functioning assessments. The system also penalizes providers who score low in these areas by reducing their payments.

In addition to helping clients achieve better outcomes during treatment (Anker et al., 2009; Lambert & Shimokawa, 2011; Lambert et al., 2003) and creating an opportunity for greater connection between the therapist and members of the couple or family unit, including feedback into your clinical routine has other potential benefits. First, it can serve as a preventive measure in treatment as well by helping to reduce early termination and signal potential warning signs (Shimokawa et al., 2010; Westmacott et al., 2010). Westmacott et al. (2010) found that when clients initiated early termination, therapists were generally not aware of clients' dissatisfactions and true thoughts about the therapy. When it comes to being accurate assessors, the client truly does know best! Helmeke and Sprenkle's (2000) "pivotal moments" research looked at the difference in what the therapist perceived as watershed moments in treatment compared to what the clients in the system actually thought made the most difference. Tryon and Winograd (2011) noted the importance of clinicians attending to clients' concerns and clarifying these concerns through agreed-upon treatment goals and therapeutic tasks. This can be crucial, because clients typically do not voluntarily report lack of improvement, and therapists are commonly overly optimistic in their assessment of client progress (Harmon et al., 2007; Walfish et al., 2012). Further, sharing the feedback information with the client can enhance user involvement and treatment engagement (Anker et al., 2009; Lambert & Shimokawa, 2011). The dialogue that occurs after the therapist reviews client feedback is critical to allowing clients to be heard and for therapists to demonstrate responsiveness to client needs. Lastly, in couple and family therapy specifically, tracking the therapeutic alliance is essential in order to prevent against a "split alliance" (see Chapter 9).

Because integrating feedback routines into your practice also constitutes research data, research becomes a valuable part of clinical practice. It narrows the often-mentioned practice–research gap and helps you to become a research-informed clinician (Karam & Sprenkle, 2010).

The benefits of tracking client feedback have been most studied almost exclusively in individual therapy, whereas use of feedback in relational therapies has only recently been addressed (Anker et al., 2009; Reese et al., 2010). One of the reasons why feedback differs in a CFT setting compared to an individual therapy setting is that each member of the system may experience the process of the therapy differently. Couples and families are undoubtedly more complex as they often comprise members with different motivations and at potentially different stages of change. Therefore, each member of the system may have different perceptions of the therapy, as well as different individual outcomes. Despite these crucial differences between individual therapy and CFT, feedback still appears to be beneficial in systemic modalities. For example, Anker et al. (2009) found that couples who participated in the feedback treatment group experienced greater gains than the control group, and those benefits were maintained at 6-month follow-up. Reese and colleagues (2010) conducted a follow-up study attempting to replicate Anker et al.'s findings with a US population. Results indicated that couples in the feedback group improved at a quicker rate than couples in the treatment as usual group. Even when feedback from different clients from the same system differs, the therapeutic conversation between the therapist and these clients provides the opportunity to bring members onto the same page through reframing or reconsidering therapy goals and tasks.

Types of Client Feedback in CFT

Unsolicited Client-Initiated Feedback

Sometimes clients will tell you about how an aspect of therapy is going without you even asking for it. This type of unsolicited feedback should always be welcomed, even if what a member of the client system is saying is not complimentary of your performance. From talking too much (or not enough) to mislabeling feelings and offering unsolicited advice, therapists may get feedback about unintentionally upsetting their clients in various ways. A client may start by saying, "I'd like to discuss how I feel therapy is going" or "Your recommendations aren't particularly helpful to me". Before airing their grievances, clients may also feel the need to say something positive, as a way to protect the therapist's feelings and balance the feedback.

It is important to let each member of the client system know from the onset of therapy that you welcome verbal feedback and that they don't have to wait for you to ask for it. This entails setting a culture of feedback from the start of therapy; that is, all feedback is welcomed.

Nonverbal Client Feedback

Although the emphasis in the therapy room is sometimes placed on verbal interactions, an estimated 60% to 65% of interpersonal communication is conveyed via nonverbal behaviors (Burgoon et al., 2016). Blanchard and Farber (2016) found that 72.6% of psychotherapy clients had lied about their therapy experience. Common lies included pretending to agree with the therapist's suggestions, pretending to find treatment helpful and masking their true opinion of the therapist. Reading nonverbal feedback is akin to a therapy lie detector test, as many nonverbal behaviors are automatic and may represent a more accurate depiction of the client's true attitude and emotional state. Being sensitive to a client's nonverbal shifts in facial expression, posture, tone of voice and other areas is certainly important in establishing and maintaining the therapeutic relationship. Drawing attention to a client's nonverbal forms of communication and pointing out possible contradictions between the client's expressed words and what is conveyed without words can also help a person increase awareness of how nonverbal communication is used in personal interactions both inside and outside of the therapy room. For instance, if clients verbally assent to a directive you give while nonverbally disagreeing by looking dismissive or despondent with their body language, it's important to pick this up immediately and address the incongruence.

Therapist Solicited Feedback

If you really want to find out how clients have experienced your service, there's nothing better you can do than actually talk to them! Initiating a dialogue about your performance as a therapist is a crucial skill in the training and development of a CFT. As therapists practice and become more comfortable soliciting feedback and talking to the entire system about their experience in therapy, they are gradually making the smooth transition between session content and the overall process of the therapy relationship. Obtaining feedback will be much easier and much more authentic if the therapist established a culture of feedback early on. Soliciting client feedback can help you identify and resolve sources of client dissatisfaction with the therapy process in the moment and before they disengage. Haber et al. (2014) proposed that after each session, family therapists should elicit information from all family members regarding their feelings about the session, what they learned in the session, what they did not like about the session and what they wished would have happened in the session. They suggested that regular assessment of client feelings, learning, dislikes and wishes will benefit the family therapy process by signaling potential warning signs of treatment failure and enabling the family therapist to proactively make necessary adjustments, thereby taking some of the guesswork out of whether or not clients will choose to return.

The following language can easily be integrated in your opening session routine to set up a culture of feedback:

From time to time in this therapy, I will be asking you questions about how things are going for you and in general about our process. This feedback is essential to the ultimate outcome of our work and helps me customize this therapy to each one of your needs. Please be honest, as you will not offend me with your opinions about me and the way I am structuring this therapy. Your role in this therapeutic relationship is important, so how you all feel about the therapy process is valid and very important to me!

The Common Factors Feedback Interview is set of questions we have designed to help the therapist become better attuned to the entire client system's experiences and perspectives. It can be used at any point in the treatment as a conversational tool that creates a dialogical space, in which the family members and the therapist can together reflect on the process of therapy, including important client, therapist, alliance and extratherapeutic factors. The hope is that a thoughtful and collaborative therapeutic dialogue will increase client system engagement. If they are not satisfied, the therapist can use this vital information to make necessary adjustments and better customize the fit to the client system.

COMMON FACTORS FEEDBACK INTERVIEW

Eliciting client feedback is an important skill to master for CFTs. The following questions can be used at any time with a client system to understand more fully the client, therapist and relationship common factors.

Client Questions

1. *Initially, how motivated were you to confront the issues that brought you to therapy? How has your motivation changed throughout our work together?*

2. *How well do you think I have balanced my relationship with you compared to your other loved ones in this therapy?*

3. *What are your personal strengths that you have brought into this therapy? What are the strengths of your other loved ones in this therapy?*

4. *What has been the pivotal moment or most important part of this therapy for you thus far?*

5. *What about my therapeutic style or approach works well for you?*

6. *What have we done in this therapy that hasn't worked as well for you? Why not?*

7. *If you felt misunderstood in this therapy, how would you address it with me?*

8. *How did I describe your relational couple/family problem cycle to help you see the issues that brought you to therapy more clearly? Do you agree with my conceptualization of the cycle?*

9. *How has my selection of homework fit with the goals and reasons you came to therapy? What are your thoughts about how I follow up on and review the homework?*

10. *How has this therapy helped you change the "doing" (behavior) around your problems?*

11. *How has this therapy helped you change the "thinking" (cognitions) around your problems?*

12. *How has this therapy helped to facilitate healthy emotional expression and regulation around your problems?*

_____
_____
_____
_____

13. *How has this therapy infused hope into your relationship/s?*

_____
_____
_____
_____

14. *What do your friends and family think about this therapy? How do you decide what or what not to share with them?*

_____
_____
_____
_____

15. *Is there anything else that I am missing that you would want me to know about this therapy?*

_____
_____
_____
_____

Formal Standardized, Proprietary Feedback Systems

In traditional practice, CFTs may evaluate therapeutic progress informally, but numerous studies have proven the benefits of using feedback in a more intentional and formalized manner. The term *formal* in this case refers to using validated tools for eliciting client feedback about their perception of the alliance and treatment progress and outcomes. Anker and colleagues (2009) conducted a randomized clinical trial of couples therapy in which clients were randomly assigned to either a feedback group (in which the therapist would obtain session-by-session feedback from clients using a brief alliance measure and an outcome measure) or to a treatment as usual group. All of the therapists believed they were already acquiring outcome and alliance feedback from their clients without the use of a formal feedback process and that formal feedback would not improve their effectiveness. In contrast to those pre-study beliefs, the data revealed that 90% of the therapists improved their outcomes with clients after integrating formal client feedback measures. This finding illustrates the tendency for therapists to assume that their informal method of checking in with clients is as useful as a formal feedback process.

In couple and family modalities, we are always dealing with multiple voices in the room. Many times, those softer voices may not be as honest in their verbal feedback or even speak up at all for fear of repercussions from more controlling or dominant system members. Forms completed individually provide clients a degree of privacy from other system members and an opportunity to express any thoughts or feelings that they might – for whatever reason – be reluctant to convey verbally in session, especially in the presence of their significant other, family member or therapist.

Feedback systems are designed to be integrated flexibly into a therapist's traditional way of working. These systems provide empirical feedback (i.e., numbers and graphs) that tell a clinician what sorts of problems and strengths exist in each case, where change is happening and, just as important, what is deteriorating in the client or therapeutic system. At the heart of the empirically informed therapist movement is the idea that feedback helps both therapists and their clients to make better decisions. The information provided by these feedback systems is not prescriptive, in that it does not tell the clinician what to do. Rather, the information offered is descriptive, providing a clearer, data-driven picture of the client system that is incorporated directly into therapeutic conversations with clients. Popular feedback systems have existed in individual therapy for the past 2 decades.

Lambert et al. (2001) developed the Outcomes Questionnaire 45 (OQ45) and pioneered its use as an instrument for regular, and ongoing, feedback regarding clients' general individual functioning. The OQ45 has since been utilized in numerous studies to monitor client outcomes. Shimokawa et al. (2010) utilized progress feedback and administered the OQ45 (Lambert et al., 2001) to identify an early warning system of treatment failure in a community sample of individual clients. Thus, clients at risk of dropout but who may benefit from longer doses of treatment are identified and retained through regular monitoring.

Another widely used method of assessing and obtaining formal client feedback includes the concurrent use of the Session Rating Scale (SRS; Duncan et al., 2003, 2011; Miller et al., 2006) and the Outcome Rating Scale (ORS; Bringhurst et al., 2004; Duncan, 2011; Miller et al., 2003). The SRS uses quantitative feedback from clients to assess the strength of the therapeutic relationship. The ORS assesses clients' perceptions of therapy outcomes periodically during treatment and asks clients about certain individual measures in therapy, such as their well-being, interpersonal relationships and social relationships (Miller et al., 2003). The OQ, ORS, and SRS have all been found to improve treatment outcomes in individual therapy. A license to use the ORS and SRS in paper-and-pencil format is available for free to individual practitioners. Licenses for paper-and-pencil use of the ORS and SRS are provided to group practices, agencies and behavioral health organizations for a fee.

CFTs may be better suited for the Systemic Therapy Inventory of Change (STIC), an online, multisystemic and multidimensional measurement and feedback system (Pinsof et al., 2009). The STIC includes six system scales that measure adult, child/adolescent, family and couple functioning, as well as three scales for measuring the alliance in family, couple and individual therapy. Clients fill out all demographically appropriate scales before the first and all subsequent sessions, regardless of the type of therapy. These measures, although good, are not easily accessible to clinicians or agencies.

No matter the form of formalized feedback used, it is essential that the feedback be used as a springboard to a therapeutic conversation. The therapist reviews the feedback each week and is especially interested in changes to the feedback from week to week, as even small shifts in the feedback may be indicative of unhappiness on the part of the clients. In terms of creating a culture of feedback, it is important that the therapist be eager to discuss both positive and negative feedback and that the therapist be responsive to the feedback to shift the direction of therapy.

Barriers to Integrating Formal Standardized, Proprietary Feedback Systems

We acknowledge that the notion of using a form to obtain client feedback can create resistance among some therapists. Barriers to integrating formal feedback systems into clinical practice are present from both logistical (e.g., financial burden, time, administration, training, turnover) and philosophical (e.g., clinical utility, relevance, professional concern) levels (Boswell et al., 2015; Hatfield & Ogles, 2004). A study by Sharples et al. (2017) focusing on clinicians' attitudes toward and facilitators and barriers to implementing feedback systems identified training, practical experience and ongoing support as crucial facilitators of the use of feedback systems at both the clinic level and the individual therapy session level. The same study also highlighted the balance between the mandatory use and consistent use of feedback systems, showing that clinicians reported struggling with standardized use of feedback in sessions when it was viewed as a distraction or not deemed appropriate. Another study highlighted that providers thought that this formalized feedback technology could help in the monitoring of, reflection on and evaluation of progress, while also perceiving disadvantages mainly concerning time and effort, concerns about how information would be used and fears about therapists being evaluated (Norman et al., 2014).

There are also logistical difficulties in collecting and analyzing client system feedback via paper-and-pencil format. Anyone who has administered and hand scored an outcome measure during a therapy session is well aware that this method is difficult to keep up with at the individual level, much less when trying to combine, compare and make sense of these data with multiple members in the same family system and a full caseload outside of that. With the advent of technology platforms that ease the burden of collecting, scoring and managing these feedback data, private practices and mental health agencies are now better able to utilize these feedback systems that had previously been time-intensive and not user-friendly.

Although these concerns are understandable, it is important to remember that client feedback tools are not for assessment alone in the traditional sense. Rather, they are primarily dialogue tools. The aim is to open constructive conversation and enfranchise the client system to express their experience of the therapy and whether progress is being made. This in turn enables the therapist and clients to work collaboratively to make adjustments and customize the treatment delivery.

Designing Your Own Feedback Survey

We believe that when confidently explained to clients, carefully designed feedback forms can provide an important perspective of an overall picture that will be useful to CFTs both for their own professional development and to improve the service offered to clients. Although these feedback forms should not replace the informal verbal feedback received during the session, they may provide a number of advantages over verbal feedback alone. If you do not want to dedicate financial resources to use one of the proprietary systems above, we suggest creating your own common factors–inspired feedback survey.

How Should I Format My Questions?

In designing your own client survey to track client progress and satisfaction, it is important to ask questions that are relevant to therapy outcomes and require minimal effort on the part of client (in answering them) and the therapist (in recording the data). A client survey should generally begin with a brief introduction stating how the information will be used and outlining relevant confidentiality protocols. The introduction should also contain simple, straightforward instructions on completing and returning the survey. The layout of the survey should be easy to follow, as a visually confusing or badly formatted questionnaire can contribute to missed questions and incomplete data.

Closed-ended questions require clients to choose from a preselected number of responses. When designing closed-ended questions, make sure that categories do not overlap. For example, the question, "How many times in the past month did you experience the problem that brought you to therapy: 1 to 3 times, 3 to 6 times, or more than 6 times?" does not give a clear choice of category to select if the answer is "3 times." Remember to cover all possible responses. For example, the statement, "My therapist was responsive to my phone calls: *always, sometimes, rarely?*" does not allow for the possibility that the therapist was *never* responsive. Also, include a balanced number of favorable and unfavorable response categories on rating scales. For example, the response scale *completely agree, agree, neither agree nor disagree, disagree* should also contain the possibility *completely disagree*. Lastly, use the same response categories across questions if possible. It is easier and less confusing to clients if response categories are consistent and do not change from question to question.

Although most questions will likely be closed-ended, it can be quite useful to include a few open-ended, qualitative questions that may give more insight into the therapeutic process. It is especially useful to ask for explanations of negative ratings to provide insight and suggestions for corrective actions. It is also good practice to end a client survey with a question like, "Is there anything else you would like to tell me about the therapy you received that wasn't already captured in this survey?" These qualitative responses not only may help you to interpret the findings from the responses to your closed-ended questions but may also demonstrate additional patterns in your practice that can be developed into closed-ended questions for use in future iterations of your survey. It is suggested to limit the survey to one to two pages, as clients may refuse outright or need more incentive or motivation to complete a longer questionnaire. The client survey should conclude with a way to contact the therapist about additional questions and a statement of appreciation for participation.

How Often Should I Track?

Data that describe your practice patterns as a whole and are taken from your previously existing paperwork (i.e., modality percentages, average number of sessions, types of presenting problems, etc.) could be aggregated once or twice per year as needed and could be used as reference points for future years. The most efficient way to do this is to audit each client file (both electronic and physical) to collect desired information before subsequently entering the data into a new spreadsheet. While we can discern many interesting patterns about our clients by reviewing intake data (i.e., presenting problem, previous experience with therapy, use of medication, etc.), other information may only be beneficial if it is collected during or at the conclusion of treatment. This type of data could be collected in the form of a client satisfaction or progress survey. As termination is not always planned, some therapists make it standard operating procedure to mail this survey out with a final letter before they officially "close" a case. Others may elect to call the client on the phone to collect relevant info, including why the client terminated and whether they experienced relief from the problems that initially brought them to therapy.

Data may be the most useful, however, if they are collected on a regular basis from clients, in order to give therapist feedback to make modifications in the treatment if needed. *Continuous outcome assessment,* or client feedback, refers to using a psychotherapy outcome measure every session rather than in a typical pre–post outcome format (Lambert et al., 2001). Research strongly indicates that outcomes improve when therapists receive formal and consistent, real-time feedback on client progress (Lambert, 2010a, 2010b). It is ideal for clients to receive the same assessment weekly. It is the tracking of data over time that allows the therapeutic system to track client and therapist progress. Fluctuations in the ratings over time indicate points that require therapeutic conversations about the progress of treatment. Feedback provided to therapists regarding client progress has also been found to reduce rates of client deterioration and can improve treatment outcomes, especially for clients predicted to be poor responders or potential treatment failures.

How Do I Analyze My Feedback Data?

When it comes to ease of use in analyzing feedback data, computer manipulation is usually preferred. While data may be tabulated "by hand", this approach is usually only feasible if the size of your caseload is small and the number of questions is limited. Although it minimizes the use of technical resources, manual tabulation restricts possible analyses to simple frequency counts and some rudimentary summary statistics. A more realistic and efficient option is the use of simple spreadsheets that don't require much technical knowledge in order to organize and perform various tabulations and analyses.

One example of a simple analysis may consist of calculating the percentage of clients giving each response to each individual question. For example, if responses to the question, "How satisfied are you with the quality of this therapy?" include *completely satisfied, somewhat satisfied, not very satisfied, not at all satisfied,* and *I don't know,* the responses may be computed in several straightforward ways. Dividing the number of clients giving each response (such as for those saying *very satisfied*) by the total number of participating respondents in your caseload produces a percentage. All such percentages constitute the percentage distribution for that question. You may also choose to assign numerical values to each response to produce an average score. For example, a value of 4 can be given to all *very satisfied* responses, a value of 3 to *somewhat satisfied,* and so on. Multiplying the number of clients responding *very satisfied* by 4, the number responding *somewhat satisfied* by 3 and so on and then summing the products and dividing by the total number of respondents results in an average score that can range from 1 to 4. In this case, the higher the number, the higher the level of client satisfaction. These data are the easiest to interpret when formatted as simple graphs or tables. These calculations also provide a single number that serves as an outcome indicator that may be used in future promotional materials for your practice.

Although these kinds of simple analyses can be done routinely without much previous experience, common neophyte fears surround the inability to use technology or compute statistics. If you are overwhelmed with the prospect of designing your own spreadsheet from scratch, obtaining initial assistance from those clinicians in your network who have done this type of data analysis on their practice before, statistical consultants at a local university or your former CFT training program may be a useful first step. This assistance will help to establish a basic analytic routine to follow and a recommended format for regular reporting.

What Therapeutic Information Should I Track?

When thinking of what types of client and therapeutic variables to track, first tap into your own curiosity. What are you interested in knowing about your practice? A good place to start is to aggregate some of the objective data you already collect on clients and your practice (through routine paperwork or client intakes) into a more usable, therapist-friendly format. Some client variables that may be of interest include:

- *Age*
- *Occupation*
- *Income level*
- *Presenting problem*
- *Diagnosis*
- *Client Motivation (stage of change: precontemplation, contemplation, preparation, action, maintenance)*
- *Marital status*
- *Referral source*
- *Type of insurance*
- *Previous history with therapy*
- *Medication*

Another source that may help you discern which statistics to report on comes from potential clients and their frequently asked questions. Generally, clients want to know about the following therapist practice variables:

- *How long does therapy usually take? How many sessions do you normally see clients for?*
- *What percentage of couples and families do you see as compared to individuals?*
- *What is your average fee?*
- *What type of homework do you give most often?*

Other data should be collected directly from client self-report, as they are the true experts into the therapeutic process. Not only is the collection of client satisfaction survey data important but research has shown that clients are more accurate than therapists in representing key relationship variables like the therapeutic alliance (Horvath, 2001). Forms can ask specific questions about individual areas CFTs consider important for either theoretical or practical reasons. We suggest tracking important therapist, client, alliance and extratherapeutic common factors, as shown in our couples therapy feedback survey below.

COMMON FACTOR FEEDBACK COUPLE THERAPY SATISFACTION AND PROGRESS SURVEY

We are interested in tracking your therapy progress and obtaining your comments about the services offered to you. Your feedback helps us to improve the quality and effectiveness of our therapy services. Please place a check mark in the appropriate box for your answer. After completing this questionnaire, please return it to us personally or mail it back in the envelope provided.

At this time, my therapy

_____ is still in progress

_____ has been completed

How long have you been involved in this therapy?

_____ Sessions _____ Months

My Relationship

	Does Not Apply (0)	Completely Disagree (1)	Disagree (2)	Neutral (3)	Agree (4)	Completely Agree (5)
I have hope about overcoming the problems that brought me into therapy.						
I am motivated to be in this therapy.						
I understand my negative relationship cycle.						
I am able to slow down and process my negative relationship cycle.						
I am able to take personal responsibility for my part in the negative relationship cycle.						
I am comfortable with who I am.						
I feel understood by my partner						
My partner is open to my ideas.						

	Does Not Apply (0)	Completely Disagree (1)	Disagree (2)	Neutral (3)	Agree (4)	Completely Agree (5)
I am able to "soften" and be calm around my partner.						
I feel emotionally connected to my partner.						
I feel physically connected to my partner.						
I am proud of my relationship.						
If there is a problem, we can talk it through.						
My partner accepts me for who I am in this relationship.						
I trust my partner.						
I am fully committed to this relationship.						

My Therapist

	Does Not Apply (0)	Completely Disagree (1)	Disagree (2)	Neutral (3)	Agree (4)	Completely Agree (5)
My therapist projects confidence in their ability to help with our relationship problems.						
My therapist's approach seems credible to me.						
My therapist's style motivates me.						
My therapist frames our negative relationship cycle in a way that is fair and acceptable to both my partner and me.						

(continued)

My Therapist (Continued)

	Does Not Apply (0)	Completely Disagree (1)	Disagree (2)	Neutral (3)	Agree (4)	Completely Agree (5)
My therapist helps me to slow down and process my negative relationship cycle.						
My therapist teaches me skills that are relevant to me and my learning style.						
My therapist is nondefensive and open to my feedback.						
My therapist actively solicits feedback from me during our sessions.						
My therapist is prepared for each session.						
My therapist conveys a sense of hope about my relationship.						
My therapist focuses on behavioral techniques to improve my relationship.						
My therapist focuses on emotional expression and regulation techniques to improve my relationship.						
My therapist focuses on cognitive techniques to improve my relationship.						

Therapeutic Alliance

	Does Not Apply (0)	Completely Disagree (1)	Disagree (2)	Neutral (3)	Agree (4)	Completely Agree (5)
My therapist collaborates with me and my partner on the goals of this therapy.						
Therapeutic goals are concretely defined and able to be measured.						
My therapist gives me and my partner regular feedback on the progress made toward our goals.						
I believe my therapist genuinely cares about my relationship.						
I feel accepted by my therapist.						
My partner feels accepted by my therapist.						
I trust my therapist.						
My partner trusts my therapist.						
My therapist is fair and impartial.						
My therapist and I are in agreement on the structure and tasks of this therapy.						
My therapist designs homework and other therapeutic tasks that are good fit for me.						

Overall Satisfaction

	Extremely Dissatisfied (1)	Dissatisfied (2)	Neutral (3)	Satisfied (4)	Extremely Satisfied (5)
Please rate your current overall satisfaction with yourself.					
Please rate your current overall satisfaction with your partner.					
Please rate your current overall satisfaction with your therapist.					
Please rate your current overall satisfaction with this therapy.					

Helpful Feedback

What do you find is the most helpful about this therapy?

_____
_____
_____
_____

What do you find is not very helpful about this therapy?

_____
_____
_____
_____

If you could change anything about this therapy, what would it be?

_____
_____
_____
_____

What other feedback or information would you like to share about this therapy?

_____
_____
_____
_____

Thanks for your participation!

Conclusion

In this chapter we have argued that it is essential for CFTs to use the common factor of feedback (both formal and informal) as a standard part of their clinical repertoire. Even among top-performing therapists, there are likely to be certain client systems or populations who, for various reasons, do not respond well to your delivery. The ability to identify these groups accurately is the first step in better understanding how you can adjust your approach to meet client needs. Feedback routines help the client system and the therapist establish and repeatedly recalibrate a shared understanding of the treatment. They also aid in the identity of a co-constructed therapeutic reality and the development of strategies for solving presenting problems together (Pinsof et al., 2011). Feedback and the conversation about that feedback are recognized as possible powerful interventions (Pinsof et al., 2012). In conclusion, please remember that becoming a feedback-informed clinician is an ongoing journey that cannot be completed solely by creating a simple survey or reading an introductory chapter in a book. Be curious not only about your client outcomes and practice patterns but also about all the good that can come from using feedback to enhance the therapeutic conversation!

References

Anker, M. G., Duncan, B. L., & Sparks, J. A. (2009). Using client feedback to improve couple therapy outcomes: A randomized clinical trial in a naturalistic setting. *Journal of Consulting and Clinical Psychology, 77*, 693–704.

Blanchard, M., & Farber, B. A. (2016). Lying in psychotherapy: Why and what clients don't tell their therapist about therapy and their relationship. *Counselling Psychology Quarterly, 29*(1), 90–112.

Boswell, J. F., Kraus, D. R., Miller, S. D., & Lambert, M. J. (2015). Implementing routine outcome monitoring in clinical practice: Benefits, challenges, and solutions. *Psychotherapy Research, 25*(1), 6–19.

Bringhurst, D. L., Watson, C. W., Miller, S. D., & Duncan, B. L. (2004). *The reliability and validity of the Outcome Rating Scale: A replication study of a brief clinical measure.* Air Force Institute of Technology.

Burgoon, J. K., Guerrero, L. K., & Floyd, K. (2016). *Nonverbal communication.* Routledge.

Centers for Medicare & Medicaid Services (CMS), HHS. (2016). Medicare Program; Merit-Based Incentive Payment System (MIPS) and Alternative Payment Model (APM) incentive under the physician fee schedule, and criteria for physician-focused payment models. Final rule with comment period. *Federal Register, 81*(214), 77008–77831.

Duncan, B. L., Miller, S. D., & Sparks, J. A. (2011). *The heroic client: A revolutionary way to improve effectiveness through client-directed, outcome-informed therapy.* John Wiley & Sons.

Duncan, B. L., Miller, S. D., Sparks, J. A., Claud, D. A., Reynolds, L. R., Brown, J., & Johnson, L. D. (2003). The Session Rating Scale: Preliminary psychometric properties of a "working" alliance measure. *Journal of Brief Therapy, 3*(1), 3–12.

Haber, R., Carlson, R. G., & Braga, C. (2014). Use of an anecdotal client feedback note in family therapy. *Family Process, 53*(2), 307–317.

Harmon, S. C., Lambert, M. J., Smart, D. M., Hawkins, E., Nielsen, S. L., Slade, K., & Lutz, W. (2007). Enhancing outcome for potential treatment failures: Therapist–client feedback and clinical support tools. *Psychotherapy Research, 17*(4), 379–392.

Hatfield, D. R., & Ogles, B. M. (2004). The use of outcome measures by psychologists in clinical practice. *Professional Psychology Research and Practice, 35*(5), 485–491.

Helmeke, K. B., & Sprenkle, D. H. (2000). Clients' perceptions of pivotal moments in couples therapy: A qualitative study of change in therapy. *Journal of Marital and Family Therapy, 26*(4), 469–483.

Horvath, A. O. (2001). The alliance. *Psychotherapy, 38*, 365–372.

Karam, E. A., & Sprenkle, D. H. (2010). The research informed clinician: A guide to training the next generation MFT. *Journal of Marital and Family Therapy, 36*, 307–319.

Lambert, M. J. (2010a). *Prevention of treatment failure: The use of measuring, monitoring, and feedback in clinical practice.* American Psychological Association.

Lambert, M. J. (2010b). Yes, it is time for clinicians to routinely monitor treatment outcome. In B. L. Duncan, S. D. Miller, B. E. Wampold, & M. A. Hubble (Eds.), *The heart and soul of change: Delivering what works in therapy* (2nd ed., pp. 239–268). American Psychological Association.

Lambert, M. J., Hansen, N. B., & Finch, A. E. (2001). Patient-focused research: Using patient outcome data to enhance treatment effects. *Journal of Consulting and Clinical Psychology, 69*(2), 159–172.

Lambert, M. J., and Hawkins, E. (2001) Using information about patient progress in supervision: Are outcomes enhanced? *Australian Psychologist, 36*, 131–138.

Lambert, M. J., & Shimokawa, K. (2011). Collecting client feedback. *Psychotherapy, 48*(1), 72–79.

Lambert, M. J., Whipple, J. L., Hawkins, E. J., Vermeersch, D. A., Nielsen, S. L., & Smart, D. W. (2003). Is it time for clinicians to routinely track patient outcome? A meta-analysis. *Clinical Psychology: Science and Practice, 10*(3), 288–301.

Lappan, S. N., Shamoon, Z., & Blow, A. J. (2018). The importance of adoption of formal client feedback in therapy: A narrative review. *Journal of Family Therapy, 40*, 466–488. https://doi.org/10.1111/1467-6427.12183

Miller, S. D., Duncan, B., Brown, J., Sorrell, R., & Chalk, M. B. (2006). Using formal client feedback to improve retention and outcome: Making ongoing, real-time assessment feasible. *Journal of Brief Therapy, 5*, 5–22.

Miller, S. D., Duncan, B. L., Brown, J., Sparks, J. A., & Claud, D. A. (2003). The Outcome Rating Scale: A preliminary study of the reliability, validity, and feasibility of a brief visual analog measure. *Journal of Brief Therapy, 2*(2), 91–100.

Miller, S. D., Hubble, M. A., Chow, D., & Seidel, J. (2015). Beyond measures and monitoring: Realizing the potential of feedback-informed treatment. *Psychotherapy, 52*(4), 449–557.

Norman, S., Dean, S., Hansford, L., & Ford, T. (2014). Clinical practitioner's attitudes towards the use of routine outcome monitoring within child and adolescent mental health services: A qualitative study of two child and adolescent mental health services. *Clinical Child Psychology and Psychiatry, 19*(4), 576–595.

Pinsof, W. M., Breunlin, D. C., Russell, W. P., & Lebow, J. (2011). Integrative problem-centered metaframeworks therapy II: Planning, conversing, and reading feedback. *Family Process, 50*(3), 314–336.

Pinsof, W. M., Goldsmith, J. Z., & Latta, T. A. (2012). Information technology and feedback research can bridge the scientist–practitioner gap: A couple therapy example. *Couple and Family Psychology, 1*(4), 253–273.

Pinsof, W. M., & Wynne, L. C. (2000). Toward progress research: Closing the gap between family therapy practice and research. *Journal of Marital and Family Therapy, 26*, 1–8.

Pinsof, W. M., Zinbarg, R. E., Lebow, J. L., Knobloch-Fedders, L. M., Durbin, E., Chambers, A., Latta, T., Karam, E. A., Goldsmith, J., & Friedman, G. (2009). Laying the foundation for progress research in family, couple, and individual therapy: The development and psychometric features of the initial Systemic Therapy Inventory of Change. *Psychotherapy Research, 19*(2), 143–156.

Reese, R. J., Toland, M. D., Slone, N. C., & Norsworthy, L. A. (2010). Effect of client feedback on couple psychotherapy outcomes. *Psychotherapy: Theory, Research, Practice, Training, 47*(4), 616–630.

Sharples, E., Qin, C., Goveas, V., Gondek, D., Deighton, J., Wolpert, M., & Edbrooke-Childs, J. (2017). A qualitative exploration of attitudes towards the use of outcome measures in child and adolescent mental health services. *Clinical Child Psychology and Psychiatry, 22*(2), 219–228.

Shimokawa, K., Lambert, M. J., & Smart, D. W. (2010). Enhancing treatment outcome of patients at risk of treatment failure: Meta-analytic and mega-analytic review of a psychotherapy quality assurance system. *Journal of Consulting and Clinical Psychology, 78*(3), 298–311.

Tryon, G. S., & Winograd, G. (2011). Goal consensus and collaboration. In J. C. Norcross (Ed.), *Psychotherapy relationships that work* (2nd ed., 653–672). Oxford University Press.

Walfish, S., McAlister, B., O'Donnell, P., & Lambert, M. J. (2012). An investigation of self-assessment bias in mental health providers. *Psychological Reports, 110*(2), 639–644.

Westmacott, R., Hunsley, J., Best, M., Rumstein-McKean, O., & Schindler, D. (2010). Client and therapist views of contextual factors related to termination from psychotherapy: A comparison between unilateral and mutual terminators. *Psychotherapy Research, 20*(4), 423–435.

11
COMMON FACTORS SELF-SUPERVISION AND TREATMENT PLANNING

Overview

In this chapter, we encourage systemic therapists to synthesize learning from previous chapters and integrate established common factors and empirically supported principles of change into their self-supervision and professional preparation routines. Self-supervision is an intentional, reflective process that therapists use to enhance their self-awareness and to monitor both therapist and client system growth. The ideas presented in this chapter may be used when (1) supervision is required but there are no available supervisors or (2) in combination with other more formalized supervision structures if you are a young professional still in a training program or working toward licensure.

Common factors self-supervision would fall under the general domain of deliberate practice (see Chapter 8), a term introduced by K. Anders Ericsson and colleagues (1993) in the science of expertise designed to improve specific aspects of an individual's performance through repetition and refinement. Professionals from a wide range of fields, from athletics to acting, rely on deliberate practice to achieve expert performance (Ericsson & Pool, 2016). There is a current trend in our profession to explore how deliberate practice can improve the effectiveness of training and supervision (e.g., Chow et al., 2015; Rousmaniere et al., 2017; Tracey et al., 2015). Of particular importance for couple and family therapists (CFTs), deliberate practice requires several processes that are not present in traditional continuing education (CE) endeavors: observing your own work, repetitive rehearsal of skills and continuously assessing performance (Ericsson, 2006).

In CFT, as in many other professions, it is important to be able to critically evaluate how you performed. In this way, you can identify any areas that may require change. Awareness in these growth areas will enable you to choose appropriate training activities to fill any identified skill or knowledge gaps. Along with evaluating your effectiveness at different stages of the therapy process, common factors self-supervision can be an immensely motivating practice to

DOI: 10.4324/9781315542737-11

keep pushing yourself and challenging the ways in which you provide therapy to family systems.

Given that therapy and supervision are viewed as isomorphic (Andolfi & Menghi, 1980; Liddle & Saba, 1982; Minuchin & Fishman, 1981), the more self-supervisory practices empower therapists to look at the strengths they have from their own common factors infused CFT practice, the more therapists will be able to do the same with their clients.

There are a number of self-reflective practices that can be implemented to assist you in monitoring and/or improving the way you integrate the common factors into your clinical work. To consistently facilitate this integration into your everyday practice, be deliberate about self-supervision at regular intervals during your (1) pre-session preparation/planning and (2) post-session review/reflection. Below we focus on simple strategies that we use both in our own practices and with our students in master's and doctoral CFT training programs.

To practice these strategies, pick a stuck or challenging family system from your current caseload. While we believe you can also learn much about potentiating the common factors from cases that are going well, research indicates that therapists typically avoid planning and have a particularly strong blind spot regarding their own cases that are at risk of deterioration (Hannan et al., 2005; Hatfield et al., 2010). Focusing on our weaknesses has an added benefit of guarding against overconfidence. Remember, with self-evaluation comes personal growth. Given that all psychotherapy is a failure-driven progression, we should not be afraid to make mistakes, because we are perpetual learners. That's why all forms of effective self-supervision, in addition to intentionality, require self-compassion and patience.

Pre-session Preparation

Common Factors Treatment Plan and Assessment

Creating and reviewing a treatment plan in essential in the early work with a new client system. Every mental health discipline uses treatment planning as a tool to assess, track progress and keep an organized record of client care. Therapists have their own preferences when it comes to the structure of their assessment and treatment plans. Some may have found that informal treatment plans are more effective, whereas others prefer to work with clients in a more orderly fashion. Traditional psychotherapy treatment plans often contain the following:

- History, assessment and demographics
- Presenting problem

- Strengths
- Treatment goals
- Objectives
- Interventions
- Progress and outcomes

In addition to including all of the above information, we suggest infusing the common factors into your current way of treating planning by adding important CFT-specific client cycle elements, alliance dimensions and extratherapeutic dimensions (i.e., hope, expectancy, client worldview). Using the following template, formulate a common factors treatment plan within the first one to three sessions, paying careful attention to collaborating with the client system on its creation. Always use client feedback throughout the therapy to update and modify the plan if necessary. Reviewing the treatment plan, from time to time, in your pre-session ritual of preparation is also essential to common factors self-supervision.

COMMON FACTORS OPENING ASSESSMENT AND TREATMENT PLAN

1. *Initial engagement*
   a. Who constituted the direct client system for the first session?
   _____
   _____

   b. Who constituted the indirect client system when the therapy started?
   _____
   _____

   c. What is the presenting problem?
   _____
   _____

2. *Family membership*
   a. List all relevant family system members, indicating their age, race/ethnicity, family position and occupation or grade in school.
   _____
   _____

   b. How many total sessions have you conducted with this client system?
   _____
   _____

3. *Description of client system's health and strength*
   a. Briefly describe the client system's physical appearance and manner of relating.
   _____
   _____

   b. What do you feel in their presence?
   _____
   _____

   c. Provide a description of client system strengths.
      i. Individual strengths
      _____
      _____

ii. Couple strengths

   iii. Family strengths

4. Stage of change
   a. What stage of change (precontemplation, contemplation, preparation, action, maintenance) is each member of the client system currently in?

5. Expectancy/previous experience with therapy/hope
   a. What is each member of the client system's previous experience with therapy?

   b. What is each member of the client system's expectation for this therapy?

   c. Describe each member of the client system's sense of hope about this therapy?

6. Relational problem cycle
   a. How does each member of the system describe the problem?

   b. What is the frequency, intensity and duration of the problem?

   c. What is the time and context of onset of the problem?

d. What are the family members reactions to the problem?

e. What are the patterns of agreement and disagreement on the problem by members of the system?

f. Why is the client system seeking treatment for the problem now?

g. What are other, nonpresenting problems in the system?

h. Is there evidence of:
   i. Substance abuse

   ii. Physical, psychological or sexual abuse

   iii. Suicidality

   iv. Major psychiatric disorder

   i. How did you frame the problem cycle to the client system in relational terms to promote fairness and engagement?

7. Therapeutic goals
   a. Outline the goals of therapy in clear operationalized and measurable terms.
      i. Individual level

ii. *Couple level*

iii. *Family level*

8. Interventions
   a. *Describe techniques used to disrupt the client system's dysfunctional relational patterns.*

   b. *Describe your intervention plan to address each goal for therapy.*

   c. *How/why did you decide to implement each intervention?*

   d. *How do these interventions fit with the client system's worldview?*

   e. *Will the direct client system need to be expanded to address the presenting problem and therapeutic goals?*

9. Alliance
   a. *Describe the fit you have on the tasks dimension with each member of the client system.*

   b. *Describe the fit you have on the goals dimension with each member of the client system.*

c. Describe the fit you have on the bonds dimension with each member of the client system.

_____
_____
_____

  d. Describe your alliance with the indirect client system.

_____
_____
_____

10. Intervention evaluation

  a. What method(s) will you use to evaluate client progress on therapeutic process, goals and alliance?

_____
_____
_____

Review Ritual

What do you do to adequately prepare for an upcoming session? Between writing a progress note, returning a phone call and taking a restroom break, most therapists lack the time or inclination to do much else. Common factors self-supervision is based on the belief that session preparation should be intentional and deliberate. Rather than focusing on mastering a specific model, the common factors framework is used primarily to get systemic therapists comfortable with hypothesizing and conceptualizing about the various client, therapist and relationship factors at play in a particular case (Karam, 2011). Practice preparing in advance for a session in a "review ritual" by reflecting on the following common factors inspired questions:

COMMON FACTORS PRE-SESSION PREPARATION INVENTORY

1. Was a feedback measure given after the last session? If yes, review the following questions:

   a. How did the alliance change since the last measurement point? Are there any data that would suggest a split alliance or rupture within the system?

   b. Is there any significant change on any individual or relationship variable since the last measurement point that could impact the therapy?

   c. How did client responses either confirm or disconfirm your clinical impressions of what is going on in the therapy?

   d. How will these feedback data inform your planning for the upcoming session?

   e. What feedback data will your introduce into the upcoming session with the client system?

2. Was homework given at the end of last session? If yes, review with the client system at an appropriate point in session, paying careful attention to explicitly link homework to the specific task and goals of the therapy.

3. What are the client system's strengths (self-identified vs. other identified) that you want to highlight in this session?

4. How do you see each member in the system contributing to the problem cycle? How will you conceptualize difficulties in relational terms and make the cycle explicit for the client system during the session?

5. What techniques and interventions will you use to disrupt the client system's dysfunctional relational patterns during the session?

6. How will you convey a sense of hope during the session?

7. What verbal feedback did the client system give you in the last session? What modifications will you make in this session because of that feedback?

8. What feedback did you share with client system in the previous session? What did you neglect to share but, upon review, think is important to share in the upcoming session?

9. Who are the important players in the indirect client system? What, if anything, do you need to know about members of the indirect system for the upcoming session?

10. Who else should be involved directly in the therapy? Why now?

We believe that reflecting on this question will both increase your awareness and prime you to potentiate the common factors in the subsequent session. Although this process may feel time-consuming at first, we believe the more you stick with this deliberate practice and engage in the iterative process, the quicker and more efficient you will become at it! In fact, we have gotten feedback from some of our students that this review process becomes nearly automatic after regular incorporation into one's pre-session routine.

Post-session Review and Reflection

Reviewing Session Recordings

While other mental health disciplines may find this practice "foreign", or out-of-place, CFTs have understood the importance of recording their work since the inception of our storied profession. Although video recording is now widely acknowledged as invaluable for enhancing the effectiveness of clinical training (e.g., Bernard & Goodyear, 2014; Ellis, 2010; Friedlander et al., 2012), not many CFTs will elect to do so once they leave the friendly confines of their graduate training program or postgraduate supervision required for licensure as a licensed marriage and family therapist. Most of us therefore rely solely on our mental recall when trying to review a session. Attempting to critically evaluate your performance with a couple or family session from memory alone, however, is akin to practicing a musical instrument without being able to hear what you sound like playing it – it can be done, but it's not very effective! Therefore, if you want help identifying your blind spots (which we all have) in common factors self-supervision, you will have to watch your work.

Maybe you remember watching your first recordings as a therapist-in-training – not confident in what to present during supervision or unsure of how to analyze the session recording. Maybe you didn't know how to determine whether your interventions had been helpful or not with the client system. But, you might ask, what should you watch for from a common factors perspective? At first, we recommend pausing the recording at particularly challenging moments in the session – places to repair the therapeutic alliance, nurture hope, facilitate client motivation and give direct feedback. Special attention should also be given to moments when you are explaining therapeutic tasks, conceptualizing client difficulties in relational terms or hypothesizing about dysfunctional relational patterns and cycles. In these moments, ask yourself:

- *Where did I go wrong?*
- *Did members of the client system understand what I was attempting to do?*
- *What should I have said or done differently?*
- *Did I create enough space and ask for client feedback?*

After you answer these questions, practice an improved response or adaptive therapeutic behavior before resuming the recording. For example, rehearse explaining the problem cycle in straightforward, nonpathologizing language to obtain buy-in from each member of the client system. By examining "raw data" from actual sessions, you can also track behavioral, cognitive and affective components of your interventions, as well as other important alliance, therapist and client common factors.

What does it look like in the session when you are in the flow and truly letting your self-of-therapist qualities (humor, warmth, curiosity, etc.) shine through? Therapists can either be in the moment and genuinely engaged with the humanity of the client system or removed and detached when distracted in the therapy room. If you are anxious and trying too hard to make up for your perceived inadequacies, you may lose the ability to remain present, relaxed and responsive to the needs of the client system. Therapists like this start to view their clients like case studies in their textbooks, rather than real people who may have many of the same fears and insecurities as they do. In order to help you gauge your authentic "way of being" (Fife et al., 2014), select segments of the session recording where you felt fully present and connected with your clients. Conversely, you may also highlight portions of the session where you were too much in your head, overly focused on your anxiety or performance instead of connected to the client's experience. Also, pay close attention to see whether your way of being changes via a function of the modality of the therapy. For example, a therapist who is in a comfort zone while working with individuals may become more reticent or removed from the hyperstimulating experience of conducting couple or family therapy.

By repeatedly practicing this self-supervisory process of reviewing challenging therapeutic moments with the recording paused, over time you will increase the speed of answering those questions and formulating appropriate responses. Once you have a sense of what you need to do, you may feel comfortable with a more advanced modification. Start self-correcting while the video is running. Don't criticize yourself, just say the right things over top of existing session audio. This way, you'll be responding in real time with the recording. This process will build your confidence to intervene more confidently and persistently in future sessions.

The following worksheet is designed to be used to evaluate the common factors with any recorded or live therapy session that you are observing. We use it to review our own sessions in private practice and again in CFT group supervision to either help our students with their own sessions or facilitate them giving feedback to their peers from a common factors perspective.

BRINGING THE COMMON FACTORS TO LIFE

Complete this worksheet as you review a session recording of yourself, a master clinician or peer conducting systemic therapy.

Therapist Factors

1. What makes this therapist effective?

___

2. How does the therapist adapt to client values and preferences in this session?

___

3. What does the therapist do that doesn't work in this session?

___

Client Factors

4. What are the client strengths being mobilized in this session?

___

5. How motivated are the clients to deal with the issues that brought them to therapy?

___

Hope

6. How do the clients connect to a sense of hope during the session?

_____
_____
_____
_____

7. How does the therapist convey a sense of hope during the session?

_____
_____
_____
_____

8. What makes you hopeful while watching this session?

_____
_____
_____
_____

The Expanded Therapeutic Alliance

9. How does the therapist work to address the alliance (tasks, goals, bonds) during the session?

_____
_____
_____

10. Are there any potential tears in the alliance in any part of the system? If so, how does the therapist address them?

_____
_____
_____
_____

11. How does the therapist address the alliance with the indirect system during the session?

_____
_____

The Couple/Family Cycle – Conceptualizing Difficulties in Relational Terms

12. How does the therapist help the clients understand their "cycle" in systemic, relational terms?

13. How does the therapist help the couple slow down, develop a self-observing stance and take personal responsibility for their own part in the couple/family cycle?

Changing the Doing, Thinking and Feeling

14. What is the therapist doing to intervene on a behavioral level?

15. What is the therapist doing to intervene on a cognitive level?

16. What is the therapist doing to intervene on an emotional level?

Feedback

17. What feedback does the therapist share with the client system during the session?

18. How does the client system respond to therapist feedback?

19. What feedback does the client system share with therapist about the therapeutic process and about pivotal moments in the session?

Common Factors Journaling

Journal writing by a therapist enhances self-awareness and is a way of witnessing the work that is an integral part of reflective practice. Not limited by the constraints of formal recordkeeping, it allows the therapist to delve deeper into the common factors that underly systemic therapeutic practice. Different than a progress note that becomes part of the clinical record, these private, informal psychotherapy notes typically include the therapist's observations and any thoughts or feelings they have about the client system. These notes are always kept separate from medical records and billing information, and providers are not permitted to share them. Even members of the client system do not have the right to access these personal notes.

A common factor–focused journal serves as both a type of personal note and an example of autoethnography, an autobiographical method of research (Patton, 2002). Thus, the therapist serves as the instrument of data collection. The data come from your lived experience as a CFT in the form of these self-reflective journal entries. The process of writing these common factors entries helps to boost creative thinking around therapeutic options. Writing something down, whether electronically or on paper, also helps you to renew focus on the therapeutic issues at hand. The entry should be about a session with a client system that is either particularly challenging or productive. Prompts focus on therapist, client, alliance, pivotal moments, hope and feedback common factors. During the journaling process, additional connections are often made – many of which may have been stimulated by reading this book. As the connections and feelings emerge, there is a sense of space, which often brings new perspectives to the problem and increases your investment in the therapeutic process.

COMMON FACTOR JOURNALING SELF-REFLECTION

By recording and describing experiences, feelings and thoughts around the common factors, therapists can develop new perspectives that can guide future clinical actions. After reflecting, it is not unusual to realize exactly what we want to bring up next time. Often, though, if we don't make notes, we forget by the time our next session arrives! Fill out the following template with prompts within 24 hours after the therapy session so that your memory is still current.

Date:
Client System:
Self of Therapist:
Alliance:
Hope:
Pivotal moments:
Things to mention next time:

Before your next session, check-in with yourself and review this entry. Consider how you want to use the information around the common factors with the client system.

Conclusion

Believe it or not, just accumulating thousands of hours of face-to-face time with couples and families does not automatically improve your clinical effectiveness (Tracey et al., 2015). To the contrary, a study examining the outcomes of 170 therapists at a large university counseling center found that the average therapist actually had a small but statistically significant decrease in effectiveness over time (Goldberg et al., 2016). Why aren't we getting better? Most of us get no CFT supervision after licensure. Most of us do not videotape our work after we leave our training programs so that we can study it. Most of us do not have a ritual of review and preparation before each session. Most of us are afraid to hear from our clients about our shortcomings or invest the time and money in feedback tools. Most continuing education offerings focus on the learning of trendy, specific interventions that don't work for everyone, instead of refining the powerful commonalities that bind us together as relational healers. Most of us are not reading books like this one. These are the things that must change in our field if we want to start seeing meaningful growth in our identity as systemic therapists and improvement in overall effectiveness. Improving effectiveness requires intentionality in the form of deliberate practice through CFT common factors self-supervision: observing your own work, getting expert feedback and continuously assessing performance (Ericsson, 2016).

We started this book with one central question in mind: What do systemic CFTs need to know in order to grow throughout their careers, remain clinically relevant in the marketplace and think critically about what really works in therapy? In an attempt to respond to this question, we have given specific examples throughout this book of how CFT common factors could be infused throughout a reflective, intentional systemic practice. We acknowledge that competent integration only comes about after years of clinical work, practical application of multiple theories with different clients, strong supervision, self-of-the-therapist work and countless other formative experiences. For this reason, we believe in using the "both/and" approach of integrating common factors alongside specific models for systemic therapists when planning and reviewing their work. If instilled early in your professional development process, this approach can lay a strong foundation for personal integration and critical thinking that will deepen as you mature, keeping both the individual and our great profession responsive to change and vital for years to come!

References

Andolfi, M., & Menghi, P. (1980). A model for training in family therapy. In M. Andolfi & I. Zwerling (Eds.), *Dimensions of family therapy* (pp. 239–259). Guilford.

Bernard, J. M., & Goodyear, R. K. (2014). *Fundamentals of clinical supervision* (5th ed.). Merrill.

Chow, D. L., Miller, S. D., Seidel, J. A., Kane, R. T., Thornton, J. A., & Andrews, W. P. (2015). The role of deliberate practice in the development of highly effective psychotherapists. *Psychotherapy, 52*(3), 337–345.

Ellis, M. V. (2010). Bridging the science and practice of clinical supervision: Some discoveries, some misconceptions. *The Clinical Supervisor, 29*, 95–116.

Ericsson, K. A. (2006). The influence of experience and deliberate practice on the development of superior expert performance. In *The Cambridge handbook of expertise and expert performance* (pp. 685–705).

Ericsson, K. A. (2016). Summing up hours of any type of practice versus identifying optimal practice activities: Comments on Macnamara, Moreau, and Hambrick (2015). *Perspectives on Psychological Science, 11*, 351–354.

Ericsson, K. A., Krampe, R. T., & Tesch Romer, C. (1993). The role of deliberate practice in the acquisition of expert performance. *Psychological Review, 100*, 363–406.

Ericsson, K. A., & Pool, R. (2016). *Peak: Secrets from the new science of expertise.* Houghton Mifflin Harcourt.

Fife, S. T., Whiting, J. B., Bradford, K., & Davis, S. (2014). The therapeutic pyramid: A common factors synthesis of techniques, alliance, and way of being. *Journal of Marital and Family Therapy, 40*(1), 20–33.

Friedlander, M. L., Sutherland, O., Sandler, S., Kortz, L., Bernardi, S., Lee, H. H., & Drozd, A. (2012). Exploring corrective experiences in a successful case of short-term dynamic psychotherapy. *Psychotherapy, 49*(3), 349–363.

Goldberg, S., Rousmaniere, T. G., Miller, S. D., Nielsen, Whipple, J., S. L., Hoyt, B., & Wampold, B. E. (2016). Do psychotherapists improve with time and experience? A longitudinal analysis of real-world outcome data. *Journal of Counseling Psychology, 63*, 1–11.

Hannan, C., Lambert, M. J., Harmon, C., Nielsen, S. L., Smart, D. W., Shimokawa, K., & Sutton, S. W. (2005). A lab test and algorithms for identifying clients at risk for treatment failure. *Journal of Clinical Psychology: In Session, 61*, 155–163.

Hatfield, D., McCullough, L., Frantz, S. H., & Krieger, K. (2010). Do we know when our clients get worse? An investigation of therapists' ability to detect negative client change. *Clinical Psychology & Psychotherapy, 17*, 25–32.

Karam, E. A. (2011). Integrating common factors into a MFT curriculum. *Family Therapy Magazine, 10*(5), 32–34.

Liddle, H. A., & Saba, G. W. (1982). Teaching family therapy at the introductory level: A conceptual model emphasizing a pattern which connects training and therapy. *Journal of Marital and Family Therapy, 8*(1), 63–72.

Minuchin, S., & Fishman, H. C. (1981). *Family therapy techniques.* Harvard University Press.

Patton, M. Q. (2002). *Qualitative research and evaluation methods.* Sage.

Rousmaniere, T., Goodyear, R. K., Miller, S. D., & Wampold, B. E. (Eds.). (2017). *The cycle of excellence: Using deliberate practice to improve supervision and training.* John Wiley & Sons.

Tracey, T. J. G., Wampold, B. E., Goodyear, R. K., & Lichtenberg, J. W. (2015). Improving expertise in psychotherapy. *Psychotherapy Bulletin, 50*(1), 7–13.

INDEX

Page numbers in italics refer to figures. Page numbers in bold refer to tables.

abstract thinking 156; *see also* thinking skills
accountability 153, 172
acting-out adolescent 25
action, stages of change 108
allegiance 82–83
alliances: appraisals 195; approaches to building 27, 106; relationships 182
alliance skill building in CFT: bond dimension 184; curiosity for members of client system 184–185; nurturing bonds 183–184; therapeutic role 184
ambivalence 22, 102
American Association for Marriage and Family Therapy (AAMFT) 174
Anderson, H. 124
Anderson, T. 155–156
Anker, M. G. 203, 208
anxiety 120, 129, 181, 202
APA Presidential Task Force 9
aspiration, rituals 133; *see also* rituals of renewal
assessment mechanism 46–47
assimilative integration 80
attention deficit hyperactivity disorder (ADHD) 45
attention problems 17
attitudes of openness 95
authentic appreciation, rituals 133
awareness, self-supervision and treatment planning 224–225

Bachelor, A. 114
Baker, K. A. 168
Baldwin, S. A. 77
Bateman, A. 169
behavioral skill building 38
biases and values 167–168

Blanchard, M. 204
Blow, A. 15, 51, 145, 157–158, 167–168
Bohart, A. C. 15, 123, 148
bona fide approaches 9, 152
bonds, nurturing 183–184
Bordin, E. S. 11–12, 181, 190
Bowen, M. 23, 150
brief strategic family therapy (BSFT) model 106–107
Butler, M. H. 193
"buy it to sell it" mentality 130

Carter, B. 66–67
Catherall, D. R. 182
Cecchin, G. 193
CFT *see* couple and family therapy (CFT)
change: assumptions about 6–9; client factors/extratherapeutic events 11; common factors unique to CFT 13; expectancy, placebo and allegiance 12; factors of 10–11; in human behaviors and conditions 7; in meaning 28; models/ techniques 12; therapeutic alliance factors 11–12; therapist effects 9, 12–13
changing the doing 15, 18, 38, 238
changing the feeling 18, 39, 238
changing the viewing, therapeutic effects: behavioral skill building 38; conflictual marital relationship 25; engagement in treatment 26–28; experiencing 39; meaning 28; problem, shared view 26; safety in therapy 28–30; shared sense of purpose 30–31; strategies 31–38
child/children: behavior 173; demotivated teenager 99; protective services workers 71; in stepfamily 49–50
circular questions 37–38, 58, 61, 103

client and contextual factors: context 114–117; couple's continuum 102–103; expectations 121–123; extratherapeutic events, opportunities 117–119; healing potential 90–92; innate healing of systems 119–121; learning client preferences/worldview 123–124; motivation 92–101, 104–107; stages of change 107–114

client feedback 204; formalized feedback 210; questions 206–208; session-by-session feedback 208

client survey 211; Closed-ended questions 211; feedback data analysis 213–214; format question 211–212; therapeutic information tracking 214–215; tracking 203, 212–213

client systems: benefit, therapist system 149; and therapist 127

coaching couples 132

cognition 127

cognitive changes 28

collaborative partnership 27

commitment 92, 102

common factors: direct treatment system, expansion 70–74; disrupting dysfunctional relational/systemic patterns 57–58; family process 58–67; feedback couple therapy satisfaction and progress survey 216–220; focused journal 239; informs intervention conceptualization 54–55; initial conceptualization 55–57; self-supervision and treatment planning 224–242; systemic conceptualization of problems 46–47; therapeutic alliance, expansion 67–70; training and model selection checklist 80–81; *see also* conceptualization

Common Factors Couple's Continuum 100–101

Common Factors Feedback Interview 205

common therapeutic effects 11

communication in CFT 131–132

community: cultural context 26; groups 117; practice 6, 153; resources 117; stakeholders 71

competent therapist 147

comprehensive systemic conceptualization 48

conceptualization: contextual information 55; informs intervention 54–55; initial 55–57; model-derived 83; pantheoretical 181; problem 40; relational 47; systemic 48–49, **49**, 55, 57

conceptual thinking 70–71

concurrent training 79

confidence 77, 138, 198, 235

conflictual marital relationship 25

confrontation 103

conjoint sessions 179

consciousness 95, 109, 139

consent and rationale 72

contemplation 108, 110; *see also* precontemplation

contemporary literature 70

contextual information, conceptualization 55

continuing education (CE) endeavors 224

continuous feedback mechanisms 28

continuous outcome assessment 213

conversation of therapy 26

cotherapy in therapy relationship 150

couple and family therapy (CFT) 6, *24*; alliance skill building in 183–185; common factors feedback 201; complexity in practice 182–183; differentiation of self 23; effects in *24*; growth and development 4–5; meta-analyses 10; rituals 132; therapist 179; training practices 21; *see also* common factors

couples: connection 132; thinking 18

Couple Therapeutic Alliance Scale–Revised 182

couple therapy 18, 145–146, 216–220; emotionally focused 18; in-depth training 145–146; integrative behavioral 78

Crane, D, R. 123

creating credible tasks 185–186

criticisms 96, 103

cultural awareness 167–168

curiosity for members 184–185

deliberate practice (DP): to enhance core skills 159–164; reframing 161; self-supervision and treatment planning 224; into supervisory activities 175

demotivated teenager/child 99

depression 8, 129, 181, 202

dialectical relationship 129

didactic lectures 17

differentiation of self 23

direct therapeutic system 149, 182

direct treatment system: build alliances 73; collaboration 73–74; community stakeholders 71; conceptual thinking

70–71; consent and rationale 72; indirect client system 70; indirect therapeutic system 71; medical family therapists 71; multiple partners 71
discernment counseling 100
discrepancies in motivation 100
discrepant motivations in couples 99–101
disengagement 95
dispersion of motivation 97–98
disrupting dysfunctional relational/systemic patterns 57–58
distal outcomes 19–20, 38
divorce 102
Doherty, B. 99
dose effect 97
drug abuse 181
dysfunctional relational patterns 58, 234
dysthymia 129

ear and repair, therapist misuses 194–195
early therapy sessions, motivation 96
EFT *see* emotionally focused therapy (EFT)
emotionally focused therapy (EFT) 18, 26, 78, 145, 185
emotion/emotional 121, 127; burden 140; family process 61, 66; reactivity 23; responses 129; strain and scheduling challenges 46
empathy 148–149
engagement and motivation 26–27, 106–107
engendering hope 131
Ericsson, K. A. 224
evidence-based models 78, 97
evidence-based movement 171–172
evidence-based practice 9; clinical work 21; medicine 21; practitioners 9; systemic therapy 155; theory 90–91; therapists 146
expanding the system 72
expansion of the therapeutic alliance 67–70
expectancy 10–12, 226, 228
expectations 122
experience and learned skills 148
externalizing the problem 22
extratherapeutic events 11, 118–119

facilitative interpersonal skills 155–156
family: couple systems 93; -focused problem 26; functioning 58; -of-origin work 71; polarizations 95–96; rituals 132; therapists 71

family process: behavioral shifts 65; cognitive interruptions 66; communication 61; content 58; definition 58–61; dysfunctional relational patterns, disruption of 58, **59–60**; emotions 61, 66; illumination and use of the here and now 61–65; interrupt without alienating system 65–66; intervention 66–67; process-oriented therapists 61
family therapy: literature 132; trainee 79; *see also* couple and family therapy (CFT)
Family Therapy Alliance Scale–Revised 182
Farbe, B. A. 204
feedback: barriers to integrating 210–211; client questions 206–208; common factors feedback interview 206–215; designing your own feedback survey 211–215; formal standardized, proprietary feedback systems 208–210; forms 211; informed treatment 201; nonverbal client feedback 204; overview 201; routine 201–203; systems 210; therapist solicited feedback 204–205; treatment group 203; unsolicited client-initiated feedback 203
feelings sharing 90
Fonagy, P. 169
forgiveness 140–141
formalized feedback 210
Friedlander, M. L. 27–29
functional family therapy 26–27, 96

"ganging up" on therapist 166
genograms **49**, 51, 167
goals: attainment 127; development 28; -setting phase 186
goodness-of-fit 186
Goolishian, H. 124
Gottman method 78
gracious ending, rituals 133
Great Psychotherapy Debate 10
Greenberg, L. S. 148
group–therapist 182
group therapy 45

Haber, R. 204
healing: contextual variables 91–92; couple and family-level strengths 91; evidence-based theory 90–91; individual characteristics 91; individuals and family systems 90
Helmeke, K. B. 91, 202
Henry, W. P. 95

"here and now" acceptance framework 131
heterosexual couple 90
homeostasis 6–7
hope: CFT hope history interview 133; forgive, don't relive 140–141; mentors 138; "hope language" 130; hopelessness 130, 134; "hope merchant" 130; in my control self-reflection 133–137; as natural complement to CFT 128–129; research on 128; rituals of renewal 132–133; spiritual resources 139–140; threats to 129–130; *see also* hopeful therapist
hopeful therapist 130–132
hope mentor 138
Horvath, A. 114
Hubble, M. A. 124

identified skill or knowledge gaps 224
Imel, Z. 11–12, 152–153
inability to concentrate 45
increasing reflective functioning 168–170
independent relationships 68
in-depth assessment 99
in-depth training, couple therapy 145–146
indirect client system 70
indirect therapeutic system 71, 190–191
indirect therapist system 149
individual psychotherapy 154; *see also* therapists
individual relationship 68
inherent talent *versus* learned skills 158–159
innate healing of systems: capacities 90; posttraumatic growth 120–121; resilience 119–120
integrative behavioral couple therapy 78
Integrative Problem Centered Therapy 20
integrative psychotherapy alliance 182
integrative training 80
intellectual thought processes 23
intention for rituals 132
internet branding 146
interpersonal skills 159; difficulties to therapists 145–146; factors, client engagement 130
interpersonal violence 23
interrupting patterns 66–67
interrupting the process 65–66
intimacy, in marriage 190

Jenkins, P. 21
Johnson, S. M. 185
journal writing 239–241

Karam, E. A. 157–158
Keith, D. V. 78
knowledge: acquisition 17; learned serving 17; therapists 171–174

Lambert, M. 10, 127, 209
Larsen, D. J. 131
laughter 132
"leaning in" partner 100
"leaning out" partner 100
learning: contexts 17; disabilities 17; goal 17; methods 17; models 78–79
Lebow, J. L. 21
licensed marriage and family therapist 234
life stress 8
linking tasks, goals and bonds 190
loneliness 130

maintenance 11, 55, 72, 108, 111, 130, 182
management skills, therapists 155
marital-family therapy 158
Masten, A. S. 120
McGoldrick, M. 66–67
medical family therapists 71
Menninger, K. 127
mental health: discipline 78; marketplace 202; problems 47
mentalization-based treatment 169
mentors and hope 138
Merit-Based Incentive Payment System (MIPS) 202
Milan approach 150
mindfulness practice and therapist effectiveness 170–171
Minuchin, S. 150
mixed agenda couples 99
models: client system's worldview 83–84; concurrent training 79; -derived conceptualization 83; importance 76–77; integrative training 80; learning 78–79; selection and empirical evidence 77–78; selection and worldview 82–83; self-reflection 84–88; -specific techniques and interventions 79; training and model selection checklist 81
motivation: client and contextual factors 92–101; commitment 92; criticisms and 96; demotivated teenager/child 99; discrepancies in 100; discrepant motivations in couples 99–101; dispersion

of 97–98; early therapy sessions 96; engagement and 106–107; family/couple systems 93; functional family therapy 96; increasing 93–96; parental subsystem 98–99; questions to assess and enhance 104–107; sustaining client motivation 97; therapist skills 93; understanding 92–93; viewing of problem 96; willingness 95
multiple partners, direct treatment system 71

narrow common factors 11
negative thoughts 140
negativity, in family members 27
negotiation 93
Nelson, T. 171
neutrality 193
Niebuhr, R. 134
nodal events 51
noncompliant 183
non-therapy factors 10
nonverbal client feedback 204
nonverbal communication 131–132
nonverbal responses 46
"no secret" contracts, signing 48–49

O'Hara, D. 129
one-on-one relationship 68
online: group interaction 17; platforms 173
opening assessment and treatment plan, self-supervision 227–231
operationalizing and collaborating on goals 186–188
oppression 129
optimism 127, 130–131; see also hope
Orlinsky, D. E. 149
Outcome Questionnaire 173
Outcome Questionnaire 45 (OQ45) 173, 209
Outcome Rating Form 173
Outcome Rating Scale (ORS) 209
outcome-related therapist factor 158
overconfidence 225; see also confidence
over-functioning parent 98–99

pantheoretical conceptualization 181
parental subsystem 98–99
pathways, therapeutic effects 20–21
patient-focused research 201
Patterson, J. E. 21
personal difficulties 185
personality differences 148
personal responsibility 23

personal self-of-the-therapist work 166–168
Philadelphia Guild Guidance Clinic 78–79
Piercy, F. P. 171
Pinsof, W. M. 69, 182, 191
pivotal moments research 202
placebo 12
play therapy 45
polarizations 95–96, 98–99
political context, therapist 167–168
positive connotation 22
post-session review and reflection, self-supervision 234–235
posttraumatic growth 120–121
poverty/illness 129
practice couple and family therapy, therapists in 154–158
precontemplation 108–110
precontemplators 113
preferred learning style 17
preparation (planning for change) 108
prescribing of symptom 22
presence and participation, rituals 133
pre-session preparation, self-supervision 225–226, 232–233
principles of change: for couples and families 41; personal family backgrounds 40; problem conceptualization 40; see also change; changing the viewing, therapeutic effects
problems: developmental history 50; relational conceptualization 47; systemic conceptualization 48–49, **49**
process: developmental 7; family therapy 112; intellectual thought 23; self-supervisory 235; skills 157–158; see also family process
Prochaska, J. O. 107–109
professional ethics and reputation 145
progress research 201
proximal outcomes 19–21
psychiatrist 46, 71, 149
psychoanalytic therapist 55
psychotherapeutic change 7
psychotherapy 10, 127, 152; individual 154; skill-enhancing methods to 159–160; training, concurrent model 79

qualities, therapists 146, 151, 156, 159, 165, 235

Rait, D. S. 69, 165
reasonable hope 128–129

INDEX

reassurance 93
Reese, R. J. 203
referrals 145–146
reflective functioning/mentalization, therapists 168–170
reflexive questions 103
reframing 22, 99, 161–163
relational conceptualization 46–47
relationship: -building differences 148; happiness 18; threats to 52
repeated failed attempts 129
resentment 140
resilience 119–120
resistance: to engagement 106; to pull of the system 165–166
responses 48
review ritual, self-supervision 231
rewriting one's life story 22
rituals of renewal 132–133
Rousmaniere, T. 161, 173, 224
routine outcome monitoring 201
ruptures 191–192

safety in therapy 28–30
Santisteban, D. A. 106
Satir, V. 78, 150
Schwartz, R. C. 23, 130
self-awareness: self-supervision 224; therapists 167–168
self-defeating internal talk 129
self-differentiation 100
self-efficacy 127
self-empathy 149
self-exploration 95
self-of-therapist qualities 164–165, 235
self-responsibility 100
self-supervision and treatment planning, common factors: awareness 224–225; bringing common factors to life 236–239; deliberate practice 224; identified skill or knowledge gaps 224; journal writing 239–241; opening assessment and treatment plan 227–231; post-session review and reflection 234–235; pre-session preparation 225–226, 232–233; review ritual 231; self-awareness 224; therapy and supervision 225
self-therapist 182
Sells, A. P. 190
session-by-session progress 173
Session Rating Form 173

Session Rating Scale (SRS) 209
sexual minority 114–115
Shadish, W, R. 77
shared sense of purpose 30–31
Sharples, E. 210
skilled couple and family therapist 69
skill-enhancing methods to psychotherapy 159–160
S.M.A.R.T.E.R. goal statements 187–189, **189**; attainable 187; equitable 188; measurable 187; rational 188; relevant 187–188; specific 187; timebound 189
Snyder, C. R. 127
social connection 130
social constructivist approaches 83
social functioning assessments 202
social support 117
softenings 18, 19
solution-focused therapy 128
spirituality 139
spiritual resources 139–140
split alliance 182, 202
Sprenkle, D. 13, 15, 47, 57–58, 71, 91, 202
stages of change: assessment 110–112; definition 107–108; discrepancies within a client system 109; matching client readiness 108–109; specific interventions in systems 112–114; therapy questions 110–111
Stege, R. 131
stress 7–8, 36, 40, 45–46, 53–54, 73, 134, 139
structural family therapy 79
Strupp, H. H. 95
subsystem relationships 68
suicide 129
supervision 174–176
supervisor–therapist relationship 175
sustaining client motivation 97
systemic circular questions 103
systemic conceptualization 47, 55; determining 53; of problems 46–47
Systemic Therapy Inventory of Change (STIC) 210
Szapocznik, J. 155–157

Talitman, E. 185
talk therapy 45
Tallman, K. 15, 123
tear and repair 191–198; acknowledge the tear 195; detect the tear 194; feelings underneath the tear 196; modification

based on feedback 197–198; potential parallel processes 196–197; space/safety to express feeling 195–196; type of tear 194
technical eclecticism 80
termination 108
theoretical allegiance 145
theoretical integration 80
theory: of alliance 11–12; evidence-based models 172; hope 127; knowledge of 53; theoretical integration 80; theory of change 2, 83–84, 124, 153; therapist's belief 171–174; Weingarten's theory 128–129
therapeutic alliance 11–12; CFT, alliance skill building in 183–185; complexity in practice 182–183; connection 67; credible tasks 185–186; curiosity for members 184–185; definition 68, 181–182; expansion 67–70; goals 67; indirect system 190–191; mismanagement 180; multifaceted relationship 180; nurturing bonds 183–184; operationalizing and collaborating on goals 186–188; overview 179–181; pantheoretical conceptualization 181; role 184; S.M.A.R.T.E.R. goal statements 186–189; task linking 185, 190; tasks of therapy 67; tear and repair 191–198; therapeutic relationship, interpersonal levels 68–69
therapeutic change 6
therapeutic effects: changing the viewing 24–31; common factors position in CFT 22; definition 15–19; desired outcomes 19; as distal (ultimate) outcomes 20; kinds 19–24; pathways 20–21; principles of change 39–41; as proximal (close or intermediate) outcomes 20; relationship, therapists in 148–149; rituals 132
therapists 192–193; approaches therapy 124; in change 151–154; deliberate practice (DP) to enhance core skills 159–164; effectiveness 145; evidence-based therapists 146; facilitative interpersonal skills 155–156; "gang up" on 166; inherent talent *versus* learned skills 158–159; internet branding 146; knowledge 171–174; management skills 155; mindfulness 170–171; personal self-of-the-therapist work 166–168; position 150–151; in practice couple and family therapy, effectiveness 154–158; process skills 157–158; professional ethics and reputation 145; qualities 151; questions about 146; referrals 145–146; reflective functioning (mentalization) 168–170; resisting pull of the system 165–166; role 147; self-of-the-therapist 164–165; skills, motivation 93; supervision 174–176; system 149–150; in therapeutic relationship 148–149; therapist system 149–150; thinking skills 156–157
therapy killer 191
thinking skills 156–157
"think on one's feet" 157
Timm, T. M. 51, 167
toxic conditions 115
transparency, therapists 174
treatment planning *see* self-supervision and treatment planning, common factors
troubled adolescents 26
Tryon, G. S. 202

undisciplined therapy 77
University of Rhode Island Change Assessment (URICA) 110

validation 93
values and perspectives 27
viewing of problems 28, 96
vulnerability 132

Wampler, R. S. 47
Wampold, B. 10–13, 152–153
Weingarten, K. 128–129
Westmacott, R. 202
Whitaker, C. A. 78, 150
whole-system relationship 69
willingness 95, 110, 111
Winograd, G. 202
within-system relationships 69, 182
work and social problems 181
worldview: client system's 83–84, 123; model selection and 82–83; personal 76; self-reflection 84–88; therapists' awareness 164, 167